BUILDING YOUR

SPIRITUAL LIFE

Grove booklets are fast-moving explorations of Christian life and ministry. They have been described by Archbishop Rowan Williams as 'a unique combination of scholarship, accessibility, relevance and careful, original thinking.' Each of the chapters in this book started life as booklets in the Spirituality series.

New titles are published every month, covering issues in the Bible, Christian ethics, evangelism, pastoral ministry, spirituality, renewal and worship. For more information, visit the Grove website www.grovebooks.co.uk.

BUILDING

YOUR

SPIRITUAL

LIFE

THE BEST CONTEMPORARY WRITING ON CHRISTIAN SPIRITUALITY

IAN PAUL

GRAND RAPIDS, MICHIGAN 49530 USA

We want to hear from you. Please send your comments about this
book to us in care of the address below. Thank you.

GRAND RAPIDS, MICHIGAN 49530 USA

WWW.ZONDERVAN.COM

Dedicated to my fellow builder, Maggie –
a very suitable partner

CONTENTS

O Christ, the Master Carpenter,
who at the last, through wood and nails,
purchased our whole salvation;
wield well your tools in the workshop of your world,
so that we who come rough-hewn to your bench
may here be fashioned to a truer beauty of your hand.
We ask it for your own name's sake.

GEORGE MCLEOD, IONA COMMUNITY

FOREWORD

George Carey

In the thirty years since their first publication, Grove booklets have acquired an enviable reputation for contemporary, thoughtful and thought-provoking comment. This collection, drawn from the Spirituality series (one of seven booklet series now in print), gives some indication as to the reason for this. The range and variety, the richness and depth, testify to the strength and confidence of evangelical spirituality – a confidence that has itself developed considerably in the thirty years of Grove's life.

Alister McGrath has defined Christian spirituality as 'the search for an authentic expression of what it means to live as a disciple of Christ.' The prayer 'O Christ, the Master Carpenter' (on the previous page and alluded to in the cover illustration for this book) from the Iona Community holds two essential aspects of such spirituality together: a focus on the finished work of Christ on the cross and in his resurrection, and the continual and unfinished quest to see that work expressed in lives that have been fashioned after him and by him. It expresses a passion to be reworked again and again by the hand of Christ until a faithful image of the maker can be seen.

The contours of an evangelical spirituality are expressed with similar emphasis in this rich anthology of Grove Books writers. Each chapter, at once rooted and shaped by reflective engagement with Scripture, at the same time seeks to make the truths found there relevant for the contemporary life of prayer, with its struggles and its joys. A wide range of experience, of the authors themselves and of the saints they reflect on down the ages, is harnessed for this task. As with other Grove booklets, these chapters are confidently evangelical, expressing a settled conviction of scriptural truth that also incorporates a generous hospitality to the wisdom and experience of other traditions in the faith. Each chapter seeks not simply to speak to these other traditions, but to engage with and learn from them too. And there is a passion here, a vitality, which reflects the excitement of discovering new depths in the ongoing journey of faith.

My prayer is that the material gathered together so helpfully in this book will both stimulate you to new reflection and equip you for your praying and your living. I commend it to you as a rich resource that will assist you in the life-long task of building your spiritual life.

Dr George Carey
Former Archbishop of Canterbury

INTRODUCTION

Ian Paul

It was dark. A ringing sound dragged me up from the depths of sleep. I fumbled for the alarm clock and managed to silence its irritating call. My roommate hit the light switch and the glare made me squint with discomfort. I peered at the clock – 4.30 a.m. A few weeks ago I had not known that such an hour existed, but now it marked the beginning of my working day. We pulled on rather shoddy and functional work clothes – drab colours further faded at knees and elbows – and trudged up the hill in the dark, navigating by the lonely lights that peeped out from behind buildings and through leafy branches. There was no sound except the footfall of our boots and the low rustle of the trees in the gentle breeze.

We reached the communal kitchen and exchanged grunts of recognition with our fellow volunteers. We each grabbed a brown paper bag, hastily stuffing it with some bread, an egg and a tomato, in anticipation of our breakfast stop in two hours' time. Then we crammed ourselves into the back of an old van which had had its front axle removed to convert it into a makeshift trailer. The stuttering engine of the tractor broke the silence of the dawn, and we eased off down the muddy track that wound its way between expanses of brown furrows. As we bumped along, the smooth stillness of the unbroken puddles on either side, full from the previous day's rain, reflected the growing light in the east ahead of us. Though my body still longed for the warmth of my bed, this was the moment when my spirit came alive.

Peering out of the glassless windows, I could see across the flatness of the valley, with its freshly ploughed fields and ordered lines of cypresses enclosing groves of citrus trees. On every side were the rounded hills of lower Galilee, strewn with rocks and boulders – the kind of satisfying roundness found in every child's picture book. And as we made our slow and sleepy journey, in my mind's eye I could see Jesus, perhaps with his co-workers, making his own early morning journey to seek the 'calm of hills above', as John Greenleaf Whittier put it:

> Where Jesus knelt to share with thee
> The silence of eternity,
> Interpreted by love.

Later in the morning, we sat at a rickety wooden table drinking thick Turkish coffee, peeling freshly picked grapefruit and enjoying our paper bag provisions, while the dew which had soaked our clothes evaporated from the trees around us. And I could again see Jesus and his disciples on the hill top – this time surrounded by the crowds who were seated in rows in this sort of inverted auditorium in the growing heat of the Mediterranean day.

As we repeated our journey to the citrus groves of the kibbutz day by day, I found that my reading of the Bible and my praying began to change. The past had broken into the present in a way I had not experienced before. Reading the stories of Jesus in the New Testament had once been a rather vague and random exercise of the imagination; now it became a vivid encounter in places I knew. The reality of prayer pressed home to me as I remembered seeing the places where Jesus had prayed.

In today's world, we are so preoccupied with our immediate concerns that we have become trapped in the poverty of the present moment. We desperately need to experience this breaking through of the past into the present – and not just the past of the biblical narrative. Since then there have been 2,000 years of faithful (and not so faithful) journeying by those who have gone before. Their legacy to us is a rich understanding of what it means to encounter God by word and Spirit, to struggle in prayer, to look forward to the coming of God's kingdom in all its fullness – in short, what it means to build one's spiritual life.

DISCOVERING DEPTH

We desperately need this wisdom, for at least three reasons. First, we live in a culture that has lost its sense of discipline and structure. We have lost many of our corporate disciplines and shared patterns of life – any day of the year is good for shopping, Sunday is no longer special, and even the shared daily rhythm of life is being left behind in the journey towards a 24-hour society. We have lost an understanding of personal discipline; eating disorders and obesity, even among the very young, are on the rise as we struggle to control what we put into our bodies. We are forgetting the disciplines of relating to one another, manifested in the extremes of the latest 'rage' (road rage, air rage, and so on), but also in the profound anxiety many new parents face in raising their children. The wealth of inherited wisdom has been lost in the shifting sands of the arguments of 'experts', and this has left us with an empty uncertainty. In the absence of natural disciplines, ever-widening areas of life have to be regulated. Patterns of trust and mutual understanding have been replaced by legislation and bureaucracy in education, medicine and politics.

Second, we have become obsessed with the present, and have developed a love-hate relationship with the past. Fascination with the past is evidenced by the welter of television programmes on some aspect of history. Yet disdain for the past is continually fed by political calls for 'more change, faster reform'. It seems impossible to imagine an area of public life where those in office might say out loud, 'Actually, they used to do it better than we do now' (though plenty of people whisper it in private). Can it really be true that we are so much wiser than our predecessors? If this is so, why do we seem to have even more insuperable problems? Why is our society marked by more crime and violence, less trust, more suicide and less hope? And why is the Church in decline like never before?

Third, we seem to have little hope for the future. This is partly a function of material wealth – when we have all we want early in our lives, what is there to hope for? But it is also a sign of failure of imagination. Many cannot imagine a better world; there appears to be no alternative to what we have now. It is all so inevitable.

THE DESERT OF THE IMMEDIATE

The decade in which I was born, the 1960s, was seen as a time when the stultifying constraints of the traditional ways of doing things were thrown off. No doubt some of these traditions were oppressive and deserved to be questioned, but along with these, all sorts of accepted ways of living and behaving were also jettisoned. Alongside the sexual revolution, respect for authority figures and institutions, and the ways of life they represented, were pushed aside. We are still feeling the effects of these changes – perhaps more powerfully than ever. The people who questioned traditional values in the 1960s had themselves been brought up in them. Their children might have been raised without believing these values, but they could still see them in their parents' (and grandparents') lives. But now these children have become parents themselves, and many search in vain for a framework of values in which to raise their children.

More than 20 years ago, Richard Foster wrote a book entitled *Celebration of Discipline*, and if that title sounded strange then, it seems almost incomprehensible now. At the beginning of the book he comments, 'Superficiality is the curse of our age,' and that is more true now than ever. When we lack discipline, we lack depth. And when we lack depth, we find it impossible to cope with the increasing pressures of contemporary life. When we cannot draw on the wisdom of the past, we have to tackle each problem we face from scratch – and there are too many of them.

Discovering something of our Christian heritage is therefore enormously refreshing. In the desert of the immediate, we stumble across an oasis of discipline and structure. In our undisciplined world, these disciplines are surprisingly welcome. It is often suggested that the future of church lies in mid-week meetings, as the traditional pattern of Sundays has been lost. Yet I have recently noticed how people coming to church for the first time – or coming back after many years' absence – are drawn to the rhythm of making Sunday special again. When I spoke to our young people's group about developing a 'rule of life' (see Chapter 4), they were amazed to discover that such thinking existed and were very much attracted to it. When we have been starved of the nourishment of such wisdom, it is only when we encounter it that we realize how hungry we have become.

On one occasion in the Gospels, Jesus sees the crowds coming to him and sees that they are like 'sheep without a shepherd' (Matthew 9:36). The phrase comes, as do so many in the New Testament, from the Old Testament. Moses warned that this is what would happen if there was a failure of leadership (see Numbers 27:17), and the phrase is picked up precisely as a criticism of Israel's religious leaders in the prophets (see Ezekiel 34:8f.). What is Jesus' response? Having compassion, Matthew tells us, he commissions and sends out the Twelve for pastoral ministry, deliverance and healing as signs of the kingdom coming among them (see Matthew 10).

By contrast, Mark records Jesus making this observation about the crowds as he and his disciples come back to them after a time away by themselves (Mark 6:34) – and Mark also notes something distinctive about Jesus' response. As he saw the crowd helpless, in his compassion he 'began teaching them many things'. Jesus' answer to the needs of the crowd was not simply to offer healing, but to offer them new understanding.

SAFE DWELLING PLACES OF UNDERSTANDING

Jesus talks of himself in John's Gospel as the 'good shepherd' who is the 'gate for the sheep' (John 10:7,11). A key job for the first-century shepherd would have been to lead his sheep to a safe place at night. Ideally this would have been a pen formed by a drystone wall, usually circular, with a gap in it through which the sheep passed. Thorns round the top of the wall prevented animals or people climbing over, and the shepherd himself would have slept across the entrance to stop anyone or anything coming in that way. In teaching the people about the love of the Father and the coming of the kingdom, Jesus was providing just such a safe dwelling place – a dwelling place of understanding.

Many Christians today live in flapping tents of understanding: they have little grasp of the breadth and depth of what God has in store for them, because they are ignorant of the riches of Scripture and the riches of spiritual practice from the saints down the ages. As a result they are easily blown about by the winds of hardship or frustration; the thieves of doubt and wrong belief come in and steal away hope.

The idea of a dwelling place, or building, is again linked with the growth of our understanding in Paul's discussion of spiritual gifts. He groups gifts of teaching, revelation, knowledge and prophecy together as those that 'build up' the people of God (1 Corinthians 14:1-6). The word he uses, *oikodome*, literally means the erection of a household dwelling. The English word 'edify', used here in some translations, comes from the same root as the word 'edifice', a building. These are gifts that help to provide safe dwelling places of understanding for the household of God, and so we are to value them.

The notion of dwelling place recurs elsewhere in Paul's writings in a personal sense. He likens our mortal bodies to mere 'tents' in comparison with our resurrection bodies, our 'heavenly dwelling' (2 Corinthians 5:1-4; see also 2 Peter 1:13). In doing this he is reminding us that all our efforts at understanding the spiritual life are but a preparation for what is to come.

THE FRAGILE PRESENCE

Paul's use of the imagery of tents was perhaps suggested by his own trade as a tent-maker (see Acts 18:3), but the idea has a long pedigree. The people of Israel were tent-dwellers, both as the family of Abraham and hundreds of years later as the pilgrim people on their wanderings to the Promised Land. The particulars of their situation shed light on a universal truth of human existence – that we are travellers on a journey, and even the most permanent thing we make or do is temporary in the light of eternity. It was a truth God's people could not miss in the desert. As they were confronted with their true nature – vulnerable, mobile and dependent day by day on God's blessing – so their relationship with him was at its most real and intimate. But it was a truth too easily forgotten in their settled existence in the land as the generations passed. Later prophets look back on the time in the desert not just as one of testing and temptation, but also as one of the moments of truest relating to God (see Hosea 2:14; 11:1-4). It is into the reality of their vulnerability that God enters by initiating a covenant relationship with his people. As they dwell in tents, so does he – in the Tent of Meeting, so carefully described in Exodus, Leviticus and Numbers.

God enters into the fragility of human existence in order to establish relationship. This is the pattern of his dealings with humanity, and it reaches its fullest expression in the incarnation. In his Gospel, John uses precisely this language of tent-dwelling to describe the life of the Word made flesh: he 'made his dwelling among us ... full of grace and truth' (John 1:14). 'Made his dwelling' means, literally, 'pitched his tent'. In the fragile and temporary tents of our earthly existence, God himself comes and lives in a tent like ours.

This tent-dwelling is not just a feature of God's earthly life in the person of Jesus. Remarkably, the same language is used by the John of Revelation to depict the future glory of the new Jerusalem. 'See, the home of God is among mortals. He will dwell with them ...' (Revelation 21:3 NRSV). Again, 'home' is 'tent' and to 'dwell' is to 'pitch his tent'. God's stooping to conquer by love marks his eternal relating to redeemed humanity. It is as if the fragility of personal relationship somehow co-exists alongside the certainties of the new heaven and new earth; the finality of judgement and salvation do not sweep away the need for the vulnerability and risk-taking of personal encounter.

My hope and my prayer is that in the chapters that follow you will find resources that offer wisdom, discipline and depth. I pray that the past of Scripture and Christian tradition will become refreshingly real in your present, that you will find yourself built up, that in amongst your feelings of fragility you will discover a safe dwelling place of understanding as you spend time in the presence of the Good Shepherd. And I pray that as a result God will open to you a new sense of hope for the future.

HOW TO USE THIS BOOK

The chapters of this book were originally written as booklets in the Grove Spirituality series. For the most part each author wrote with one eye on what had been written earlier in the series, but without necessarily assuming knowledge of previous titles. So although each chapter is distinct, they all fit together rather like pieces of a jigsaw. It is therefore possible to take any one chapter and read it on its own – as well as seeing where it fits in the wider picture. The only possible exception to this is Chapter 1: as an overview of prayer it is a good place to start, and it will provide a framework within which the ideas of subsequent chapters fit.

Because they were written as short booklets, the chapters also contain a lot of information and are therefore excellent resources. The earliest were written nearly 20 years ago; I have lived with some of them since they were first written and I continue to return to their wisdom, their ideas and their imagery. They can be used in a number of different ways.

For individual study

The most obvious way to use these chapters is to read them by yourself. As you do so, you may like to make a note to yourself of anything that is new, that strikes you as strange or interesting, that challenges your present way of doing things. Perhaps the most important thing you could note down is what you are now going to do differently. What new practice are you going to incorporate into your devotional life? What can you use that will enable you and your household to walk more closely with God?

For group study or teaching

This is how many of these chapters started life – as teaching sessions or courses originally put on by the authors. So why not use them like this? Many of the chapters contain material that suggests individual or group exercises. For example, the section on meditative prayer in Chapter 1 gives some verses to meditate on, and you could quite easily do this in a group. Chapter 4 offers a framework for developing a 'rule of life'. After a suitable introduction, members of a group could begin to work on this together, helping each other to discover appropriate patterns of living. Or you may like to spend time together writing your own spiritual autobiographies after looking at the examples from Chapter 7. If you are not involved in leading a group in your church (such as a home group), you could suggest this to someone who is. There is no need for anyone to feel embarrassed about using someone else's teaching material; after all, most of the chapters are borrowing wisdom from saints who have gone before!

As material for a service of worship

I once used Chapter 2 to lead a service based on the Psalms. All the hymns and songs we sang were based on different psalms, and the material in the chapter provided readings, reflections and teaching scattered throughout the service in place of a sermon. Why not have a service using teaching from the English mystics, with complementary Bible readings? Or one that explores the place of silence in Scripture and in our lives? Or a whole service on the theme of forgiveness and how it works? There are endless creative possibilities.

My time on a kibbutz in Israel was something of an adventure. It was the first time I had travelled alone. I was going to a place where people spoke a different language, had different customs and ate different food. The climate was different, and the work was demanding. It required of me courage, persistence and determination. At times it was very hard going. And yet it was a fantastic adventure – an adventure of discovery and an adventure of *self*-discovery. If you take the chapters that follow seriously, you too will embark on a journey into what may feel like a foreign country, and at times it will demand courage and perseverance. But it will also become an adventure of discovery – about yourself, about the world, and about God.

PART 1

PRAYER

CREATIVE PRAYER

Jane Keiller

Why is it that, for many Christians, the practice of prayer seems to be so difficult? We do not want to deny, of course, that prayer is the most important dimension of the Christian life, but there is undoubtedly a blatant 'contrast between the great support for the idea of prayer and the lack of support for the practice of it'.[1]

There are at least three identifiable factors underlying the problem. The first and most basic of these revolves around the individual's wish to pray, or lack of it. The Prayer Book collect for the third Sunday after Trinity speaks of 'an hearty desire to pray'. Perhaps the first step for many of us is to admit that it is easier to go to a meeting or to clean the house than to be alone with God.

Second, the harassment of our daily lives further compounds the problem. Western civilization applauds the activist. It is good to be busy, and thus a successful church is seen to be one that provides plenty of events for every age group. All too soon we discover that we no longer step back to rest, to reflect upon what lies behind our ceaseless activity, and to pray.

But what do we do when we finally manage to stop still? The tremendous breadth of classical literature on prayer can be somewhat daunting, and we are left with the third factor: where do we begin?

To lay a foundation for building our spiritual worlds, this chapter aims to encourage those who feel dissatisfied with the present state of their prayer life. It is for those who would like to be able to say with Frederick Faber, 'Only to sit and think of God, Oh what a joy it is!' but who feel that at present such sentiments are indeed remote.

THE DESIRE TO PRAY

> O God, the Triune God, I want Thee: I long to be filled with longing: I thirst to be made more thirsty still.[2]

For years I felt guilty that my prayer life was not 'good enough'. I searched fruitlessly amongst other people's techniques and devotional patterns in an attempt to discover some method that would instantly transform me into a woman of prayer. What a relief it was to realize that prayer is God's gift to us, that it is initiated in heaven and not on earth. 'No-one can come to me,' said Jesus, 'unless the Father ... draws him' (John 6:44). It is the Holy Spirit who enables our hearts to cry out, 'Abba! Father!' And so he can be asked to teach us to pray, to give us the desire to pray, or even to give us the desire to want to pray.

Perhaps one of the most fundamental hindrances to this desire is the idea that prayer is simply something Christians 'do'. This cultivates an attitude of duty, turning prayer into a burden. If it is seen as communication, however, as the response of the beloved to the lover, the concept of prayer is transformed. If God has made each one of us to respond to himself, it follows that there must be a means of communication that is individually appropriate. Moreover, one can assume that this will change and develop with the years and with circumstances.

Scripture makes it clear that God intends us, wants us, to know himself (see John 17:3). This process of knowing, of developing the relationship, is carried out by means of our minds, our wills and our emotions. Jesus himself ratified the command to 'Love the Lord your God with all your heart and with all your soul and with all your strength and with all your mind' (Luke 10:27). A deeply satisfying human relationship is more than simply communication between two minds. Should we really be surprised that this is also the case in the human-divine relationship? There are few pursuits more creative than that of developing a friendship; for many Christians the discovery that this is true also for their relationship with God is both exciting and liberating.

Scripture encourages us to describe our knowledge and communication with God in terms of human knowledge and communication. 'Taste and see that the LORD is good,' urges the psalmist (Psalm 34:8). 'Do you not know? Have you not heard?' God asks Israel (Isaiah 40:21). These and other such verses point to a spiritual counterpart to those physical faculties (of taste, sight, hearing, and so on) with which we comprehend the physical world. It is, however, only God the Holy Spirit who can quicken these faculties latent within us. As we have already seen, it is he who gives us the desire to pray, and he who gives us all we need to satisfy that desire.

Nevertheless, having said that prayer is God's gift of grace and love, the gift must be received, the grace appreciated, and the love responded to. The desire to pray and the capacity to do it 'is the gift which they receive who seek the Lord with love and singleness of vision'.[3] It is possible to 'cultivate' the gift of inward awareness.

Besides the joy of recognizing that God is offering us the inestimable privilege of his love and friendship, there are at least two other factors which seem to be fundamental to a life of prayer.

A recognition that prayer changes us

'The prayer of a righteous man is powerful and effective' (James 5:16). A belief in the underlying value of prayer as the most important factor in an individual's walk with God is a vital stimulus to the desire to pray. It is often slow and painful for the truth to penetrate that there is nothing in the way of learning, gifts or hard work which can make up for a lack of prayer.

Many who visit the late Mother Teresa's Missionaries of Charity are surprised that every lunchtime they leave their life-sustaining work in the dispensaries and in the home for the dying. Why go back so soon? They go back to pray. They have learnt that to work without prayer is to achieve only what is humanly possible, and their desire is to be involved in divine possibilities. It was the same desire that caused Charles Simeon to pray from 4 to 8 a.m. and John Wesley from 4 to 6 a.m. Luther's saying on this subject – that he had so much to do he could not manage without spending three hours each day in prayer – is legendary.

There is a danger that those of us who find prayer difficult may be overwhelmed by even the attempt at such daily marathons.

Their challenge may lead to a type of piety where prayer is no longer 'an expression of faith in God's grace, but a monument erected to attract his attention'.[4] It is a danger worth risking. There seems to be no doubt at all that those men and women who have most illustrated Jesus Christ in their character, who have most affected the world for the extension of his kingdom, have 'spent so much time with God as to make it a notable feature in their lives'.[5] As we read their biographies and journals, it soon becomes apparent that their prayer was no attention-attracting exercise; it was the delight of their hearts.

A knowledge that prayer increases the desire to pray

Paul's assertion that 'we, who with unveiled faces all reflect the Lord's glory, are being transformed into his likeness with ever-increasing glory' (2 Corinthians 3:18) presupposes that we are taking time to gaze upon the Lord, that it is something we delight to do, and that it is a continuing and ever-increasing process. It is this ability to gaze in wonder that is the transforming agent of an individual and of his or her walk with God.

We come back to the gift of the relationship extended to us, for it is seeing and loving which moves us to a deeper level of spiritual experience. This is why it is not so much a question of form and pattern, but a learning to love. 'The great of the kingdom have been those who loved God more than others did,'[6] and who loved sufficiently to want to do something about it, to organize their lives in such a way that prayer could become 'a notable feature'.

FINDING SPACE

The Gospels do not provide us with a detailed description of Jesus' prayer life, but they do make clear the fact that he chose to retreat from the crowds on a number of occasions. It was in the desert that he was prepared for active ministry (see Mark 1:12), and there he found a place of quiet communication with his Father throughout the following three years (see Mark 6:46). Before major decisions, such as the calling of the Twelve (see Luke 6:12), he was in the hills all night, and after an extremely busy day he was found early next morning praying in a solitary place (see Mark 1:35). If

Jesus, the Son of God, needed 'desert space' to be with the Father, we may safely assume that we do too. We may be tempted to think it was easier for Jesus because of who he was, but there is no reason for believing that his divinity helped him to get up in the morning! Jesus knew what it was to be very tired.

The concept of such space was very much the basis of the spirituality of the Desert Fathers and Mothers. Their lifestyle and teaching may sound somewhat extreme to twenty-first-century Christianity, but they did learn the lesson that 'solitude is the furnace of transformation',[7] that this is where the manipulative powers of society can be shed and where the heart can meet with the Risen Christ. 'Flee, be silent, pray' was the command given to Father Arsenius,[8] and various prayerful people have attempted to incorporate 'desert space' into modern-day living.

The desert of solitude

'To create a desert means to seek solitude,'[9] writes Carlo Carretto, one of the Little Brothers of Charles de Foucauld, who has himself spent many years in the Sahara learning to pray. The setting aside of space to be with God alone will involve different things for each one of us. As we will see, it does not necessarily require a geographical spot, but what may be described as a 'desert state of mind and heart' is usually achieved through making physical space a part of personal discipline.

Catherine de Hueck Doherty develops this theme using the Russian concept of *poustinia*.[10] *Poustinia* means 'desert', but it can also refer to a hermitage. Russian *poustiniks* are those who find a truly isolated place, and then spend their lives seeking God in solitude, silence and prayer. *Poustinia*, as Doherty has interpreted the concept in Ontario, 'is simply that secret room the Lord has told us of, where the Father will reward us with himself in secret, if we only go there in faith'.[11] Individuals are encouraged to enter 'physical solitude' by spending 24, 36 or 48 hours in their chosen place. It may mean going away from one's home or finding a room within it. There is a Bible to read, bread to eat and tea, coffee or water to drink. There are no set rules for using this 'space', but *poustiniks* are encouraged to walk if they feel like it, to sleep, to read the Scriptures and to open their hearts to God, whose Son is the living Word and who longs to reveal himself to us.

It is here that the importance of silence emerges. The witness of those who have made it their business to spend time silently in the 'desert' seems to be the ability to have within themselves 'an infinite space into which anyone could be invited'.[12] It is as if the physical solitude and silence becomes a tangible part of the individual as he or she returns to the busyness and clamouring demands of daily living. 'Desert space', in the sense of being physically apart in a *poustinia* or other place of retreat, seems to be the foundation for the growth of inner silence and solitude which no longer requires a geographical spot. It is from such inner space that the heart is released to reach out in love to all around. Here lies the secret of those extraordinary people who never seem flustered; who, no matter how busy they are, always have time; who can go on and on absorbing pain and giving love – 'for a silent heart is a loving heart, and a loving heart is a hospice to the world'.[13] 'Desert space', then, is not an escape from the world, for it immediately sends the praying person back to love and to work amongst those men, women and children whom Jesus died to save.

The search for silence

In recent years monasteries and convents have become increasingly popular, amongst clergy and laity alike, as places where individuals or small groups can go in search of silence.[14] Indeed, a few days once a year may prove easier to find than a short space every day.

The pressures of a busy life tend to mean that a regular time for prayer is the first to disappear from the daily programme. We need to be realistic in our attempts to establish a specific time of prayer. If we fix a space to begin with which is on the shorter side, we are far less likely to fail. Five minutes' prayer no matter what happens is a good deal more satisfactory than any number of good intentions to pray for longer periods of time which, if not kept, only lead to a sense of failure, frustration and guilt. There really is no alternative to finding a time for daily prayer; if we begin realistically, the time will grow quite naturally as the relationship deepens.

Finding time is never easy and we may need to look ruthlessly at our daily routine. Our own 'natural clocks' will have something to say; for some people the early morning is less than useless. It is advisable to avoid family 'pressure times'. We may need to question our motives if we choose the moment when the children require maximum attention to disappear to a 'quiet place'! It can also be harmful to a marriage if one partner insists on rising an hour earlier than the other. Nonetheless, an Indian friend of mine recalls with great pleasure that her mother was always the first up in the household and the children would wake to find her praying at their bedside. Some mothers find that the best time is at the beginning of the day, once everyone else has left the house. Men and women who go out to work, particularly those who commute or for some other reason leave the house early, may feel the need to be somewhat more flexible in finding a suitable time. For those who are unmarried the early morning is perhaps the first place to look, for there is far less chance of disturbance from the telephone or doorbell. Whether or not one is able to claim the earliest part of the day for prayer, it is still possible to learn to turn one's thoughts towards God on waking. Jack Winslow's first words each day were 'Good morning, Lord!' – a simple prayer and yet symptomatic of a life focused on God, open to his voice and desiring to spend that day in his presence.

Those who meet with God in solitude and silence at specific times soon find that daily living can be transformed, for that silence can be taken to work and found in the office, the church, the classroom, the meeting. I have been greatly helped by the idea of 'little solitudes', 'odd desert places' which are sprinkled throughout every day. Sometimes these can be consciously built in. Many people have solitude while travelling to work, and this can be especially easy if one drives alone and makes the decision to switch off the radio. Sometimes solitude can be salvaged by choosing to walk part of a journey, getting off the bus or train a stop earlier than necessary, or by cycling. Those at home may find a time of solitude in certain tasks – the ironing or the mending, for example. 'These "little solitudes" are often right behind a door which we can open, or in a little corner where we can stop to look at a tree ...'[15]

It is here that the question of loving God becomes so important. A man or woman 'in love' does not stop to ask whether there is time to think of the beloved; nor is there any reason why expressions of love for God cannot become a regular and natural part of an individual's praying day. A heart that loves God can learn to turn even mundane tasks into an intrinsic part of the walk with God.

The sacrament of the present moment

Many of those who have been responsible for teaching others to pray have stressed the powerful reality of allowing God to meet with us wherever we are and whatever we are doing. Jean-Pierre de Caussade, a Jesuit priest (1675-1751), described such an approach to life as 'the sacrament of the present moment'.[16] Interestingly, he described the present moment as 'a desert in which simple souls see and rejoice only in God, being solely concerned to do what He asks us'.[17] The desert of each 'now' is grasped as the individual realizes that God is indeed everywhere; he is at every moment available and is particularly easily received in all that is lowly and simple. The great joy of discovering God in ordinary things is that one is released from the pressure to account for the use of one's time. The earnest desire to love God in everything, to respond to his will for us, means that we are allowing him to make us instruments of his purpose. Such teaching seems to me to have far-reaching implications in our present society, where high unemployment has made the question 'What do you do?' in many cases inappropriate.

Such living requires patience, for it can only spring from a loving heart and, as in all relationships, such love takes time to grow. Yet while it remains true that prayer is a gift to us, the finding of space, the setting aside of time and our willingness to use odd moments are all indications of the degree of earnestness with which we seek that gift.

PLACE AND POSTURE

Accounts of the devotional lives of Christians down the centuries seem to indicate that wandering thoughts and lack of concentration are the major problems for those seeking after God. Prayer can, of course, be totally absorbing, but even those whom one might term 'professionals' in the monastic orders write of their continual battle to focus on God. It is for this reason that an important part of learning to pray involves putting ourselves physically and psychologically in a position which will most facilitate concentration. Both place and posture can help or hinder the proceedings. My hope is that some of the following suggestions may help some people. If something does not help, please simply accept that, rather than feeling that it ought to be useful to you or it is not useful to anyone.

Place

The divine attribute of omnipresence means quite obviously that there is no place where God is not. In terms of distance, we cannot speak of being nearer to or further from God. Yet why is it that people everywhere do not express their knowledge of the divine presence? A. W. Tozer suggests that the Presence and the manifestation of the Presence are not the same and that, although God is here whether we are aware of him or not, he is manifest only when we are aware of his presence.[18] For most of us this will require a place where distraction of eyes and ears are at a minimum, or where there is a conscious seeking after God through the use of our senses.

An example of the latter would be to go for a walk with the explicit intention of turning the heart and mind towards God. This can be of special value in times of stress when we may find staying still difficult. The walk does not need to be along a river bank, seashore or country lane in order to speak to us of our Creator. A dandelion poking up between paving stones, the sound of rain on an umbrella, crowds of people milling along a street – any or all may prove to be 'triggers' that will focus our hearts towards God. An eye attuned to God's Presence in his world will learn to see his glory in new ways and unexpected places, so that indeed, in George Wade Robinson's words, 'Heaven above is softer blue, Earth around is sweeter green.'

Most people, however, want a place indoors for their regular time of prayer. In a busy household this is easier said than done. Richard Foster writes of a family who have a prayer chair, and everyone knows that an individual sitting there does not want to be disturbed.[19] The repeated use of the same place has the advantage not only that others refrain from coming to us, but also that we ourselves are in 'the place where we pray'. In times of darkness, dryness or sheer exhaustion, the simple act of putting ourselves in this place can be the act of self-offering necessary for the nearness of God's presence to be made manifest to us.

Susannah Wesley, with 19 active children including John and Charles, managed an hour of daily devotions in spite of the fact that she had no specific place. Her secret was to pull her apron over her face whenever she wished to pray. Every child knew that she was not to be disturbed when her head was covered!

Wherever we choose to pray, it is a good idea not to be facing a pile of unwritten letters or anything else that will serve only to remind us of all the jobs we have not finished. If the place where we pray is at least relatively tidy, we are less likely to be distracted. Some people find a position by a window helpful, although this depends on the view, and whether our curiosity concerning the people in the house opposite is greater than our ability to concentrate on God.

It is worth experimenting in order to find the place where we will be least distracted and which we personally find most conducive to prayerful attention. Place is, of course, closely dependent on the time when we pray. Those who leave home very early or who want to pray later on will need to find some other place. We have already considered the use of a car or a bicycle; others may take the opportunity to enter a church during a lunch hour or on the way home. Wherever we choose, I suspect that it is best to avoid our beds! However good our intentions and however hard we struggle, the battle with sleep is almost inevitably a losing one.

Posture

'The important thing is that we should realize that we are little and must help ourselves in little ways.'[20] The posture we adopt for prayer may seem to be unimportant, but if we are relaxed and comfortable (but not so comfortable that we are likely to doze off) we discover that prayer becomes much easier. There are biblical precedents for sitting (Luke 10:39), standing (Luke 18:11), kneeling (Psalm 95:6), lying prostrate (Ezekiel 1:28) and even moving around (2 Samuel 6:14). Many people appreciate the use of a prayer stool or small cushion to take the weight off the calves and heels while kneeling.[21] As with place, it is worth experimenting with posture. Sometimes it can be beneficial to adopt different positions for different types of prayer or circumstances. For example, lying prostrate on the floor may be appropriate for a time of confession, while standing may help to ward off tiredness. Some of us have lost our nerve about the intrinsic validity of praying with our bodies and tend rather to dump them as a more-or-less living sacrifice. Paul tells us to present them (Romans 12:1)!

There is evidence to indicate that early Christians were sometimes extremely energetic. When Johannan of Ephesus was staying in a certain Syrian monastery he heard a tremendous noise from the room next door all night, 'as if there were three workmen beating hammers on the floor'.[22] It was the monk who lived there prostrating himself by first throwing his hands on the floor, then his knees, and finally his head. If this sounds a little too much, a simple movement of the hands or bowing of the head may be a useful exercise. Many people find that the combination of a simple prayer and an action adds a new dimension to the Father-child relationship. A missionary, imprisoned for he knew not how long, found that by cupping his hands together each morning it was easier for him to pray, 'Lord, may I receive everything that comes to me today as from your hands.' Even if we feel far too self-conscious to move about very much, it is the experience of an increasing number of Christians that a single tentative action can sometimes express the desires and thoughts of our hearts in a way that is impossible for words alone. Moreover, the position we adopt in prayer says much about our inward attitude.

Space, place and posture all provide us with 'little helps' to quieten ourselves as we prepare to come before God in prayer. But where do we go from here? Amongst evangelicals there has long been a reticence about thinking creatively about the devotional life. Although many types of prayer are recognized, intercession has often been stressed to the neglect of other types. During recent years, however, there has been a growing desire to draw from a wider circle of traditions in the search for a closer walk with God.

> I take my help where I find it and set my heart to graze where the pastures are greenest. Only one stipulation do I make: my teacher must know God, as Carlyle said, 'otherwise than by hearsay', and Christ must be all in all to him.[23]

And so, with that proviso, let us consider three types of prayer – meditative, contemplative and vocal.

MEDITATIVE PRAYER

The primary aim of meditative prayer is to draw the praying person nearer to God in love. Meditative prayer is a means of opening ourselves to the concrete expression God himself has given us, particularly through his word. The meditative prayer of the Christian has nothing to do with transcendental meditation. The aim of the latter is self-awareness rather than God-awareness, and there is a vast difference between the two.[24]

The Bible speaks many times of the joys and benefits of meditation. We are told in Genesis 24:63 that Isaac 'went out to the field one evening to meditate'. The Lord commanded Joshua to 'meditate on [the Book of the Law] day and night' (Joshua 1:8). In a number of his teachings Jesus asked his followers to 'consider' (e.g. Luke 12:27), and Paul bade the Philippians 'think about' those things that are true (Philippians 4:8).

The Psalms make frequent reference to this type of prayer, and they provide us with three main topics for meditation:

- The law or decrees of God (Psalm 1:2; 119:15, 23, 48, 78, 97, 99)
- The qualities of God (Psalm 48:9; 119:148)
- The deeds or works of God (Psalm 77:12; 119:27; 143:5; 145:5)

Scripture therefore provides us with vast resources for meditative prayer. This may involve immersing ourselves in a situation covering a substantial passage (an incident from a Gospel, for example), or it may mean taking one verse or phrase. Meditation on God's deeds may be encouraged by the use of some aspects of his creation – the sky at night, or some natural object such as a tree or flower. It may involve a conscious remembering of the deeds of God in our own life. All these can lead to a more intimate knowledge of the Lord and his ways. Such prayer does involve discipline of mind and will, and it is expected to lead to some kind of response on the part of the one meditating – perhaps wonder, love and praise; perhaps a deeper sense of unworthiness and more vivid recognition of the need for forgiveness; perhaps intercession; perhaps a practical response in the form of a letter written or a visit made.

The prayer of one word

A degree of determination is required. The Desert Fathers knew well the problems of distraction. 'The devil of the noonday sun' is their description of the feeling of listlessness in prayer. It causes boredom and apathy, an inability to train and to remain disciplined, because the praying person has given him- or herself over to feelings – a 'demon' no doubt familiar to most of us. We have considered already how we can begin to combat this by careful use of place and posture. It seems, however, that those early seekers after God found that they were helped by the use of 'monologistic' prayer – prayer of one word or thought – and the main concentration was on the name of Jesus. The idea behind this comes from Paul's invocation of his name (e.g. 1 Corinthians 1:10; 6:11; Philippians 2:10). It may well be that what has become known as the Jesus Prayer developed in the desert of Egypt. Certainly Abba Philemon, an Egyptian hermit, provides us with the first explicit reference to this prayer from some time in the sixth or seventh century.[25] The prayer 'Lord Jesus Christ, have mercy on me' aimed to combine the importance of the name of Jesus with the command to pray continually (see 1 Thessalonians 5:17; Ephesians 6:18).

This prayer has become an integral part of Orthodox Christianity and is perhaps most clearly explained in *The Way of a Pilgrim*.[26] Meditation on such a simple prayer is described as a way of moving from prayer with the mind to prayer with the heart. The repetition of words aloud and silently in the mind gradually becomes a part of the praying person's life. This may particularly be the case if it is prayed in connection with one's breathing. 'Lord Jesus Christ' might be prayed on the intake of breath, and 'have mercy on me' on the exhalation. We may be far from wanting to repeat this 6,000 times daily, as the pilgrim tells us he prayed; nevertheless, it can be an important aid to prayer preparation. This is particularly the case in its shortest forms: 'Lord', or simply 'Jesus'. The mystics of the Middle Ages referred to such preparation as 'recollection'; Richard Foster calls it 'centring down'. The prayer is explored further in Chapter 3.

Whatever type of prayer we feel suits us best can be transformed by taking a few minutes quietly resting in God's presence. Some people find it helpful to use their imagination and to picture the cross in their mind's eye; in this case the use of the Jesus Prayer would be a most appropriate 'centring down' exercise. Others may feel in need of sensing more closely the Lord's love, and can be much helped by imagining themselves seated on the Lord's knees like a small child. Here the single word 'Jesus' may become an aid to concentration. Still others may not want to imagine anything, but the repetition of 'Abba' or 'Father' may still the mind and body and prepare for a greater openness to whatever is the chosen subject for meditation. This is the time for the praying person to ask God to speak by the power of his Spirit and to remove all thoughts that are not from him. As the verse or verses of Scripture are pondered with a receptive heart, 'the Holy Spirit takes the written word and applies it as the Living Word to the inner being',[27] so that it becomes, in reality, a vital part of the one who is praying. As well as being good preparation for further prayer, it can also help us to concentrate if we wish to make use of an odd few minutes to focus on God in the middle of a busy day.

Spiritual exercises

The spiritual masters of the past have given us a number of different types of meditation. One example comes from Ignatius Loyola (1491-1556), who suggests the use of five methods in his *Spiritual Exercises*. His first, for those who are unable to read, involves choosing a subject (such as the Ten Commandments) and then speaking about it as a child with his father. In the second method, each word of a prayer (such as the Lord's Prayer) is reflected upon. The third is like the second, only set to a rhythm by saying a word between each breath. During the breath the meditator thinks of the meaning of the word, or of the person to whom he or she is speaking, or of the state of his or her own life, or of the contrast between God and him- or herself. The fourth method involves taking an instance in the life of Christ and applying each of the five senses to it – sight, hearing, smell, taste and touch. The fifth, which might be described 'Ignatian proper', requires by way of preparation that the passage of Scripture be read the night before and reflected upon. One or two points are chosen for meditation and these are then focused on immediately the next morning. Again a theme is imagined and a significant aspect of it brought to mind. The praying person asks to know, love and follow the

Lord. Memory and understanding are applied to the scene, and then finally the will, so that some action or resolve may be the response.

The methods of the seventeenth-century French masters, such as Francis de Sales (1547-1622) and those from the Oratory of St Sulpice, Paris, are quite similar in many details, but include the notion at the end of the meditation of 'the spiritual nosegay' – a thought from the meditation carried through the day.

Campbell McAlpine's *The Practice of Biblical Meditation*[28] is a useful handbook for those wanting practical advice on how to set about meditating on Scripture today. He explains the need for the individual to become still before the Lord, to pray that God might show if there is anything that is cutting that person off from himself, and then asking God to teach from his word. McAlpine stresses the importance of meditation always leading to a response of some kind, and it may well lead to intercession. He suggests four questions that can be asked at the end of a time of meditation:

- What did I learn of God today?
- What did I learn about myself?
- What did I praise him for?
- What and whom did I pray for?

Meditation is, therefore, an exercise of the mind to draw closer to God; by it we learn, if we are patient, to hear God speaking to us. And yet meditation becomes more than something we think. Psalm 19:14 speaks of the 'meditation of my heart'. The biblical meaning of 'heart' is the central organ of our life, and so prayer of the heart is prayer from the very centre of our being; as we direct ourselves towards God, our whole person is affected. This does not necessarily mean we will experience more 'feeling' in our prayers (though it may), but it will mean that our whole lives will be moulded by the prayer we are offering. The process has been likened to that of a tap dripping slowly but steadily into a dirty cup. Gradually the cup fills and is cleansed.

It is in this way that not only our minds, but also our wills and desires can be brought by God more closely under his sovereign will. This was the truth discovered by Richard Baxter (1615-91), a chaplain in Cromwell's army who was obsessed by the question 'How can I know I have saving faith?' in *The Saints' Everlasting Rest*. He claimed that regular meditation on Scripture would give assurance of mind and purpose. The method he advocated can be traced back to the sixteenth century and the teaching of Ignatius Loyola.

CONTEMPLATIVE PRAYER

Evangelicals have often been somewhat suspicious of this type of prayer, because the mystics tended to stress the passivity of the soul in contemplation. They speak of the fading away of the mind, the imagination and the knowledge of the objects of God's creation. Nonetheless, those who have had some of the most profound experiences of God during times of contemplative prayer have been those most keen to stress that an individual must never seek such experiences for their own sake. Many of them are also anxious to check everything against the truth of Scripture. The French mystical theologian Richard of St Victor (d. 1173) said, 'Every truth that the authority of Scripture does not confirm is suspect to me.'[29] John of the Cross (1542-91) was steeped in the Bible. 'If we take Scripture as our guide, we do not err,' he declared.[30] Moreover, many contemplatives have pointed to the fact that, as with meditation, a response is required on the part of the praying person. This may be a response of contrition, intercession or outward action, as well as adoration and praise.

Contemplative prayer usually flows from meditative prayer. It seems to be the common experience of those earnestly seeking to know God that they reach a point when they are aware only of the wonder of God's presence. If meditation helps us to hear God's voice, contemplation refers to sight – the gaze of the heart on the glory of God. The English mystics Richard Rolle (c.1295-1349) and Julian of Norwich (b. 1342) illustrate the emphasis on sight. Rolle speaks of the 'inner eye' contemplating the things that are above, and Mother Julian refers to her 'spiritual eye'. This idea is picked up by others from a very different theological persuasion. Francis Rous (1579-1669), an ardent Puritan, believed that there is 'something divine which is the eye of the soul which unites us to God himself when touched by his word'.

Such concepts do not seem to be so very far away from the kind of things the Wesleys advocated. Samuel Wesley's dying words to John were, 'The inward witness, son, the inward witness, that is the proof, the strongest proof of Christianity.'[31] And what is this inner eye gazing upon God if not the inward witness that is the gift of God's Holy Spirit? For John Wesley it was his contact with the Moravians that provided the spark of this inner dynamic – the spark that convinced him that justification by faith and living by faith could become inward realities rather than doctrinal concepts. He writes of 'a more extensive knowledge of things invisible, showing what eye has not seen, nor ear heard, neither could it before enter into our hearts to conceive. And all these faith shows in the clearest light, with the fullest certainty and evidence.'[32]

Certainly the things Tozer describes in *The Pursuit of God*, *The Divine Conquest* and *Knowledge of the Holy* are very reminiscent of earlier mystical writers. He writes, 'Hearts which are "fit to break" with love for the Godhead are those who have been in the Presence and have looked with opened eye upon the Majesty of the Deity.'[33] His suggestion that by means of the gaze of the 'inward eye' we should 'push in sensitive living experience into the Holy Presence'[34] will remind anyone who has read *The Cloud of Unknowing* of that unknown author's direction to allow all our distractions, all the things we have forgotten, all our worries, to be covered by a thick cloud of forgetting and look up to the peak where God involves himself in a cloud of unknowing which cannot be penetrated by our reason alone, but only by a 'sharp dart of longing love'. Tozer, like Wesley, stresses the role of the Holy Spirit in making possible the 'divine gaze'. It is when the Spirit illuminates the heart that 'a part of the man sees which never saw before: part of him knows which never knew before'.[35]

It is Tozer's contention that such an experience of God is possible for every one of his children who will seek it. However, the veil of self – self-righteousness, self-pity, self-confidence and self-sufficiency – can keep us outside God's presence. Perhaps this is what earlier mystical writers meant when they spoke of the need for everything but the desire for God to fade away.

VOCAL PRAYER

So far we have considered aspects of prayer which help us to focus on the person of God. We have examined the need to wait for God to warm our hearts; we have looked at ways of helping us to listen to his voice and to gaze in wondering love. In many cases silence and the vocalizing of words may be intermingled. Meditation begins with the focus on the word, which may be silently absorbed, but it may well also be spoken, particularly as we begin. Contemplation is more often a silent prayer, and yet this may be greatly enhanced by the occasional crying out: 'Dear Lord!'; 'Jesus!'; 'Father!'

Nonetheless, however deeply we may go into silence, there is always the need for specific vocal prayer. John Cassian went to the Desert Fathers and, although he learned much from their use of silence, he was equally convinced that we never move beyond the need for vocalized prayer. This does not mean the use of the spoken word alone, but also of song and of speaking in tongues for those who have this gift (see 1 Corinthians 12; 14). As we have seen already, silent meditation and contemplation may well lead directly into specific spoken prayers of praise, thanksgiving, confession or supplication. It may also happen the other way round, for word and silence feed each other in our prayer life, just as they do in the context of human friendship.

Praise

> Let us continually offer to God a sacrifice of praise – the fruit of lips that confess his name. (Hebrews 13:15)

This is a vital part of life, for it is God's purpose for us. As Paul writes, 'We who first hoped in Christ have been destined and appointed to live for the praise of his glory' (Ephesians 1:12, paraphrase). This is not so surprising when we read Revelation and see that worship is the activity of heaven. Learning to praise God here on earth is preparation for eternity.

The Psalms can teach us much about praising God. Forty-one of them tell us to 'sing to the Lord'. Singing is meant to move us into praise and it can be a most important aid – a favourite hymn or chorus may lift us above the immediate concerns of the day and enable us to focus on the wonder of God. Those who feel inhibited by the awful possibility of others hearing them may still be helped by reading aloud a hymn or chorus of praise, or by using some of the psalms themselves (e.g. Psalm 95:1-6; 148). These may simply be read as an expression of love and worship, or one or two stanzas may be taken and used meditatively. Some find it helpful to keep a notebook in which to make a collection of favourite psalms, songs, hymns and choruses. The addition of postcards or pictures of views and natural objects can provide further stimuli to praise. Those who commit verses from psalms of praise to memory find that they have a wonderful source of worship ready to well up from the heart. Those with less good memories may prefer to listen to recordings of sung psalms, or indeed other kinds of devotional music.

There are many people who have a gift of speaking in tongues and yet fail to use it, either because they do not know how it should be used, or because they are unable to understand its purpose. God only gives good gifts (Luke 11:13) and if he has seen fit to give tongues, one may safely assume that he intends them to be used. They may be a public gift requiring interpretation, or a private gift for the building-up of the individual, which will, of course, affect the larger body in turn. A private gift of tongues is a wonderful God-given way by which an individual may respond to the Holy Spirit, free from the constraint of temporal concerns and bodily needs. As in the case of all prayer, it 'improves with practice' and the individual cannot go wrong if he or she begins by asking for God's protection to say only that which is pleasing to him. The one who asks for understanding may find that a time of praising in a tongue leads immediately into praise in human language. 'So what shall I do? I will pray with my spirit, but I will also pray with my mind; I will sing with my spirit, but I will also sing with my mind' (1 Corinthians 14:15).

Thanksgiving

'Always giv[e] thanks to God the Father for everything.'
(Ephesians 5:20)

Thanks and praise are not synonymous, although they are closely related. Ole Hallesby provides us with a helpful differentiation: 'When we give thanks we give God glory for what he has done for us; and when we worship or give praise, we give God glory for what he is in himself.'[36] It certainly seems true that a heart that finds worship a natural activity is usually a thankful heart. The Gospels provide us with a number of examples of Jesus giving thanks to his Father (see John 11:41; Mark 8:6), and Scripture provides us with direct commands that we too should express our gratitude to God.

Specific thanksgiving as a vital element in our prayer life is something that we can cultivate. In much the same way that children learn to say 'thank you', so we can train ourselves to praise God. I heard recently of an elderly lady who had transformed her devotions with the use of a 'blessings book'. She began by jotting down her material blessings, and the list grew to include so much more – friendships, answered prayers, spiritual gifts, and so on. She soon discovered that we often have very short memories and many expressions of God's love and mercy towards us pass by with no sign of gratitude on our part.

There is a Hebrew proverb that says, 'He who eats and drinks but does not bless the Lord is a thief.' Saying grace at mealtimes is another way of training ourselves to give God the thanks due to him. Some people find this an easy and natural expression of gratitude; for others the family situation makes a spoken prayer inappropriate. There is nothing, however, to stop anyone from turning silently towards God. In this way we not only express our thanks and praise, but also acknowledge our Father's sovereign power and our dependence on him. As we begin by thanking him for physical and material blessings, so we are drawn into a closer awareness of his faithfulness. This in turn leads us on to worship and provides further encouragement to persevere in prayer for other people and concerns.

Confession

> If I had cherished sin in my heart,
> the Lord would not have listened. (Psalm 66:18)

In confession we acknowledge before God what we are, not because God needs to know, but because we need to remind ourselves. This is often the most difficult kind of prayer and there are ways we can help ourselves. Confession is often stimulated by worship, for, as Anthony Bloom has written, it is 'not the constant thought of their sins, but the vision of the holiness of God that makes saints aware of their own sinfulness'.[37] The more aware we are of God's holiness, the clearer will be the view of our own thoughts and hearts.

It can be helpful to ask for a keener conscience so that we will find it easier to know when we are doing, saying and thinking those things that God finds displeasing. It is better to make an act of confession as soon as we are aware of the need than to wait until a specific time of day or later in the week. There is, however, much to be gained from setting the time aside to examine carefully the different areas of our life and relationships, and to admit failures, weaknesses and sheer sinfulness.

It is only as we do this that we can experience the joy of forgiveness. We know that we cannot expect our devotional life to develop if we are behaving disobediently, if we are refusing to forgive others, if we are harbouring resentments or bitterness – and yet how often we need to be reminded of this. So many of us are tied up with people and incidents from the past, and we not only cripple ourselves, we also tie up others in the process. The simple act of bringing someone who has hurt us to God in prayer, forgiving him and releasing him from our judgement can have profound effects in our own lives as we become free to receive the forgiveness God offers to us. I do not understand why this should have such far-reaching ramifications. I only know that it is so.

Confession in the presence of another, as is the case with other forms of prayer, can be especially beneficial. This is not because we are unable to receive God's forgiveness by ourselves, but we do not like to admit the truth about our own nature and we may be unable to forgive ourselves. The fact that another human being has heard what we are like and still accepts us can be an enormous release. Mark Morton explores this further in Chapter 12.

Supplication

> You do not have, because you do not ask God. (James 4:2)

Supplication includes petition as we come to God with the needs and desires of our own hearts, and intercession as we bring others before him. Neither of these types of prayer involves 'twisting God's arm' or reminding him of something he has forgotten. To ask, however, indicates our desire, and it seems that there are some things that we need to want enough to request before God grants them to us. It seems also that he wants us to share in the blessing of answered prayer.

The problem when 'no' is the answer, particularly in the case of healing, and the question of discovering how we can pray 'according to his will', are beyond the scope of this chapter. Nevertheless, our ability and our desire to intercede grow with our love for God. It is as we learn to spend time in his presence that bringing others there becomes a natural response. As we grow to love and trust more fully, it becomes more natural to ask for those things which we need ourselves, and by so doing we express our dependence on our heavenly Father.

Intercession, more than any other kind of prayer, is in the most danger of becoming little more than the recitation of a shopping list. Yet Paul told the Christians in Rome, Ephesus, Philippi and Thessalonica that he remembered them in his prayers, and so we too can exercise responsibility in deciding for whom we should pray. Time spent in working out some kind of daily plan over the period of a week can be of great benefit to us as it avoids time being wasted while we worry about people and needs we might have forgotten. I have also found it helpful to stick up photographs of friends and relatives above my desk and in the kitchen as reminders for intercession.

There are occasions when we simply do not know how to pray. Such times are usually those when we find it most difficult to listen for the guidance of God's voice, and so we need as many 'aids to concentration' as possible. Holding one hand upwards as if reaching for God's hand, and holding the other out to grasp, in the imagination, the hand of the one for whom we are praying may be a helpful focus. Some people are able to see the person concerned in their mind's eye, and then simply picture them before the cross. In our ignorance and helplessness, the gift of tongues may be a particularly appropriate form of prayer; by it we pray the request without floundering for the answer.

CREATING A PATTERN OF PRAYER

At the beginning of this chapter I suggested that the life of prayer is something which grows and develops in much the same way as we long for a valued human relationship to deepen. It follows that, just as we do not always meet our friends in the same place nor speak the same words, we can work towards a prayer life which is multifaceted. When we pray, how we pray, what happens when we pray, need not be the same year in, year out. God's gift of prayer is living and will change as it changes us, but this reminds us that our Father deals with each of his children as individuals, and prayer which carries one person closer to God need not necessarily benefit another.

The important thing is that we begin where we are. 'Pray as you can and not as you can't' was the wise advice of Abbot John Chapman in his *Spiritual Letters*. We can read books about the subject, we can go on retreats, we can listen to talks and sermons, but in the end there is no alternative to getting on with it ourselves and risking mistakes and false starts. This is echoed time and again by the spiritual masters who insist that, although prayer is a gift, it is also something to be learned.

There is no reason why the learning process should be limited to individual methods of prayer; we can also experiment with the ways in which we create a pattern. Dick Eastman in *The Hour that Changes the World*[38] gives suggestions for dividing one hour into twelve separate five-minute slots. He provides a mixture of silent and vocal prayer, time for praise, thanksgiving, intercession and confession. He includes Scripture meditation and singing. Some people may prefer not to sing, but would like to meditate for longer. The plan is in no way intended to lay down rules, but it does put together a variety of types of prayer in a balanced manner. Those who feel intimidated by such a programme may wish to pray in different ways at different times throughout the day, making use of those 'little silences' referred to earlier. This can be a helpful step towards integrating our heavenly citizenship and earthly life.

Prayer does not need to be complicated; it is simply being with God. As Bishop Ramsey said, 'To be with God wondering, that is adoration. To be with God gratefully, that is thanksgiving. To be with God ashamed, that is contrition. To be with God with others on the heart, that is intercession.'[39] It is the testimony of those who have persevered in prayer that time spent in a conscious attitude of openness to God, in spite of wandering thoughts, periods of blankness and even boredom, yields the immeasurable reward: knowing the love of Christ which surpasses knowledge so that we may be filled with all the fullness of God (Ephesians 3:19).

Praise

Send forth your light and your truth,
let them guide me;
let them bring me to your holy mountain,
to the place where you dwell.
Then will I go to the altar of God,
to God, my joy and my delight.
I will praise you with the harp,
O God, my God.   PSALM 43:3-4

Ascribe to the LORD the glory due to his name;
worship the LORD in the splendour of his holiness.

PSALM 29:2

The LORD is in his holy temple;
let all the earth be silent before him.

HABAKKUK 2:20

When you exalt him, summon all your strength,
and do not grow weary, for you cannot praise him enough.

ECCLESIASTICUS 43:30 NRSV

You are worthy, our Lord and God,
to receive glory and honour and power,
for you created all things,
and by your will they were created
and have their being.   REVELATION 4:11

Thanksgiving

Every good and perfect gift is from above, coming down from
the Father of the heavenly lights, who does not change like
shifting shadows.   JAMES 1:17

I will praise you for ever for what you have done.

PSALM 52:9

I am the vine; you are the branches. If a man remains in me and I in him, he will bear much fruit; apart from me you can do nothing.　JOHN 15:5

Let the peace of Christ rule in your hearts ... And be thankful.　COLOSSIANS 3:15

Thanks be to God! He gives us the victory through our Lord Jesus Christ.　1 CORINTHIANS 15:57

Confession

My transgressions are multiplied,
O Lord, they are multiplied!
I am not worthy to look up and see the height of heaven
because of the multitude of my iniquities.

PRAYER OF MANASSEH, V. 9 NRSV

You were bought at a price. Therefore honour God with your body.　1 CORINTHIANS 6:20

Why do you call me, 'Lord, Lord,' and do not do what I say?

LUKE 6:46

I tell you that men will have to give account on the day of judgment for every careless word they have spoken.

MATTHEW 12:36

Who can discern his errors?
Forgive my hidden faults.　PSALM 19:12

As a father has compassion on his children,
so the LORD has compassion on those who fear him.

PSALM 103:13

If we confess our sins, he is faithful and just and will forgive us our sins and purify us from all unrighteousness.

1 JOHN 1:9

Intercession

> Let us then approach the throne of grace with confidence, so
> that we may receive mercy and find grace to help us in our
> time of need.   HEBREWS 4:16

> O LORD my God. Hear the cry and the prayer that your
> servant is praying.   2 CHRONICLES 6:19

> Ask and it will be given to you; seek and you will find; knock
> and the door will be opened to you.   MATTHEW 7:7

> Carry each other's burdens.   GALATIANS 6:2

> If we ask anything according to his will, he hears us.
>   1 JOHN 5:14

SUGGESTIONS FOR FURTHER READING

General

Anthony Bloom, *Living Prayer* (DLT)
Sheila Cassidy, *Prayer for Pilgrims* (Fount)
Richard Foster, *Celebration of Discipline* (Hodder and Stoughton)
Richard Foster, *Prayer* (Hodder and Stoughton)
Mark Gibbard, *Guides to Hidden Springs* (SCM)
Kenneth Leech, *True Prayer: An Introduction to Christian Spirituality*
    (Sheldon)
Richard Lovelace, *Dynamics of the Spiritual Life* (Paternoster)
Simon Tugwell, *Prayer – Volumes 1 and 2* (Veritas)
J. Neville Ward, *The Use of Praying* (Epworth)

Silence and space

Carlo Carretto, *In Search of the Beyond* (DLT); *Letters from the
    Desert* (DLT)
Jean-Pierre de Caussade, *The Sacrament of the Present Moment*
    (Fount)
Brother Lawrence, *The Practice of the Presence of God* (Hodder and
    Stoughton)

Michael Mitton, *The Wisdom to Listen* (Grove Books)
Henri Nouwen, *The Way of the Heart* (DLT)
Wendy Robinson, *Exploring Silence* (Fairacres)

Meditation and contemplation
Edmund P. Clowney, *Christian Meditation* (IVP)
R. M. French (trans.), *The Way of a Pilgrim* (SPCK)
Mark Gibbard, *Prayer and Contemplation* (Mowbrays)
Campbell McAlpine, *The Practice of Biblical Meditation* (Marshall, Morgan and Scott)
A. W. Tozer, *The Divine Conquest* (STL); *The Knowledge of the Holy* (STL); *The Pursuit of God* (STL)

Books of prayers and meditations
George Appleton, *Journey for a Soul* (Fontana)
John Baillie, *A Diary of Private Prayer* (OUP)
Brother Kenneth CGA, *Private Prayers* (Hodder and Stoughton)
Mark Link SJ, *You: Prayer For Beginners and Those Who Have Forgotten How* (Argus); *Breakaway: Twenty-Eight Steps to a More Reflective Life* (Argus)

Notes
1 Henri Nouwen, *The Way of the Heart: Desert Spirituality and Contemporary Ministry* (DLT, 1981), p. 72.
2 A. W. Tozer, *The Pursuit of God* (STL Books, 1981), p. 20.
3 Carlo Carretto, trans. Sarah Fawcett, *In Search of the Beyond* (DLT, 1975), p. 72.
4 Richard F. Lovelace, *Dynamics of Spiritual Life: An Evangelical Theology of Renewal* (Paternoster Press, 1979), p. 154.
5 E. M. Bounds, *Power Through Prayer* (Marshall, Morgan and Scott, 1970), p. 19.
6 Tozer, *The Pursuit of God*, p. 40.
7 Nouwen, *The Way of the Heart*, p. 25.
8 Benedicta Ward (trans.), *The Sayings of the Desert Fathers* (Mowbrays, 1975), p. 9.
9 Carretto, *In Search of the Beyond*, p. 19.
10 Catherine de Hueck Doherty, *Poustinia* (Fount, 1977).

11 Ibid., p. 13.

12 Nouwen, *The Way of the Heart*, p. 33.

13 Doherty, *Poustinia*, p. 21.

14 For those seeking a suitable place, see Geoffrey Gerrard, *Away from it All: A Guide to Retreat Houses and Monastic Hospitality* (Lutterworth Press, 1978).

15 Doherty, *Poustinia*, p. 22.

16 Jean-Pierre de Caussade, *Self-Abandonment to Divine Providence*; see Kitty Muggeridge (trans.), *The Sacrament of the Present Moment* (Fount, 1981).

17 Ibid., p. 25.

18 Tozer, *The Pursuit of God*, p. 64.

19 Richard Foster, *Celebration of Discipline: The Path to Spiritual Growth* (Hodder and Stoughton, 1980), p. 93.

20 Carretto, *In Search of the Beyond*, p. 95.

21 See Michael Mitton, *The Wisdom to Listen* (Grove Pastoral Series No. 5, 1981), p. 14.

22 Simon Tugwell, *Prayer: Volume 2. Prayer in Practice* (Veritas Publications, 1974), p. 29.

23 A. W. Tozer, *The Divine Conquest* (STL Books, 1979), p. 13.

24 See Edmund P. Clowney, *Christian Meditation* (IVP, 1978).

25 Urban T. Holmes, *A History of Christian Spirituality: An Analytical Introduction* (Seabury Press, 1981), p. 35.

26 R. M. French (trans.), *The Way of a Pilgrim* (SPCK, 1930).

27 Campbell McAlpine. *The Practice of Biblical Meditation* (Marshall, Morgan and Scott, 1981), p. 75.

28 Ibid.

29 Holmes, *A History of Christian Spirituality*, p. 63.

30 Ibid., p. 99.

31 John and Charles Wesley, ed. Frank Whaling, *Selected Prayers, Hymns, Journal Notes, Sermons, Letters and Treatises* (SPCK, 1981), p. 5.

32 Ibid., p. 128.

33 Tozer, *The Pursuit of God*, p. 42.

34 Ibid., p. 43.

35 Tozer, *The Divine Conquest*, p. 78.

36 Ole Hallesby, *Prayer* (IVP, 1948), p. 116.

37 Anthony Bloom, *Living Prayer* (Libra DLT, 1966), p. 11.

38 Dick Eastman, *The Hour that Changes the World* (Baker Book House, 1979).

39 Michael Ramsey, *Be Still and Know* (Fount, 1982), p. 74.

PRAYING THE PSALMS

John Goldingay

I was once in a church meeting that was discussing replacing Morning Prayer with Holy Communion as the church's main Sunday service. I allowed myself the opinion that an advantage of this would be that we would be able to get out of singing the wretched psalms, which I viewed as the most tedious element in Sunday worship. My vicar withered me with a look across the room in a way he had perfected and barked, 'One day, my boy, you will need the psalms.' He was right. Twenty-five years later the psalms are the framework of my life with God, the part of each day's reading of Scripture that is most likely to give me matters to take up with God. They are most likely to encourage me because in their agony they so often start where I may need to start in prayer, and most likely to challenge me because they move from there into a worship whose conviction and enthusiasm I long to emulate.

Nonetheless, very few people nowadays have the opportunity to use the psalms systematically in worship and to discover the way they could draw us into praise and prayer that expresses and develops our own life with God. The Church of England once expected its worship to include an average of six psalms every day, but the requirement is now very much reduced – and is very often ignored. Where the psalms are used it can be in a rigid and traditional way, and this usually puts people off them rather than winning them over.

Of course, the problem cannot be solved by legislation. If people are not convinced that the psalms express worship and prayer that they can and need to offer, forcing them to use them is no more useful than it is practicable. My concern here, then, is to point to something of what I discovered when I began to use this indispensable resource of praise and prayer.

OUR WORD TO GOD, GOD'S WORD TO US

Sometimes the beginning of a scriptural text gives us important pointers about how to read it. The books of the prophets commonly open by providing us with information about their origin in a human author (though one who brings God's revelation) speaking to a particular audience in a particular historical context – as if to say, 'You will only understand the messages that follow against this concrete historical context.' Something similar is true of the epistles, and Luke begins his Gospel by telling us his aim in writing it, while John does something similar at the end of his Gospel.

In a parallel manner, Psalm 1 introduces the Psalter as a whole by encouraging us to meditate on God's Torah, or teaching. Where is this teaching to be found? Perhaps Psalm 1 refers to the Torah, the 'Law', and implies that only those who live by this Torah can read and use the psalms correctly – which would certainly fit what the prophets have to say about the relationship between worship and life. Perhaps it hints at the idea that the psalms themselves have become a resource for teaching as well as a hymn book, God's word to us as well as ours to God. The rest of Scripture speaks *to* us, but the psalms speak *for* us, Athanasius declared. But by being *in* Scripture, the psalms speak *to* us as well. The psalms which spoke *to* God now speak *for* God, reveal God's ways, and reveal to us the kind of prayer and praise God encourages. Praise has become teaching; the Psalter has become Torah. It is even divided into five books like the Pentateuch, with doxologies like the Gloria at the end of each (see Psalms 41, 72, 89 and 106, with Psalm 150 as a doxology to the whole).

Psalm 1 invites us to be open to God's word. Psalm 150 closes off the Psalter as a whole with a summons to praise that is unique because it gives no reasons for the praise – the reasons are contained in its 149 predecessors. At the end the Psalter can content itself with 'lyrical self-abandonment'.[1] As the Psalter unfolds, the way from the obedience of Psalm 1 to the praise of Psalm 150 goes via candour about suffering (which faces the questions left unfaced by the assurances of Psalm 1) and gratitude about hope. It is a way that has Psalm 73 (combining suffering and hope in one psalm) as a halfway staging post as it journeys between these two poles.

Individual psalms also commonly begin with some introduction, though the details of the meaning of these introductions are obscure. But what they do make clear is that the psalms have a background in the context of worship (for instance, indicating how or when to sing them). In order to connect our worship with the worship of the psalms, we need to ask a question: what are the recurrent ways of speaking to God which feature in the psalms – what different types of psalm are there, and what are their internal dynamics? The answer is that the psalms reflect three recurrent ways of speaking to God.

1. Psalms of praise and worship rejoice in who God is and what God has done to redeem.
2. Psalms of lament and prayer emerge from contexts when God does not seem to be acting in a redeeming way for an individual or a people.
3. Psalms of thanksgiving or testimony confess what God has done for an individual or a community in response to such prayer.

There are other types of psalm, such as those bringing God's word to the king, but we will focus on the first three types because of their significance for our concern with praying the psalms.

THE PSALMS AS WORLD-CREATING PRAISE

In looking at the psalms' actual worship – their praise – we may begin with the single piece of Scripture that recurs most often in the worship of the Church of England (the Lord's Prayer excepted): Psalm 95, the *Venite*. Its name comes from the first word in the Latin version of the psalm.

> Come, let us cry out to Yahweh,
> let us shout to the Rock who saves us.
> Let us come before his face with thanksgiving,
> let us shout to him in psalms.
>
> (vv. 1-2, my translation)

Its beginning is rather noisier than most translations indicate (many say 'let us sing'), and in Hebrew that line contains no word for 'joy'. The word is often smuggled in to make the psalm sound more religious than it naturally does! The *Venite* begins with an invitation to a fervent, exuberant, out-loud confession that God is God. The invitation is renewed later in the psalm, in very different terms.

> Come, let us bow down prostrate,
> let us kneel before Yahweh our maker.
>
> (v. 6, my translation)

Again the translations often make the psalm more Anglican than it is. It contains no word for 'worship' – the verbs are all body-words. Having opened like a charismatic praise meeting, the psalm continues like a Muslim observance of Ramadan.

In the psalms we relate to God as whole people, and moderation is not among the psalms' vices or virtues. They deal in extremes, and invite us to join them there. They presuppose that relating to God is not a matter of slouching or sitting but of leaping and bowing. When we come before God, we do not abandon the self-expression and body language, the enthusiasm and gloom, of the pub or the sports field. Worship is a matter of shouting and weeping.

The polemic of worship

There are several reasons why shouting and bowing down are appropriate responses to God. Most importantly, 'the LORD is the great God, the great King above all gods' (v. 3). That is a more polemical statement than it sounds. 'The LORD' here stands for the name of Israel's own God, Yahweh. (This practice of avoiding God's name originated with the scribes of the Hebrew Bible; the (New) Jerusalem Bible is the only translation to use God's name 'Yahweh' where it occurs instead of this substitute formula.) Yahweh is the only being who has divine or kingly power.

The Israelites were surrounded by people who acknowledged other gods and other kings, people who said that Baal was a great god or who acknowledged Shalmanezer as the great king. In that context, to affirm that 'Yahweh is a great God and a great king' was a bold confession, an exercise in what a sociologist might call 'world creating'.[2] To declare that 'Yahweh is a great God' is a profoundly political statement; worship is not an escape from life in the world.

Indeed, when we worship we take the world with us into the presence of God, so that we can speak God's name over it. We look the world in the face, and we look the questions that trouble us or the developments that excite us in the face – and declare over them, 'Yahweh is God; Jesus is Lord.' In the power of that confession we take the world and its questions more seriously, because it carries with it the promise that they can be faced. In worship we affirm how we believe the world to be, despite what we see. We do not create this new world: it already exists as the real world, the world of God. In the light of our affirmation, we live with that conviction in the world.

The logic of submission

We cry out our praise to God, then, because God is Creator and Sovereign. We bow down in prostration because this God is our God and we are his people or flock – the Almighty Creator, the great King, is our Maker, our Shepherd. I think I would have expected the psalm's logic to work the other way round – to offer God's almightiness as grounds for reverent submission and God's shepherdly caring as grounds for enthusiastic thanksgiving. The psalm's own logic is less predictable but more profound. We glory in the fact that God is the Creator, but then kneel in reverence in the light of the fact that this Creator and Sovereign has condescended to be our Maker and Shepherd.

God's involvement with the world and with us as Creator is actually a theme that runs through the Psalter. Psalm 104 illustrates that involvement with the world particularly well. It affirms the wonder of creation, the generosity of God that creation reflects, and the lordship of its God even over the realm of darkness. It offers a variety of models for God's relationship with nature – starting it off, being the very locus of the energy and system of nature, being personally involved in the present, acting in the manner of the 'God of the gaps', bringing about calamities and disasters. Elsewhere different psalms affirm the security of a world in which the powers of darkness cannot reassert themselves (Psalm 93). Others wonder at the way the cosmos declares God's glory and at the way the mighty Creator is involved with mere human beings (Psalms 19 and 8). They testify that the God who is the Creator is the God of every-day life and therefore of my everyday experience and need. In the psalms God is giver, healer and deliverer more than lawgiver and judge. Yahweh is not just the God of the past (history) and the God of the future (eschatology), but also the God of the present, of worship and everyday life.

PRAISE AND COMMITMENT

The first part of the *Venite* is a hymn of praise, comprised of an invitation to worship and the reasons for worship – the two features of a hymn of praise in the Psalter. The *Jubilate*, Psalm 100, has the same two features, and even the same double structure – invitation, reasons, renewed invitation, further reasons. It also has much of the same imagery.

Then, however, the *Venite* and the *Jubilate* diverge, because the latter has nothing corresponding to the last part of the *Venite*. Psalm 95 stops being a hymn and becomes a kind of prophecy. So far it has been doing what the psalms normally do, speaking Godwards. The last stanza of Psalm 95 reverses this movement. Instead of addressing God, we find ourselves being addressed in God's name: 'If only you would listen to him now!' For seven verses we have been making God listen to our voices, telling God how enthusiastic we are and how willing to prostrate ourselves. Then God speaks back.

How did the *Venite* come to have this form? I like to imagine that verses 1-7 once existed on their own as a perfectly good hymn of praise, used year in, year out in the temple for generations. Then on some specific festival occasion, perhaps, some priest or prophet was given a word of response to the people's worship, which then became attached to it. The divine response says, 'Oh, shut up for a minute and listen, will you? You're all enthusiasm and prostration. That talk about God being your king and shepherd – is it mere talk?' A more respectable, less romantic view of the origin of Psalm 95, I should add, is that the psalm was written that way because it linked with the kind of occasion when Israel recalled its deliverance from Egypt and its entering into covenant relations with God at Sinai. The beauty of the psalm is that it combines the worship and the commitment that are both parts of a proper response to the God of redemption.

Making the connection between worship and life

The exodus generation shouted aloud when they saw God act, but their submission to God did not carry over from words to life. The psalm does not question that people meant every hallelujah and every genuflection, but it does ask whether what they meant in worship was matched by what they did outside worship. 'Where do you place your trust? Who directs your path? I know what your words and hearts say about that, but what does your life say? If your life belies your words and feelings, you forfeit your share in God's rest.' Our worship has professed to make a link with life. Is the link real? When used in public worship, the psalm is often shortened by omitting the stanza which makes it distinctive – the words with which God responds to our worship – and adding words from the end of Psalm 96 which refer to God judging the world instead.[3]

Psalm 95's challenge to commitment links with one of the features of the psalms that often offends modern Christian readers (not ancient Christian readers, as far as I know). When things go wrong in our lives or we lose touch with God, we instinctively blame ourselves. The point is classically expressed in the question on the church poster, 'If God seems far away, guess who has moved?' The psalms view that as an open question. Sometimes they acknowledge human failure as the reason for God moving away, and pray 'out of the depths' of human sin and chastisement (see Psalm 130; compare Psalm 51). On other occasions they affirm that they have kept their commitment in the way Psalm 95 challenged them to (see, for example, Psalm 44:17-18). That is part of the basis for their appeal to God to act. In the same way, at the end of Psalm 139, after calling on God to act in judgement on the wicked who oppose his purpose (God's enemies, of course, not ours), we ask God to test our hearts and see if there is any wickedness in us. We are not saying, 'Oh dear, perhaps I should not have prayed that prayer.' We are saying, 'Look into my heart to make sure that I really meant my opposition to people who oppose you and that I am not secretly in sympathy with them.' Like Job, in affirming their commitment the psalmists are not claiming to be sinless. They are making a claim about the fundamental commitment of their lives. We have to be able to make that claim and survive the challenge of the last part of Psalm 95 if we are to be able to praise God authentically.

Life and liturgy

In our own hymn books and worship books there are prayers and praises (not least metrical versions of the psalms) which look as if they were written to order rather than because someone had met with God. Perhaps there are psalms which had an origin of that kind, when an Asaphite had to produce a new psalm for Passover because the choir was tired of the old ones. Characteristically, however, the psalms reflect real experience of God on the psalmists' part. The praise and prayer of the psalms belong first in life and only derivatively in worship.

The point can be illustrated from the occurrences of psalms and psalm-like praise and prayer elsewhere in the Old Testament. If God's people Israel comes into being (in the strict sense) in Exodus, then its prayer life begins with an agonized, helpless cry arising from a labour camp. As such, prayer belongs first in life and not in liturgy. So, too, does the praise which recognizes that God has overheard the people's cry even though that cry may not have been uttered with God in mind, but was just a helpless cry (see Exodus 2:23).

Later Hannah does pray and praise at the shrine, but she prays out of the reality of life experience, in the grief, hurt and anger of a woman who cannot have children and is despised for it. When Yahweh answers her prayer and she has her baby, she praises at the shrine out of that reality too (see 1 Samuel 1-2).

Job's prayer begins at the shrine, but when real life intervenes his prayer continues in the place of affliction itself – not least the presence of his friends. Jonah seeks to escape from the face of God, a phrase that rather implies he was in worship when he received his word from the Lord. But he found himself called to prayer on a foundering boat, drawn to praise in the midst of a large fish, and initiating a resentful conversation with God in the streets and outside the walls of a pagan city. Jeremiah, too, finds himself drawn into a prophetic ministry that requires him to declare prophecies that God is not committed to fulfilling, in his case to a people who will not listen to them because they are bent on self-destruction. The combination commits Jeremiah in turn to living between the upper millstone of danger because of the content of his words and the lower millstone of ridicule because of their emptiness. Experience is the engine of his prayer life (see Jeremiah 11-20).

Thus praise and prayer belong first in life and derivatively in worship. The same is true of our hymns. Their power and their meaningfulness derive from their having emerged from real people's personal turning to God. The record of those people's experience resonates with ours, even though we may not know precisely what their experience was. It is significant that another of the great writers on the psalms in the twentieth century, Claus Westermann, came to his study out of the context of the German Church's struggle of the 1930s. In the preface to his study *The Praise of God in the Psalms* he notes how, 'in the present transitions and disasters the church has been confronted anew with the question of the praise of God'.[4] There the Church praised God and prayed 'out of the depths' (Psalm 130). It was there that the people learned not only how to be steadfast but also how to praise.

PRAYER WHICH HOLDS TOGETHER TWO SETS OF FACTS

The psalms deal characteristically in extremes. They deal in extremes of enthusiasm and reverence which indicate that people's praise was not a matter of merely going through the motions. When other agendas dictate the nature of their prayer, they deal in extremes of dark despair, lonely helplessness, grief, anger and hurt in their relationships with other people, in their own spirits and before God. The psalms assume that when we talk to God punches do not have to be pulled nor words minced. Infinitives can be split and emotions expressed. There are hardly any feelings of pain, despair, vindictiveness or disappointment that fail to find expression somewhere among these 150 examples of things you can say to God.

One of the most powerful of those 'laments' is Psalm 22, 'My God, my God, why have you forsaken me?' It illustrates many of the characteristics of this way of praying. It naturally begins by calling on God. We may be less comfortable with the protest with which it immediately continues. The protest and expression of hurt is expressed in three directions. It laments what other people have done to us, in so far as that seems to be the problem: 'All who see me mock at me ... Many bulls encircle me ... a company of evil-doers encircles me ...' (vv. 7, 12, 16 NRSV). It draws us into acknowledging how we feel in ourselves: 'I am a worm, and not human ... I am poured out like water ... my mouth is dried up like a potsherd ...' (vv. 6, 14, 15 NRSV). But the point of deepest hurt is where the psalm starts, with what God has done or not done to us: 'Why are you so far from helping me, from the words of my groaning? O my God, I cry by day, but you do not answer ...' (vv. 1-2 NRSV). The psalm invites us into an extraordinary freedom in our speech with God. This is what it can mean to call on God as 'Abba, Father'. And though it undoubtedly makes us feel better by letting it all hang out, this is not its object. Its object is 'to summon God away from the throne [i.e. God's position in heaven which our worship celebrates], back into human life which is so hurtful and raw'.[5] Its object is to mobilize God into action.

Facts of God and facts of life

Psalm 22 also powerfully illustrates another characteristic feature of lament psalms – their recollection of God's deeds in the past and their statement of trust in God in the present. Indeed, Psalm 22's own distinctive power derives partly from the way it holds together the truths about God by which the psalmist is committed to living, and the experience of abandonment and loss which he or she currently experiences. (The 'he or she' is worth mentioning, both because the Old Testament explicitly indicates that its poetry, prayer and praise can very easily be of female authorship – consider Miriam, Deborah and Hannah – and because the psalms are in the Psalter to be used by people of either sex.)

The psalm insists on looking in the face the facts about God and the facts about one's current experience. It refuses to let the first subvert an acknowledgement of the second – unlike Job's friends, who, as Robert Davidson put it, rewrite Job's life rather than revise their theology.[6] Those involved in pastoral care often meet people who have not owned their pain or grief because it threatens their faith and their world-view.

Neither does Psalm 22 let the pains of the present permit a denial of the facts about God. People involved in pastoral care also meet much of that in hospitals and funeral parlours – and in themselves. Psalm 22 insists on looking both sets of facts steadily in the face. It alternates a sense of abandonment, insecurity and isolation with a poignant recollection of what God is, what God has been to Israel, what God has been to the particular individual who prays, and what God is going to be on the other side of this calamitous experience. 'The praise has power to transform the pain. But conversely the present pain also keeps the act of praise honest.'[7]

That is not its only function. Psalm 22 is significant in its own right, but it is also significant as the tortured lament which appears on the lips of Jesus and as one of the New Testament's key texts for an understanding of Jesus. Nor is it only Jesus who prays with the psalms of lament. Paul uses a lament such as this (actually Psalm 44) to describe his own experience in Romans 8:36. Anyone who feels the need of a New Testament warrant for taking up Old Testament spirituality has it! The psalms of lament are there for us to pray. They speak for us.

Psalm 22 illustrates at its most dialectical a regular feature of the psalms of lament. While they arise out of darkness and near hopelessness, in one way or another they reach out in hope as they contemplate past, present or future. A further feature of the way they reach out in hope is instructive for our own prayer: they are fervent and to the point, but quite unspecific in precisely how they expect God to act. Psalm 22 simply pleads, 'Do not be far from me . . . do not be far away . . . come quickly to my aid . . . deliver my soul . . . Save me . . .' (vv. 11, 19, 20, 21 NRSV). What prayer asks for is to be heard and delivered. How God effects deliverance is best left unspecified.

PRAYER, PAIN AND ANGER

When Paul uses the psalms, and when we do so, we are actually showing that we are walking in Jesus' way.

If we are to mirror God, to be in God's image, to be like God, to invite God to indwell us so that we live Christ's life ... we have to be willing to enter our individual wounds and through them the wounds of the community.

The psalms can be one of our means of doing that.

> The importance of our wounds lies in how we choose to relate to them, how we choose to enter and to integrate them into our lives ... We must never yield to the temptation to engage, in the name of 'healing', a new and often more destructive denial and repression such as T. S. Eliot describes: People change and smile, but agony abides.

We must be prepared to sit in the dark. With the laments, we must be prepared to release our tears.

> Tears are a sign that we are struggling with power of one sort or another: the loss of ours, the entering of God's.[8]

The most extreme example of this inherently extreme way of praying is Psalm 88. Claus Westermann observed that 'there is no petition that did not move at least one step on the road to praise'.[9] Psalm 88 is the nearest to an exception to this rule, for this expression of utter isolation and abandonment, a cry from the realm of death itself, contains no recollection of God's past acts of love and no statements of conviction about how things will be again.

> Your wrath lies heavy upon me ...
> You have caused my companions to shun me ...
> I am shut in so that I cannot escape ...
> Your dread assaults destroy me.
>
> (vv. 7, 8, 16 NRSV)

So it goes on, until in due course it simply stops (rather than finishes). What has gone wrong in the psalmist's life we do not know. We cannot penetrate behind the metaphorical and symbolic descriptions of the experience to the experience itself. But that is just as well. The fact that the experience is described only in metaphorical and symbolic terms makes it more feasible for us to find ourselves in these words. We too know what it is to be overwhelmed, to have things pressing down on us (demands, burdens, guilt, expectations), to feel insecure, threatened, afraid, forgotten, cut off from God, hemmed in, alone – 'not waving, but drowning'.

Entering despair

I say we know how that feels, but I must allow for the possibility that not everyone does. In studying the psalms with other people, I invite them to decide whether they find Psalm 88 encouraging or discouraging. They vary in their answers. Some find its dark despair and sense of abandonment inappropriate for a Christian. That may indicate that they are unwilling to look despair in the face, or it may indicate that they are people of particular inner resilience or spiritual resources, or people to whom life and God are especially kind, who do not need to identify with Psalm 88.

I still seek to encourage them to enter into it, for the sake of those to whom they may minister, if not for themselves. There are many in the Church and in the world who do weep, and many others who need to do so, and when the psalms of lament are not functioning as our prayer for ourselves they can become our intercession for the Church and for the world. They provide us with a way of entering into the experience of people in need and standing in their place in prayer.

Not that intercession is quite absent from the psalms. In effect, Psalm 72 is an intercession for the king. It suggests God's vision for government (in monarchic terms, though its vision is not difficult to translate into democratic terms) holding together fairness, prosperity, prayer, witness, fame and victory. It is a telling fact that the prophets' own key terms – judgement, justice, salvation, peace and blessing – all appear here.

The psalms which pray for vengeance also become our intercession as we pray them on behalf of people who need to express these feelings but are not able to do so, or who properly pray for their oppressors' forgiveness as we properly pray for their overturning. What are we to say, then, of liturgical reform,

> which deprives Christian prayer of the so-called cursing psalms, the instrument by which the poor and the oppressed denounce their historical ills, asking God to do justice by abstaining from doing justice themselves? These are psalms which, while calling on God to establish divine justice, sanction the principle of non-violence, pledging the one who prays not to yield to the temptation to render evil for evil.[10]

I find that the anger of the psalms arouses similar mixed reactions to those which apply to the psalms' hopelessness. But I also find that the people who are most offended by it are people whom I suspect to be fooling themselves about their own anger, perhaps repressing it in a very British way. Walter Brueggemann has observed that the real problem lies not in the anger in the psalms but in the anger in us, and he comments on how attuned the Psalter thus is to what goes on among us. There is 'an acute correspondence between what is *written there* and what is *practised here*'. It offers us the opportunity to face our anger, to express it in words rather than in actions, and thus to own it before God and yield it to the wisdom of the God who also knows anger and gives it expression in the pursuit of justice in history. Only when we have gone through that process 'can our rage and indignation be *yielded* to the mercy of God'.[11] If the death of Christ was God's act of judgement on human sin, it constituted a positive answer to the psalms' prayers for vengeance.[12]

Prayer and helplessness

In their despair and their anger, the psalms reflect not the shallowness of Old Testament spirituality but the depth of its grasp of what a relationship with God makes possible. The darkest of the psalms are some of God's most reassuring invitations to us.

We may often be faced in our lives and in our prayers with the agony of the silence and inactivity of God, and we may be tempted to wonder whether the actual silence reflects a metaphysical silence, a silence that indicates that there is no one there, no one to whom we pray, no one to speak. In that context, the first words of Psalm 88 take on new significance, given the cries of rejection that they introduce. There is a breathtaking illogic about its conventional opening, 'O LORD, God of my salvation . . .' How can you say 'My God' to someone you believe has turned the other way and stuffed their hands over their ears? The variety in the psalms is such that sufferers in all sorts of circumstances may be able to find themselves somewhere in them.

Whether in our pain and hurt we triumph, trust, cope, struggle or despair, there is a psalm we can use, one which begins where we are. Psalm 88 is in some ways the most precious of them, because it is the most wretched and comfortless. A person who has lost all trust, hope and faith may be able to begin their praying here. Even such a person then finds that, in articulating prayer at all, they have uttered the words 'O LORD my God'. They are not merely articulating their suffering, letting it all hang out, giving expression to it rather than bottling it up. They are doing these things, but to somebody, to someone who is there. They have not been drawn out of despair, but they have been drawn into that argument between hope and despair that is needed if they are to face both sets of facts and be true to their experience and true to the God they know. There is no overt step towards praise in Psalm 88, but there is an implicit statement of faith that catches you out when it requires you to utter it.

Psalm 88 is dominated by death. Death is a prominent feature of the Psalter – the possibility of death, the threat of death, the inevitability of death, deliverance from death, the death of someone near you. Perhaps this is another reason why we cannot cope with the psalms. Death is perceived as not merely the event that finally terminates human life when (if you are fortunate) you have had your threescore years and ten. The psalms have a slightly Johannine view of life and death. Life worth living is full life, a life that is truly alive, and when such fullness of life is taken away from us by illness, danger, fear, loneliness, oppression or depression, it is as if death reaches out and takes possession of us even in the midst of life. It is partly for this reason that the psalms talk about death so much.

> You have put me in the depths of the Pit,
>   in the regions dark and deep . . .
> Is your steadfast love declared in the grave,
>   or your faithfulness in Abaddon?
>
> PSALM 88:6, 11 NRSV

The end of death

The psalms talk as if death is the end. Christians may be inclined to find that assumption difficult to relate to, though it has several significances for us even this side of Christ's resurrection. Assuming that death is the end makes people take this life with the seriousness it deserves. It encourages us to live by reality and by evidence – for before Christ's resurrection there was no evidence that human beings would have resurrection life. It reflects the conviction that no one else is Lord of that realm. It reflects the fact that to someone who feels cut off from God, it seems as if death must be the end. It reflects the fact that death is indeed the end if people are cut off from God.

Death is the realm in which praise and prayer are neither uttered nor heard. Yet these very psalms show that it is out of death (out of the prospect of death, out of the death of someone near me, out of some experience of living death) that prayer arises at its most powerful. And because such prayers are heard, this mercifully disproves the lament they express – that prayer has no place in the realm of death. The very fact that a person is praying in such a place is one of God's wonders, and the next of God's wonders is that he hears that cry out of the place of darkness.

There is a page or two in an old book on prayer by Ole Hallesby to which I find myself coming back when I feel that in some way I have reached a cul-de-sac in prayer, when I do not know how to pray and feel spiritually dry and thus helpless.

> As far as I can see prayer has been ordained only for the helpless. It is the last resort of the helpless ... We try everything before we finally resort to prayer ... Prayer and helplessness are inseparable.

Only the person who is helpless can truly pray. If I feel sinful or abandoned, cold or depressed, doubting or dishonest, the feeling of helplessness that this awareness induces is not a barrier but my way into prayer.

> Prayer therefore simply consists in telling God day by day in what ways we feel that we are helpless.[13]

The psalms encourage this view.

THE PSALMS IN PERSONAL MINISTRY

Ideally, we are not left alone to come to terms with this helplessness. The dynamic of a prayer such as Psalm 22 presupposes that the transition from abandoned lament to anticipated thanksgiving is made possible by the ministry of someone who speaks a word from God to us.

Even if my fantasy regarding the origin of Psalm 95 is indeed mere romance, the Old Testament provides us with substantial evidence that prophets did function within Israel's worship (see especially Chronicles). When people had brought their need before God, someone brought God's word of response to them, and that made possible this transition from lament to praise. The story of Jehoshaphat threatened by invasion provides a spectacular example (see 2 Chronicles 20). The psalms themselves also provide examples of how a word from God makes possible this transition from plea to praise (see, for example, Psalms 12 and 60). In most cases in the Psalter, however, the actual word from God is not included. Of course one can never prescribe the nature of God's answer to prayer, and this is perhaps one reason for leaving empty the 'space' where one seeks for God's word. Jeremiah's experience shows how the response to a lament may be other than what one hopes for (see Jeremiah 14-15; also Hosea 6:1-6). God is free to respond in the way he wishes; we can prescribe a way for us to pray, but not a way for God to answer. 'God does speak, but he . . . almost never repeats himself.'[14]

The place of lament

I used to fret at the fact that I could not imagine how Christian worship could ever incorporate the outpouring of the laments in which individuals bring their pains to God, as they need to do. Walter Brueggemann notes how the censoring of their note from Christian worship in favour of a predominant note of praise encourages a triumphalist theology of glory and fails to witness to a theology of the cross.[15] Israel's own practice most likely points us to the resolution of this dilemma. Individuals gave voice to such laments in a context that was more like that of a fellowship or prayer group than that of temple worship. The latter may be the natural and effective context for a festival of praise, the former for prayer for healing and deliverance.[16]

The lament psalms also have a place in the ministry of individual to individual. The story of Hannah in 1 Samuel 1 again provides an illustration. She comes to pour out her heart to God in her grief, anger, pain and helplessness, praying the way the psalms of lament do. With an element of tragicomedy, Eli initially misreads the situation and upbraids her for coming near the temple in a drunken state (compare Acts 2). The celebration of the festival no doubt gave him every reason for suspicion. In due course, however, he gets his pastoral act together and brings God's word of reassurance and promise to her, in the way the psalms presuppose. After this Hannah can return home with her spirit restored, as the lament psalms again presuppose happens when a person has heard God answer their prayer.

Donald Capps has written helpfully on the use of the lament psalms in grief counselling.[17] The psalms give people the means of expressing the pain they need to express – but to God. We help them to do that, then listen to God for them. As a theological college tutor I used to have a certain amount of experience of people coming to share their pain and hurt. Having stumbled across this feature of the psalms of lament, I found myself encouraging people to use them to express their pain to God when they had explored it with me. Sometimes this was a matter of inviting them to say a particular psalm which said what they needed to say; sometimes it was a matter of me saying such a psalm for them, for saying it themselves could still be too much; sometimes it was a matter of me turning what they had been telling me into a lament-type prayer on their behalf. My task then was to change positions and listen to God on their behalf (which I found a tricky exercise, because it demands a significant move if one has truly been standing in their place), so that I could utter God's word of reassurance (or otherwise) to them. I believe Scripture provides us with a powerful pattern of ministry here.

Communal grief

Communities, too, need to express their grief. Death and mourning can be corporate realities. Changes in the economy can bring death to communities that depended for their livelihoods on one particular industry; a company or institution can feel the threat of death because of changes in the wider organization to which it belongs. The broader death experienced by the Church in Britain (the death of its old power and significance) raises similar questions. Awareness of the importance of grieving and of the nature of its stages has become part of the conventional wisdom of pastoral care since the 1990s, but an equivalent awareness of the corporate grief process also needs to develop. The psalms of lament provide resources for the expression of that corporate grief which can be the beginning of new life.[18]

Nor is it only believers who may find that the psalms speak to them and for them in this way. In 1945, a 19-year-old German soldier called Jürgen Moltmann was taken prisoner by the British and eventually placed in a camp in Sherwood Forest, where the Nottingham YMCA set him going on the theological study which eventually led to him becoming one of the great twentieth-century theologians. Having lived through the horrors of the Second World War, the collapse of an empire and its institutions, and the guilt and shame of their nation, many German prisoners collapsed inwardly and gave up all hope, some of them dying. 'The same thing almost happened to me,' Moltmann testifies – had it not been for a 'rebirth to a new life' which turned Christian faith into reality rather than formality. 'The experience of misery and forsakenness and daily humiliation gradually built up into an experience of God,' he writes.

> It was the experience of God's presence in the dark night of the soul: 'If I make my bed in hell, behold, thou art there.' A well-meaning army chaplain had given me a New Testament. I thought it was out of place. I would rather have had something to eat. But then I became fascinated by the psalms (which were printed in an appendix) and especially by Psalm 39: 'I was dumb with silence, I held my peace, even from good; and my sorrow was stirred (but the German is much stronger – 'I have to eat up my grief within myself')... Hold thou not thy peace at my tears: for I am a stranger with thee, and a sojourner, as all my fathers were.' These psalms gave me the words for my own suffering. They opened my eyes to the God who is with those 'that are of a broken heart'.

Later Moltmann adds that he does not so much want to say that this is how he found God, 'but I do know in my heart that it is there that he found me, and that I would otherwise have been lost'.[19] Moltmann's testimony may suggest that the psalms are also a neglected resource for our ministry to a lost world.

THE PSALMS AS TESTIMONY

There is a third way of speaking to God that we have yet to consider. A psalm of praise like the *Venite* or the *Jubilate* acknowledges who God is and how God characteristically behaves in relation to the world and Israel. A lament such as Psalm 22 or 88 agonizes over God's failure to act in those characteristic ways and to be that person. A thanksgiving psalm rejoices over some recent personal experience of the turning of God's face and the answering of prayer.

Laments work by their specific nature, their systematic out-pouring of the supplicant's experience, albeit described in metaphorical terms. Thanksgivings also work by their specific nature, now a systematic testifying to the worshipper's experience of deliverance. Psalm 30 illustrates what is happening when we pray a prayer of this kind. It parallels the *Venite* and the *Jubilate* in that it goes through a sequence of movements twice, in verses 1-5 and 6-12. There are four elements in the sequence.

First, I remember how things once were. 'I said in my prosperity, "I shall never be moved ..."' (v. 6 NRSV). The recollection is reminiscent of statements of a right confidence in God such as that in Psalm 62 ('God is my fortress, I shall never be shaken'), but it also reminds us of other statements that reflect rather a confidence in oneself. Is the psalmist affirming that past spiritual stance of confidence in God, or recognizing now that it reflected a foolish self-confidence? The statement itself is ambiguous, and ambiguity of this kind is an important positive feature of the psalms. There is an openness about their language. Often they do not tell us which interpretation of their words is the right one; they test us by leaving it to us to decide what we would mean by their words. The most telling example of this phenomenon is Psalm 139, 'O LORD, you have searched me and known me' (v. 1 NRSV). Is God's knowledge of us good news or bad news? The translations of Psalm 139 vary fascinatingly over the points at which they understand it one way or the other. The psalm is systematically ambiguous and puts those who pray it on the spot, because they have to decide which way they dare mean it or whether they dare say it.

Second, I remember how things went wrong and how I prayed. 'You hid your face; I was dismayed. To you, O LORD, I cried ... O LORD, be my helper!' (vv. 7-8, 10 NRSV). The prayer that is recalled further illustrates the nature of the actual plea in a lament. It is very vague compared with the specific way in which the psalm describes the situation and the need. Our prayers tend to suggest to God policies for implementing: 'Lord, make the chancellor see that increasing government spending is better than cutting taxes.' Biblical prayer, by contrast, works by describing before God the plight of the needy and then simply urging him to do something about it.

(Third,) I remember how God responded. 'You have turned my mourning into dancing; you have taken off my sackcloth and clothed me with joy' (v. 11 NRSV). Once more prayer is a matter of extremes – either lamentation and sackcloth or dancing and joy. The thanksgiving psalms have a further striking feature. Although we may give this title to them, it has been pointed out that they do not use the verb 'thank' so very often. Indeed, the word in question does not quite mean 'thank', but rather 'acknowledge', 'confess', or 'testify', and the psalms commonly go about confessing what God has done without having to say that this is what they are doing. Indeed, the word can get in the way: to say 'I thank you' puts me in the front of the sentence. To omit it offers God the glory even in the syntax: 'You have drawn me up . . . you have healed me . . . [you have] restored me to life . . .' (vv. 1, 2, 3 NRSV).

(Fourth,) I rejoice with a joy that extends to other people and to other times. What God does for me deserves also to glorify God and to build up the Church. Conversely, what God does for other people deserves also to glorify God and to build me up. So, 'Sing praises to the LORD, O you his faithful ones . . .' (v. 4 NRSV). The psalms assume that we share our griefs and hurts with each other in prayer – we have noted that people did not necessarily or ideally pray laments on their own. They also assume that we share our joys in Christ with each other. We weep with those who weep, and we rejoice with those who rejoice. As I prove that the apparent world is not the real world, I draw other people into my world-creating experience. Like praise and prayer in general, thanksgiving for what God has done for me begins in life and is initially personal to God and me, but it must become public, as confession or testimony. My confession extends to other times as well as to other people: 'You have turned my mourning into dancing . . . so that my soul may praise you and not be silent. O LORD my God, I will give thanks to you forever' (vv. 11-12 NRSV).

THE DYNAMIC CYCLE OF PRAISE AND PRAYER

In a sense, we are back where we began. We began with hymns such as the *Venite*, with a life committed to praise because of who God is and because of the mercy that lasts for ever. We crashed from height to depth in the laments, which confront a God who seems to be silent for ever. In thanksgiving we have come out the other side of that experience into a praise which breaks silence, in response to God having broken it first. The entire sequence of praise, lament and confession that characterizes the spirituality of the psalms thus appears within Psalm 30 itself (as it does also in Psalm 22).

There is more than one way to characterize their interrelationship. Claus Westermann continues his observation that 'there is no petition that did not move at least one step on the road to praise' by adding that 'there is no praise that is fully separated from the experience of God's wonderful intervention in time of need'.[20] He contrasts Egyptian psalms, which praise God only in general terms and not in relation to him actually doing anything, and Babylonian psalms, which praise God only as a lead-in to prayer, never for the sake of praise itself. In Israel, what he calls the 'vital, tension-filled polarity of plea and praise' has its centre in the thanksgiving at which we have just been looking, which looks back to lament and forward to ongoing worship of God.

Walter Brueggemann suggests a different analysis of the interrelationship of these three ways of speaking to God. In *The Message of the Psalms* (Augsburg, Minneapolis, 1984) he points out that the sequence of praise, lament and thanksgiving corresponds to three stages by which life and faith develop: orientation, disorientation and reorientation.[21] *Orientation* implies knowing who you are, knowing who God is, knowing how life works. *Disorientation* means seeing those convictions collapse through some experience of loss (or some unexpected joy). The temptation then is to seek to find our way back to the old orientation – or to give in to disorientation and yield to agnostic despair. The only truly human way out is forward, into a *new orientation* that does justice both to what was true about the old and to the experience that has exploded it. It is a renewed orientation that does justice to both sets of facts, to use the language we employed earlier. Put in worship terms, the move is one from praise to lament to thanksgiving, confession or testimony.

Paths to reorientation

To judge from the psalms, the move forward to reorientation may come in several ways. In Psalm 30 it apparently comes because God does something. In Psalm 22 there is a sudden change of mood two-thirds of the way through which seems to suggest that God has said something, perhaps through a priest or a prophet, which the psalmist has accepted, and this has changed everything. In Psalm 73, which recalls an experience of almost losing faith, the psalmist somehow sees something, and comes to another of the Psalter's extremes:

> Whom have I in heaven but you?
> And there is nothing on earth that I desire other than you.
>
> v. 25 NRSV

The breathtaking confession is only reached because of the 'Why? Why? Why?' of the bulk of the psalm. It was only when an old orientation caved in that something new could be perceived.

The two ways mentioned above of relating lament, worship and thanksgiving seem mutually exclusive, but they are both plausible. This points us to a more dialectical understanding of the relationship. Praise feeds prayer; prayer feeds praise. The relationship is a circular one in which praise can be a beginning or a climax, thanksgiving a midpoint or an end. It would be better to describe the relationship as a spiral, for yesterday's fresh new orientation is today's old inadequate one which has to be allowed to collapse. What the psalms are portraying is an ongoing pattern of life in the Spirit, one that is neither static nor circular nor linear, but spiral. They invite us to live in this dynamic cycle of worship and obedience, lament at the experiences of loss and suffering that we have ourselves and share with the Church and with the world, petition to God to turn back and act, confession that this has happened, and renewed commitment to worship and obedience which takes us full circle. To judge from individual psalms, when we need to we can enter the circle at any point and go round it as far as we wish. We will find ourselves passing places we have been before and saying words we have said before, yet meaning new things by them as we come to them out of new experiences as new people.

I cannot understand how Christians can take a superior stance in comparison to the spirituality of the Jewish Bible. The psalms do not make me think, 'Poor Jews, that they have this distant, legalistic relationship with God,' but rather, 'I wish I related to God the way these Jews did even before Jesus came.' Christians need to recover the psalms.

Notes

1 Walter Brueggemann, 'Bounded by Obedience and Praise', JSOT 50 (1991), p. 67.

2 See Walter Brueggemann, *Israel's Praise* (Fortress, 1988).

3 For example, see the Church of England's *Alternative Service Book*. The newer *Common Worship* restores the biblical text, though rather suspiciously gives the option of avoiding these difficult final words.

4 Claus Westermann, *The Praise of God in the Psalms* (Knox, 1965/Epworth, 1966; expanded edition, *Praise and Lament in the Psalms* (Knox/Clark, 1981), p. 5.

5 Walter Brueggemann, *Interpretation and Obedience* (Fortress, 1991).

6 Robert Davidson, *The Courage to Doubt* (SCM, 1983), p. 178.

7 Brueggemann, *Israel's Praise*, p. 139.

8 M. Ross, *Pillars of Flame* (SCM, 1988), pp. xvii, xviii, 124.

9 Westermann, *Praise and Lament in the Psalms*, p. 154.

10 E. Bianchi (ed. C. Duqee and C. Florestan), 'Contemporary challenges to prayer', in *Asking and Thanking* (Concilium, 1990/1993), pp. 55-56.

11 Walter Brueggemann, *Praying the Psalms* (St Mary's Press, 1982), pp. 68, 79.

12 See Dietrich Bonhoeffer, *The Psalms* (SLG, 1982), pp. 21-23.

13 Ole Hallesby, *Prayer* (IVF, 1948), pp. 11, 17.

14 J. B. Metz, in J. B. Metz and K. Rahner, *The Courage to Pray* (Burns and Oates, 1980), p. 25.

15 Brueggemann, *Interpretation and Obedience*, p. 194.

16 See P. D. Miller, *Interpreting the Psalms* (Fortress, 1986), pp. 5-7.

17 See his *Biblical Approaches to Pastoral Counselling* (Westminster, 1981), pp. 59-97.

18 See G. A. Arbuckle, *Grieving for Change* (Chapman, 1991).

19 Jürgen Moltmann, *Experiences of God* (SCM, 1980), pp. 6-9.

20 Westermann, *Praise and Lament in the Psalms*, p. 154.

21 Walter Brueggemann, *The Message of the Psalms* (Augsburg, 1984).

IN THE NAME
OF JESUS

USING THE JESUS PRAYER

Keith Hubbard

Lord Jesus Christ,
Son of God,
have mercy upon me,
a sinner.

God has reached out to us in Jesus to enable us to come to him in prayer. The following reflections play on this gospel theme to show how, by praying in the name of Jesus, the Father can become enthroned at the heart of human living.

Prayer can require considerable effort on our part amidst life's many distractions and demands, but in Christian prayer the initiative belongs to God. The Holy Spirit within us turns us to God and lifts our prayers before him (see Romans 8:26-27). Keeping sight of this big picture – a relationship with God in Christ through the Holy Spirit – should broaden our vision of where praying leads and so help us to relax more into the beauty, truth and goodness of the Father.

The Jesus Prayer provides us with a framework in which to think through the issues more fully. This prayer, in one form or another, has been part of the basic diet for disciples of the Eastern

Church for centuries. At its simplest the prayer is a plain invocation of the name of Jesus. A more formal form is 'Lord Jesus Christ, Son of God, have mercy on me, a sinner' – echoing the cry of the tax collector in Luke 18:13. In each section, I will take a word or phrase from this prayer and explore what it means to pray in the name of Jesus. This is not about the Jesus Prayer as such, but an account of what it means to pray as a Christian, letting the God of Jesus Christ shape our thought and practice.

GOD'S BEAUTY IN JESUS: 'LORD'

Prayer to Jesus begins with us confessing that he is Lord – not just our Lord, but Lord of all. Even this confession is not our own work, but the fruit of God's working in us. Right at the outset we should be encouraged; if we are able to utter this beginning of prayer, then by God's grace the dynamics of prayer must already have reached an advanced stage of development in us. Already we must have become helplessly attracted to God's beauty revealed in the face of Jesus Christ. This in turn demonstrates that God has reached out to us and stirred us inwardly to sensitize us to his beauty. This process of coming into relationship with God, in which God's initiative is increasingly realized and enjoyed, takes many forms. Here the relationship can be pictured as God drawing us out of self-involvement and reaching out in his Son, to bring us to a point where we recognize the sovereignty of God in naming Christ as Lord. In such a place we cannot help but acknowledge him to be our own Lord, and indeed at this point we are often overwhelmed by his love.

'Beauty' may not be the first thing we associate with Jesus' lordship. We more usually think of his authority, or our response of obedience. Yet the idea of God being Lord and being beautiful are linked in Old Testament worship:

> One thing I asked of the LORD,
>   that will I seek after:
> to live in the house of the LORD
>   all the days of my life,
> to behold the beauty of the LORD,
>   and to inquire in his temple.   PSALM 27:4 NRSV

God's beauty has to do with his perfection, his splendour and radiance, and so touches on the *shekinah*, the glory of God as he made his presence known in the temple. This is why the temple itself had to be a thing of great beauty, so that it was a fit place for his people to encounter the beauty of God himself. This connection between God's beauty and his Lordship has also emerged in recent worship songs, from 'Isn't he beautiful' to 'May the beauty of Jesus fill my life', along with the not-so-recent 'Worship the Lord in the beauty of holiness'.

Beauty has a strong role to play in preparing our hearts to be encountered by God in prayer. What do we usually think of when we think of beauty? The chances are that we do not think of God at first. This is not unusual; we cannot easily imagine beauty in an uncreated realm. We always see it, at least initially, exemplified in beautiful things in the world – a face, a leaf, a building. Beauty is characterized and in a sense defined for us by objects of beauty. We do not carry around with us a yardstick of beauty against which we measure any particular object that we might meet. What is more, our response to beauty is generally immediate. We have no trouble in accounting for the beauty of the world, since it seems to provide its own examples of beauty, but the question remains: how can we conceive of the beauty of God?

The neglect of beauty

The difficulties here are not helped by the fact that beauty has been neglected in much modern Protestant theology. God has more often been seen as holy, a tremendous and fascinating mystery, than as one upon whose face one could look and live, let alone love. Beauty has generally been associated with the world, a sign of God's unutterable glory. So long as the discussion takes place on the level of concepts, we are unlikely to make much headway. This is because beauty is not something one can turn into an objective and unchanging property; it has always to do with how an object is perceived or experienced. Even a building is beautiful only in relation to light or shade or to the shifting viewpoint of the onlooker. So long as theology tried to pin down God's properties from the outside by reason alone, it was bound to overlook the beauty of God.

In prayer we begin to find something analogous to the experience of beauty, and the language of beauty begins to become appropriate to describe God. In practice, especially in worship, aesthetic and spiritual experience often appear to be inseparable from one another, although it is very important not to confuse the two. When we are encountered by God in prayer, one of the first characteristics will often be what we might call spiritual or charismatic experience. This can play an important role in leading us on to a deeper level of prayerful relationship in many different ways, although it is a common mistake to think that such experience belongs only to an early stage of prayer. It should accompany us every step of the way.

One of the ways in which such experience is aroused is in a sense of indescribable sweetness being poured out in the heart of the one praying. This can be felt almost like honey which, remaining upon the lips at first, can then be traced to the region of the heart. The heart is, as it were, the place where our relationship with God flourishes as we invoke Jesus' name. Prayer is working one of its many transformations in our relationship with God. No longer is this relationship simply a verbal exchange (the primary medium of many everyday relationships), but it is heart-to-heart. This praying relationship touches the heart, where we are most vulnerable and which consequently we try to keep hidden. Addressing God as Lord can seem rather like any other conversation, in which we expect to keep certain prerogatives – but whenever prayer descends from the lips to the heart it reaches a more intimate place, where God is able to surprise, delight and jolt us away from any desire we might have to keep control.

We are not, of course, to pray for the sake of having such experiences of sweetness, and indeed we cannot. That would not be prayer, but something else. The point is that, although the depths of God's glory are inaccessible to us (see 1 Timothy 6:16), the beauty of the Father that is eternally enjoyed by and reflected in the Son is translated by the Spirit into forms that we are able to enjoy. This is what Jesus allows us to glimpse in prayer through a willingness, which is also of his making, to be open to what is both beautiful and spiritual. As we pray, God stirs our heart and opens it up so that it becomes able to catch a glimpse of the beauty of the Lord.

The desire for intimacy

Even a glimpse provides light enough for us to see that our own heart is attuned to who God is. We can no longer rest. We are not content with the beauty of the world, even though our encounter with God may also revive our aesthetic experience. We have tasted of the beauty of Jesus and we are now filled with an unquenchable thirst for more of Jesus. Invocation of the name of Jesus can therefore never be a single event. It is necessarily repeated, because part of what it means to call upon Jesus is to desire more and more of his closeness and to experience more and more of his beauty. It is not uncommon for people who have been caught up in the presence of the Lord to utter 'Jesus' constantly and, indeed, helplessly.

Often such passion characterizes the awakening of our call to Christian ministry of some kind. It is a shame when such a sense of our intimacy with Jesus becomes lost in the practice of the ministry itself and is ascribed only to the early stages of spirituality. Such intimacy invariably contributes an endless vitality to Christian thought and practice in whatever form it takes.

> We just cannot say enough about intimacy [with Jesus]. When I was a little boy I fell so insatiably in love with Jesus that I used to slip out of my bed at three or four o'clock in the morning, and I would go out into a lonely deserted field out in the country and I would hide there between the high stalks of corn or whatever was growing, and I would just call out the name of Jesus and adore him and tell him how much I loved him and ask him to speak to me. And I fell in love with the name of Jesus.[1]

One rarely hears testimonies of such passion in the Church today. Indeed, the place of giving testimonies in church has generally become less prominent, even in charismatic churches. In the charismatic movement there has been much emphasis throughout the last ten years on our need to prepare for revival. If we could cry out to God with the quality of passion being demonstrated here, and express such passion openly, then we would perhaps be in the position of being able to respond to God's desire to visit the Church with revival.

GOD'S MISSION IN THE NAME: 'JESUS'

Calling on the name of the Lord is a fitting response to God's communication of his beauty in Jesus. But what is the significance of Jesus' name for Christian mission? Sometimes it is argued that, because God became incarnate in Jesus at a particular time and place, mission cannot be carried out in Jesus' name in other cultures whose time and place have little in common with his situation. We therefore have to consider the affirmation that it is in the name of Jesus, and no other, that we must be saved (see Acts 4:12).

Calling on Jesus in prayer already says something about the place of Jesus in our lives. The grace of God has already brought us to a place where prayer is possible. This grace is at work outside the little stretches of time that we deliberately devote to praying. Similarly, invocation of the name involves more than simply uttering the word 'Jesus'. It requires a certain degree of harmony between the one being called and the expectations of the one doing the calling. In other words, Jesus is only named as Jesus when he already occupies a certain place in a person's life. This need not imply that the person is a Christian who holds to the doctrines and practices of a particular church. Nor does it mean that there is some magic cord extending between the word 'Jesus' and the living person to whom that word refers, as if a tug on the cord might instantly bring Jesus' presence to someone. The naming of Jesus always entails a real reaching out of the heart in the grace of the Holy Spirit.

The fact that Jesus cannot be proclaimed Lord without the Holy Spirit (see 1 Corinthians 12:3) again distinguishes the name of Jesus from mere words such as 'Jesus' and 'Lord', since these can clearly be abused in all sorts of ways, irrespective of the presence of the Holy Spirit. Although it is occasionally said that it is arrogant to maintain that Jesus' name is the only one in which we must be saved, this is at least in part a confusion between the word 'Jesus' and the one to whom the word points. It is clearly possible to be known by Jesus and to respond to this in a transforming way, independently of whether a person uses such a word or not. The faith of people with severe learning difficulties would be one example. Acknowledging this possibility only serves to magnify the saving power of the name of Jesus.

The word and the name

We should therefore be bold in affirming that only in Jesus can we be reconciled to God and brought into the fullness of intimacy with him, which he has prepared for us all. And although we are not simply to equate the word 'Jesus' with the name of Jesus, this does not mean that those who use it in prayer will be ignored. The word carries the same potential for naming him as it did in his earthly ministry. There is thus a certain privilege to be accorded even the word 'Jesus', although non-Christian cultures are not thereby bereft.

The powerful claim of the hymn in Philippians 2 is that at the name of Jesus 'every knee should bend' (Philippians 2:10 NRSV). This universal claim means that no human being, on recognizing Jesus for who he is (which I believe all will have to do at some point), will be able to refrain from glorifying him as Lord. The term 'Lord' in this wonderful hymn conveys this universal event of the recognition of Jesus' identity as divine. It attests that the language with which we properly glorify God is equally applicable to Jesus. It is not the outward form of the term that matters, but the dynamics of one's relationship with God in Jesus. If we keep this distinction in mind we can see how repeating the name of Jesus in prayer – voicing 'Jesus' in the context of a living faith – is the very essence of the Jesus Prayer, bringing us into Jesus' proximity.

Being close to Jesus brings a taste of eternity to the one praying, but not at the expense of a life in time. Rather, we come to relate to time in a different way, from a different perspective that has to do with sharing in God's work. We are not merely held in a warm embrace in the name of Jesus, but we are also drawn into a transformative relationship with him, in which we come to see the world of time increasingly through his eyes. There is a movement outward and to others that starts, as it were, with a movement upwards – a cry of the heart to the Lord Jesus. We become prepared for a life in time by being distanced from the everyday patterns of our own temporal existence. In adjusting to the value of God who is other than ourselves, we become better able to spend time with those whose values are other than our own. This movement into time makes us aware again of our need for God, so that we can be sent out again in his name. The dynamic of the Jesus Prayer suggests how we might live in time for the sake of mission, for in such prayer we are sent onward and outward by the one we are invoking.

Reckoning time

The repeated use of the name of Jesus can transform our relationship to time in other ways. Citizens of the modern world cannot escape having lives that are in some sense based upon the clock. We get up at a certain time and do things at various specific points in the day. The ticking of the clock suggests that every second is similarly defined, each second measuring out an identical period to the last. There is nothing in the clock to indicate that one second should be qualitatively different from any other. And there is clearly a part of us that finds this formal reckoning of time conducive to our own lifestyle. This sort of time is like a piece of cloth that we are able to cut up in various ways, a resource for our own use. We set aside a time for work, a 'quality time' for family and a 'quiet time' for God. In doing so, however, we are in danger of making ourselves responsible for arranging the shape of our lives, rather than allowing openness to God's initiative to prevail.

Repetition could be seen as the structural tissue of time, because repetition of what has gone before forms the basis of our sense of the rhythm and pace of time. The incessant ticking of the clock is one potent symbol of this. Yet the repetition of the Jesus Prayer has a different meaning, in that it is not susceptible to being structured by our own intentions. Each utterance is not simply another instance of the one preceding it, but represents a step forward in our journey with God. With each step we gain encouragement from God leading us onwards and we are dependent on him. This is of value in helping us to sense that our time is not our own but belongs to God. Time is not in fact stuff at our disposal, nor even a neutral framework in which we play out our lives; time is the expression of God's dealings with the world. When God gives himself to the world, time is what it takes. It is this endless self-giving in time that, as we shall see more and more, calls forth a like response from our own heart.

The repeating of the name of Jesus therefore opens up another possibility for transformation: we give up to God our propensity to be the lord of our own time, and we put 'our' time into God's hands for the sake of his mission. We ourselves become God's hands in our identification with God's missionary purposes in his word and his Spirit.

GOD'S TRUTH IN JESUS: 'CHRIST'

So it is that we give up to God in prayer the timing of our own projects in order that our interests may coincide more perfectly with those of God. We no longer conceive of ourselves as embarking upon a mission; rather, we are appointed agents in God's own mission. What this mission is will clearly be bound together with our view of what counts for truth.

If it is Jesus who shapes us in prayer and Jesus is truth, when we go out in his name we go out in the name of truth. This is obviously a dangerous assertion, given that historically mission has often left a trail of physical and cultural destruction in its wake. I want to stress, therefore, how the living truth we meet in prayer is intended for the anointing of the world with mercy.

In prayer the agency of the one praying can become so completely surrendered to God that the Holy Spirit can take the divine mission deeply into the heart of that person. This is another sign of our known selves becoming decentred. What we know and do, even what we are, is transformed as we enter the depths of our relationship with Christ. In him we outgrow a disposition of self-assertion and grow into one of fundamental receptivity to the mission of the Spirit. In the case of the Jesus Prayer, this reversal can be experienced in a fairly literal way. In time it is possible to become aware of the prayer being continuously repeated in one's heart, independently of one's conscious intentions to utter it. The voice of the Holy Spirit can be smothered by worldly concerns, but it is not the world itself that prevents the Spirit from acting. The Spirit is only quenched when the one praying acts out of step with the divine passion for the world.

Personal versus propositional

In this reversal of orientation, where it is no longer a case of us actively praying to God but of God praying in us, we need to discover a new conception of truth. The Christian's answer to the question 'What is truth?' must necessarily be different from that of others, because here truth is Christ himself. Truth is bound up with the second person of the Trinity, who communicates and embodies the truth of God. For the Christian, truth is not essentially a property of propositions such as 'grass is green', nor is it a property of a person, even of Jesus. Jesus did not *merely* say, 'I am truthful,' or, 'My words are true' (though he did say both of these). He said, 'I am the truth' (John 14:6). This has radical implications for the way in which truth is to be defined, discussed and lived.

We do not normally treat truth as if it were something you could parcel up in a proposition, as if the truth of assertions is all that concerns us. In fact, when we pay close attention to the way in which language is used in everyday situations, the truth of persons seems more fundamental. People are not ultimately concerned with whether assertions are true or not – although in particular cases this is obviously important – but with whether the person making the assertions is true. Furthermore, we call many expressions of a person's life 'true' that could simply not be translated into propositional form – character and attitude, thoughts and feelings, intuitions and hunches. On the one hand, the truth of particular claims is mostly used to establish the integrity of the person. On the other hand, what we know of such integrity is remembered to judge whether what is being talked about is worthy of attention. What we value in a person is their integrity, whereas we can overlook them making a certain number of erroneous claims, provided they are made in good faith.

Furthermore, we commonly refer to people as being true or false in contexts where what they have said is not at issue. We might well allow that what a person has said is true and yet remain concerned that the person herself is not. This happens in cases where there is reason to suppose that someone's motives for saying something are at variance with the context of what is being said. Whether a person is deemed true or not will depend on more subtle things such as how ready he is to be swept along by the tide of current opinion. Readiness to go along with and act on a partial truth, without taking the trouble to evaluate it, can be more indicative of a person's falsity than any incorrect assertion. Not to protest against a lie can be as much an expression of falsity as simply to utter the lie in the first place.

True disclosure

Thus we can see that truth and falsehood are personal qualities even before they are terms we might apply to particular statements. Truth may be said to consist in the capacity of people to
remember or represent things rightly. When one has discovered for
oneself the genuine character of something, then one has taken it
out of hiding, or the realm in which its value has been forgotten,
and has set forth its truth. Knowing the truth is a process of personal discovery and evaluation. The sense of the New Testament
word for truth, *aletheia*, also suggests this. The stem is the word for
forgetfulness or hiddenness, *lethe*. In the Greek mythic world-view
the River Lethe, which led to the land of the dead, would carry
away the memories of the deceased so that they might forget their
former lives. The prefix *'a-'* implies that truth resides in unforget-
fulness (remembering) or uncovering (discovering). Hence the
classical understanding of truth associates it with discovery. Truth
is in the nature of people and has to do with the integrity of their
life among other people.

When we turn to Christ in prayer we are turning to the one
who embodied truth, whose whole life enacted a discovery of a
realm that had been hidden – the kingdom of God. And yet this
truth never becomes impersonal. It is offered in human encounter
through the agency of the Christ, the one anointed by God's Spirit,
and is received by turning in faith towards the one who is and was
and is to come. This is the movement of the Jesus Prayer. In confessing the name of Christ we are freed by the truth of Jesus to live
in love for others, no longer subject to our own unaided moral dis-
positions or fixed religious ideologies.

We can only open our heart to facilitate our receptivity to such
truth, and accordingly we have to give up our own desires to establish the truth for ourselves. Jesus alone is to be identified with the
truth and is the source of all truth. Truth for the Christian therefore
has more of the character of revelation than of discovery. We cannot uncover the things of the Spirit by our own initiative. Rather,
the Holy Spirit reveals them step by step as we too live in the truth
of Christ.

Ultimately Jesus reveals our true selves to us in prayer, as
those wholly known and loved by God. The Jesus Prayer facili-
tates this by separating the conscious intentions of the one praying

from their expression. Thus the prayer can be maintained even in sleep, being perpetuated by the Holy Spirit. The prayer disarms us of our control over our intentions and subjects us to the fact that the truth of God is to be revealed to us by intentions beyond our own. The Holy Spirit, who leads us into all truth (see John 16:13), shows us that truth is to be disclosed to us only in Jesus' name. In this name we are invigorated and sent out to be effective channels of God's love, sharing in his mission in the world.

GOD'S GOODNESS IN JESUS: 'SON OF GOD'

The quest to discover truth as something to be asserted is supplanted by a humble acceptance of the revelation of truth given in the face of Jesus Christ. This prepares us for a similar reversal concerning the nature of goodness.

When we proclaim things such as 'God is good', what we mean is that God is good in a way analogous to the ways in which virtuous people are good, only at a higher level. To put it more philosophically, there is continuity between ascriptions of value to God and everyday value claims. Indeed, this is partly what offers any possibility of speaking of a God who is beyond all human definition. Yet we should note that this approach assumes that goodness may be adequately defined independently of God. Goodness can be recognized in others independently of any comparisons with the being of God.

We could argue, however, that value-expressing language might be even more comprehensively understood the other way around, as being dependent on a concept of God. God then represents the absolute standard of goodness against which all talk of good can be measured. As we saw earlier concerning truth, attention to how language is used reveals that we do in fact use terms as if they reflect something of the nature of God. As for truth, so for goodness. A good action is an unselfish one, and the reason for this is that it reflects something of the self-giving nature of God. The fact that we quite naturally value efforts to overcome selfishness cannot be accounted for only in terms of the public benefits of this attitude. We are inherently orientated in such a way that we knowingly aspire towards self-giving, and this distinguishes us from other mammals in an important respect. We are essentially ethical in our being, and this can best be accounted for in terms of the ends for which God created us.

To be made in God's image is to participate to some extent in his nature of self-giving. Such self-giving is therefore basic to our existence and runs against the impulses of our self-interest. A self-giving nature is common to all, but a Christian is someone whose own natural (though flawed) propensity for self-giving has been caught up into God's eternal activity of self-emptying in Christ and who lives his or her life in emulation of the fulfilment of this activity in Jesus' life and death.

This implies that our understanding of goodness – like our understanding of truth and beauty – is to be based on our understanding of the nature of God as exemplified in Jesus. We must focus on the meaning of God's self-emptying of his goodness if we are to understand the way in which this may be enacted in everyday life. Then we will value goodness not simply in itself, but also as something that participates in the nature of God. Here is another reversal for us: things are good not primarily because they satisfy our own criteria of goodness or that of our society, but because they reflect the goodness of God's being as one of endless giving.

Again the Jesus Prayer helps us to understand the way in which goodness – like truth and beauty – is to be authentically comprehended only in Jesus. The designation of Jesus as the Son of God points us to his relations with God as Son of the Father, by whom he is sent into the world in the communion of the Holy Spirit. Thus God's goodness can be seen as a fullness, a trinitarian event, which is dynamic and inexhaustibly full of love.

Dynamic goodness

We can expand on this theme of goodness in God. In the first centuries of the life of the Church, Christians came to see that God's life was richer than had ever been appreciated before the coming of Christ and the outpouring of the Spirit. They came to understand on the basis of their experience and the testimony of the Scriptures that God's life is characterized by what is given and received abundantly among the persons of the Trinity. 'What can be given when each is divine?' is a fair question, to which Christians can answer that divinity is not a stuff that is contained in equal measure by separable beings – divinity is in interrelationship. The persons of the Trinity are distinct but distinguished precisely in their relationships with each other. Divinity is an energetic but patterned, overflowing but balanced flux of mutuality between persons. This would be a contemporary exposition of the biblical phrase 'God is love', and its importance lies in the dynamism it injects into the notion of goodness.

God's goodness in the Son of God from eternity consists in his being sent from the Father and receiving sonship in the Spirit to return to the Father. This energy is given to the world in the incarnation of the Son. All this mutuality, this absolute reciprocity of relationship, is given to the world in the sending of the Son. His mission is to be the firstborn among many brothers, to be the firstfruits of new creation, to draw the world into the goodness of God. His goodness and loving purposes for the world are one.

Just as God's love is dynamic, it is also inexhaustible. Love is what constitutes God's very existence. Turned outwards towards the world, it is ever abundant, ever intent to give itself to the other, ever reaching out to the other. Love compels God to reach out to the world, giving it a profusion of life, in order to generate as many means as possible by which his love may be shared. It is love that compels God to throw the net of possible relationships with himself as wide as can be. God's love, then, is a giving of nothing less than his being, since his being is love. In everyday discourse we refer to 'sending' in situations where a gift is given that leaves the sender independent of the recipient. In Christ, however, there are no such distinctions. The one giving gives of him- or herself and is even defined in terms of this self-sending character. God retains the dignity of the one and only Father by divesting himself, pouring himself out in his Son in an incomparable act of self-emptying.

In such a movement of outpouring, God gives of himself without reserve and demonstrates his inexhaustible goodness. To hold anything back would contradict the fact that it is the same love involved in creation that also defines himself. There is thus an identity between the way God's being is expressed towards the world and towards himself. This self-emptying character of God's love is shown to us again and again in acts of goodness: in the foundational self-emptying of the Son of God in the incarnation (see Philippians 2:7); in the pouring out of his precious blood in the eucharistic wine (see Matthew 26:28); in God's pouring out of himself in his death, symbolized by the blood and water that poured from Jesus' side on the cross (see John 19:34); in Christ's pouring out of the Holy Spirit at Pentecost for the empowerment of us all for mission (see Acts 2:33); and in the pouring out of the Church in sacrificial emulation of Jesus' example and inspired by the Spirit (see Philippians 2:17).

Decanting the life of God

God pours out his life in these many profound ways for the sake of the world. This is God's goodness in all its fullness. God, the source of all goodness, is never diminished or exhausted in this giving. This would contradict the fact that God is infinite, for then his being would be defined by a finite measure of love. Rather, God's love is endless and superabundant, always giving more than it is possible for the world to receive. It is therefore inconceivable for the eternal being of God to be fully received by the temporal being of the world. Indeed, God's self-emptying is also a self-replenishing from the perspective of the world, as his gift to the world draws the world, glorified, into his fullness.

The one who prays to the Son of God stands before One who is prepared to pour himself into each particular creature, loving each uniquely, to raise that creature into his abundant life. However much the heart expands to make room for goodness, there is always more to receive. God is the Supreme Good, a new wine bursting old wineskins. This means that there is no end of goodness to those who live by the Spirit of the Son. The crucifixion of Christ is a vivid demonstration that even the cup of suffering and death becomes a cup of blessing poured out for others when the heart is filled with God's goodness.

GOD'S REACHING OUT IN JESUS: 'HAVE MERCY'

We have so far seen how prayer brings about a reversal of orientation in our relationships with one another, the world and God. We can leave behind the need to guard ourselves or to seek life through others as we become more able to find fulfilment in genuine mutuality. We come to be more patient and dependent on God for all things and desire to share what we have with others. In short, we come to be more and more like God in prayer.

The receptivity called for in order to allow such inner change does raise questions about how best to see prayer. It is far more than a chat between friends, however helpful telephone imagery may be for children. Prayer is primarily God reaching out in communication with us. An emphasis on reaching out, therefore, might better inform the practice of prayer. Generally we reach out for an object of some kind only when we have the confidence to do so. When we have become disorientated in ourselves, we are only capable of reaching out blindly and helplessly. The baby reaches out for its mother's breast whether it is available or not.

Our propensity to reach out for something is a vital human disposition. In reaching out we assume the existence of something other than ourselves, even though we do not always find the object which we are seeking. Reaching out assumes not only that the object sought exists, but also that it is of value. When we reach out for something, we have already grasped hold of it at some level. When I reach out for my pen, for example, I do so without needing to reflect on what I am doing. I do not pause to consider that the pen might not be what I have always taken it to be. To reach out for an object of ordinary experience implies a relationship that issues in practical activity. It is only when something goes wrong – the pen is broken, or missing – that the automatic manner of reaching out for the pen is disturbed. What should I do? Do I go out and buy a new pen, and if so, with what kind of pen should I replace the old one? Do I continue to look for it, only no longer with such immediate confidence that I will be successful in obtaining that for which I am reaching out? The absence of the pen somehow brings it into being for us.

The absent object

True prayer is perhaps more analogous to our flailing attempts to reach out for an absent object than being able to pick something up directly. We assume that we are reaching out to God in prayer, and that he is really there. We may even use various formulas of expression to ensure that we are addressing the correct object, the 'God and Father of Jesus Christ', and so on. But too often it may feel as if we are reaching out for an object easily within our grasp. The character that this prayer takes is like something on which we have already decided. Our prayer becomes automatic, and jaded. It is only when the network of our relationships comes unstuck that our reaching out becomes also a crying out to God, as the baby cries for its mother. In times of sickness, for example, when we are incapable of doing anything much and can no longer reach out for familiar objects, we are thrown back on our isolation. You cry out for God, helpless like a child. Is he there for you?

At such times we are no longer conceiving of God in any way comparable to an object of experience. We do not pray to him for his blessing on this or that project, although we may well pray for health. Yet it is precisely in such moments that God's presence comes to us. God's presence coincides with the very absence of God in the world that we have tried to arrange carefully around ourselves.

God is like the mother who cannot help but immediately responds to the cry of her child. She cannot act otherwise, or refrain from acting. Then we realize that there is something of peculiar value here that we desire to hold close to us. We have not been speaking at, to or of God – we have simply cried out, not reaching out in any definite or articulate way. At this point prayer has been permitted to take on a whole new meaning. We have given up on prayer as an initiative of our own design, on prayer as finding a tidy place in our working life, almost like a clear space on the desk. We can no longer grasp God by our own efforts. Rather we allow ourselves to be found by God and searched by God, and finally we know ourselves to be known by God.

In crying out we become aware that we can never know God in any sense that we could conceive by reason. We realize that we cannot reach out to God in any way that could give another the impression that we know precisely what we are doing. God comes to us, searches us, convicts us. In this we know God's mercy: a knowing that we are known by God and – in the face of our helplessness and nothingness – are accepted and loved by him.

GOD'S CONVICTION IN JESUS: 'UPON ME'

We have moved from our reaching out to God to our being found and searched by God, but we could only come to this by passing through a crying out for God. Such crying out is often voiced in contexts where we become somehow cut off from our everyday world. Of course, when we become ill family and friends often come to our aid and we can know God's love in their tending. I have, however, been concentrating on an interior movement where God's mercy is experienced immediately as an undeserved presence.

I would claim not only that it is right for us to enjoy a personal and inward relationship with God, but that significant aspects of our overall life with God and one another are to be nurtured here. Such inwardness has its own energy which in time turns us outwards again into the world, where our activities and relationships are invested with meaning and colour.

Let us take the example of reconciliation. A beautiful example of this can be found in David Lynch's sensitive film about old age, *The Straight Story*. This was based on the real-life story of a 73-year-old man from Iowa called Alvin Straight. After hearing that his brother has had a stroke, and realizing that he himself might not have long to live, Straight prepares himself to travel the 300 miles to see his brother by the only means of transport he has – a lawnmower. The point is that Straight's consciousness of their impending death makes him determined to see his brother, to whom he has not spoken for a decade, and be reconciled to him. The reconciliation seems to be brought about when the brother realizes that Straight has been travelling for months on end on a lawnmower just to see him.

When we ask for the mercy of Jesus Christ to fall on us, we do so from a sense of our own human mortality and frailty. It is a personal confession of need, but never an individualistic one, since we make it in solidarity with the entire human race. But more directly, this awareness of finitude brings to the fore those things that are of final value to us – things that we could not face death without having done something about – and speaks to us of the possibility of setting ourselves at rest about them. It provides us with a horizon of what is genuinely possible for us still to do and which should be done. Often this may be accompanied by a sense of regret for not having done such things earlier, just as Alvin Straight seems in the film to carry about with him a need to make up for the previous ten years with his brother, years that seem to trundle behind him like the trailer of his lawnmower.

Outward movement

Awareness of human frailty is therefore not introspective. It inevitably takes us out of ourselves in practical accountability to others. This is especially true of families and communities. Alvin Straight's awareness of his own failure to 'make peace' earlier with his brother issues in advice he gives to others, at various points in the film, that they should affirm the other members of their own families and let them know that they are valued. Especially moving is a scene set around an open fire of burning sticks, where he attempts to console a girl who has run away from her family, believing that they would reject her for becoming pregnant. His words to her are as follows:

> When my kids were little I used to play a game with them. I would give each of them a stick, one for each one of them, and I would say, 'You break that' – and of course they could, real easy. Then I would say, 'Tie them sticks in a bundle and try to break that' – and of course they could not. Then I would say, 'That bundle, that's family.'

The perennial wisdom being expressed here summarizes the sense in which an individual's integrity can only be found in relationship, in community. It is no accident that this same basic metaphor for family and friendship can be found throughout history. It is witnessed in Ecclesiastes 4:9-16, a saying of which, recorded in verse 12, provides a specific parallel to Straight's words of wisdom: 'A threefold cord is not quickly broken' (NRSV). Interestingly, this saying may also be found in the much earlier Sumerian body of epic literature that presumably fed into this Old Testament tradition. It expresses a truth at the heart of any social structure, a truth inhabited by anyone who confesses his or her radical incompleteness without God and the people of God.

Our true identity is only to be found in the family of God, the Church. Yet God's love is never lost in a crowd. He does not deal with us *en bloc*, as members of a collective, but rather as individuals, each held in being in relation to others by his love. Far from our being cogs in an ecclesiastical machine, his love and concern for each of us is a necessary condition for the Church to be a united and diverse body in which people flourish as themselves. Our integrity is to be found in our filial and ecclesial relationships as members of the growing body of Christ.

In prayer God deals with us individually, as uniquely loved members of his household of faith. He takes us into his heart so that we may know ourselves to be objects of his mercy and of infinite importance to him. This is the opposite of individualism, because it implies the resignation of our first-person perspective and the welcoming of God's universal love. We become 'me' rather than 'I', the object of love rather than the subject of choosing, the one with whom God is dealing mercifully. As that 'me' becomes our core identity, we become able to live out that identity among others, giving them the freedom from having to fulfil our need for security.

GOD'S GRACE IN JESUS: 'A SINNER'

Often this phrase of the Jesus Prayer is omitted, and in a sense it only reinforces what we have already begun to say about the identity of a praying person. Certainly 'sinner' is a name we truthfully call ourselves. As Paul says, 'all have sinned and fall short of the glory of God' (Romans 3:23 NRSV). It would be fair to say, however, that in the Eastern Church the identity of a sinner has always been seen as a cause for hope, even celebration, because it puts us in a place before God where we can be justified. Remember that the Jesus Prayer is essentially the prayer of Luke's tax collector (see Luke 18:13).

As we name ourselves sinners, our need for God's mercy is at once transparent to us. We realize that we are created out of nothing, and that we will return to nothing without the grace of God working within us. Our culture encourages its people to construct their self-identity through seeking possessions or status, but this illusion can be broken by the deliberate effort to dethrone the self. Having retracted our gaze from our preoccupations in the world, we are able to penetrate their vanity and realize that our fundamental identity cannot come from ourselves. We come to realize that all value – including any good that we may appear to do or that is ascribed to us in public – must be ascribed to the mercy of Jesus dwelling within us.

Our struggle to come to simplicity of heart reminds us that sin still overshadows our heart. Yet this is not a cause of despair, but renewed honesty in prayer. If the possibility of maintaining our own purity of heart belonged to us, then we might become an object of God's love but not of his mercy. Only in Jesus do we become an object of God's merciful love, and only in Jesus may we attain purity of heart. The penitential character of the Jesus Prayer means that we need not always make the confession 'a sinner' explicit. Only those who already know themselves to be sinners can begin to utter the prayer with conviction, although their sense of sinfulness may deepen, as does their sense of being in receipt of God's overwhelming grace.

The unspoken truth

When the Jesus Prayer is used in practice, this last phrase is often left unspoken. However, while it is true that this phrase is implied by what has come before, it clearly has an expressive value on the lips of the one who prays. It is precisely this sense of sinfulness that compels us to come back to the Lord in repentance and faith to cry out again, 'Lord Jesus,' and reiterate the Jesus Prayer again and again.

Once we have recognized our nothingness before God, this prepares us for fresh insight into the gracious character of our relationship to God. We see that we have been trying to make ourselves a place in the world that is altogether too cosy. Our mind has been preoccupied with small circles of reasoning, enough for survival in a busy and complex world. Even such a simple thought as 'Why is my pen missing?' might issue in a series of attempts to account for the fact of the pen being absent. 'Did I leave it in the other room?' 'Did someone borrow it?' None of these questions is useless in themselves, but they come to nothing when they flurry from an agitated and untranquil mind. In prayer, dissipating habits of thought can be broken as the mind comes to rest in the graciousness of God.

'Why did he choose me?' There is no reason. You are unable to account for the fact that you exist, for the fact that you are at this moment being held in being by God. The situation is not subject to your decision any more than a child should decide to be born. You know that God 'searches minds and hearts' (Revelation 2:23 NRSV). You know yourself to be searched by God and that perhaps it is already only an expression of his mercy that you are able to respond to him at all. You dare to cry out to Jesus, 'Have mercy on me, a sinner.' We discover, although it defies reason, that precisely in acknowledging our nothingness before God we find God's merciful love poured out afresh in our hearts.

In prayer our hearts echo the theme of St Paul: 'the grace of our Lord overflowed for me' (1 Timothy 1:14). Grace lies outside our control, though never outside God's; grace is nothing other than the hand of God at work. God's Spirit searches our heart, tending it with the utmost care, like a gardener not wanting to disturb the new shoots of spring as he removes some weeds from around them. Just as each flower in a garden is unique, so we know ourselves to be unique to God as he reaches through the many recesses of our hearts.

Confessing that one is a sinner is a vital, but never a final, part of praying. It is indeed frightening to admit that one is radically unfinished and in danger of being unmade, but, as Luke reminds us, the point of admitting one's lostness is the joy of being found and coming home to God (see Luke 15:7). As we have noted, the Jesus Prayer is meant for repetition – 'sinner' is never given the last word, but is always the gateway for the Lord to re-enter with beauty, truth and goodness, bringing new blessedness to those who know their need of him.

CONCLUDING REFLECTIONS

I have tried to address some images of ourselves in relation to God which may be deficient and which may consequently hinder us as we face God in prayer. I have not delved into the philosophical background of our culture, but its legacy is discernible in our assumptions about how to pray. We see ourselves as independent people who can come to grasp what God is like through conversation with him. Our focus here, however, has been on God knowing us rather than on our having knowledge of God or even knowing him. This is consistent with biblical theology. True love is to be defined not in terms of the love we may have for God, but in terms of God's love for us in Jesus (see 1 John 4:10).

Although this may sound strange, I have never wanted to know God, at least in the conditions of this life, as much as I have grown in my desire to be known by God (see Galatians 4:9; 1 Corinthians 13:12). Yet acknowledging this does not lead me to vagueness about what God is like and whether he exists. The process of prayer as I have described it brings us into an overwhelming sense of the existence of God, so great that we cease to define our place in the world by our own means and can even come to affirm our nothingness as creatures. We turn back to the world with our existence affirmed in a fresh way, for we know it to be grounded on God's own existence and held in being by his mercy.

To know oneself known by God, indeed, to know the depth of God's love, does not tally with seeing God as an object of knowledge. Throughout this reflection we have had to adapt common parlance to fit the ways in which God chooses to relate to us. Frequently this has involved a reversal of perspective to do justice to the dynamics of prayer. But as it is not just prayer that is done in the name of Jesus, I would like to end by briefly raising some implications for practical ministries such as evangelism, preaching and spirituality.

Knowledge and known-ness

Traditional modes of evangelism have tended to distinguish at once between those who know God and those who do not. This separates one set of people from the other and creates a situation where one group is 'in' with God and the other 'out'. This can cause resentment among those who are being evangelized, as they see those who claim to know God in a way they do not as smug and self-righteous. Problems like this inevitably arise when one takes a first-person perspective as a basis for describing different relationships people might have with God. On the other hand, one can hardly claim that God knows some people more than others. He knows us all inside out, and he loves us all equally. The pressing difference is that Christians have a vivid awareness of God's searching knowledge of their own heart as they call on his name in Jesus, whereas others lack this. I want others to know themselves to be searched through and through by God, and to see that they can never begin to know the reaches of their own heart otherwise. It is this that motivates me to talk to others about Jesus.

The same applies to preaching, in so far as preaching attempts to convey knowledge of God and to communicate the value of this knowledge to others. In doing this the preacher may appear to be characterizing him- or herself as a knowing subject – or as one gifted with knowledge of which others are ignorant – rather than pointing to God as the source of all knowing. Bad preachers point to themselves as a subject of interest and a source of truth. Good preachers refer to themselves only as a means of communicating the mercy of Jesus. There has been much emphasis on story-telling in recent years – whereas people used to give 'testimonies', they now relate their 'stories'. The terminology is unimportant so long as the essence of testimony is preserved. This consists in giving particular accounts of events in which Jesus' name is glorified, in using such events in order to 'confess that Jesus Christ is Lord' (Philippians 2:11 NRSV). This then can become the seedbed of evangelism and also prophecy (see Revelation 19:19).

Knowing, doing and being

Finally, we might reflect that spirituality is sometimes discussed in terms of knowing, doing and being, with each strand given varying emphasis according to whose spirituality is being discussed. For example, liberationists tend to stress the doing, evangelicals the knowing and contemplatives the being. What tends to characterize such discussions, however, is the anthropological manner in which such categories are defined. Our age has often put the emphasis on being, as if somehow our attempts to rediscover the relative importance of being could provide the basis for an appropriate Christian spirituality. In contrast to this, we might say that spirituality is not about our own doing or knowing, nor even about our being. It is rather about being known, met and led by God in his activity of reaching out to every particle of his creation.

The Jesus Prayer is not a cure-all for the misperceptions that beset our efforts to evangelize, preach and develop our spirituality. Nonetheless, it can at least open up the possibility that by praying in a trinitarian pattern we, and the ministries in which we share, will be conformed to the One to whom we pray, to the glory of his name.

Notes

1 Paul Cain, who was regarded by some as a contemporary prophet, speaking at a conference in London back in 1990.

PART 2

SPIRITUAL PRACTICES

FINDING A PERSONAL RULE OF LIFE

Harold Miller

When I was confirmed on Ascension Day 1965, my vicar handed out to all of us very official-looking confirmation cards. On one side of the card were all the details: 'Harold Miller, confirmed on 24 May 1965 by the Bishop of Connor. First Communion 27 May 1965.' That was fine, as it was all pretty objective fact, but the other side of the card horrified me:

Personal Rule of Life

To pray every day, morning and evening
To read my Bible every day
To be at Holy Communion regularly
To attend church every Sunday
To seek to do good to others when the opportunity arises

Or something like that. All the reverberations of the word 'rule' within a rather legalistic Anglicanism came through – what I could not do, feelings of failure, hopelessness and a bit of anger as well, deep down, that this had been unwittingly imposed on me without anyone saying anything about it before the confirmation service. Well, all I can say is that I tried. I was 'converted' a few months later, and that helped a little, but I always felt a pretty poor example of what a spiritual person should be. In the end, I forgot all about it, labelled the concept of 'rule' as a rather high-church and deadening practice, and entered into evangelical bondage instead!

The idea of a personal 'rule of life' did not enter my head again until I became a tutor at St John's College, Nottingham. During my first year on the staff there was a tremendous outcry from the students that, although they were receiving good academic and pastoral supervision, and had opportunities for personal growth, they did not find that they were being 'enabled' much in the area of personal spiritual growth. At that point, I determined that no student of mine would ever go through his or her time at college without an opportunity for a thorough and detailed chat about personal spirituality, and some chance to set new aims and objectives and explore new ideas in this area. The problem was that very few people knew where to start in talking about their spiritual lives, and the concept of setting goals for spiritual growth appeared to be very new. The thing which helped me to enable these students to begin to explore their spirituality in a fresh way was the age-old idea of 'rule', which had lain dormant in my life for at least 15 years.

I hope my experience and thinking over the last few years can be put across to you here in such a way that you can discover that what may appear at first to be bondage is actually freedom, and that the shape and structure placed on your spiritual life by embracing rule can be most advantageous and rewarding.

WHAT IS 'RULE'?

Rule is a means whereby, under God, we take responsibility for the pattern of our spiritual lives. It is 'rule' in terms of 'measure' or 'regulation' rather than 'law'. The Latin and Greek words from which it derives make that clear. The word in Greek is *kanon*,[1] and we apply it in English when we talk about the 'canon of Holy Scripture'. For a biblical book to be canonical means that it has been measured up against a standard, and has not been found wanting. In Latin *regula* is the word, which means, very simply, 'rule, pattern, model, example'.[2] Both the Latin and the Greek have the sense of 'rule' or 'measurement' and I think that will emerge as an important aspect of the concept. By embracing rule, we make for ourselves a standard to which we would like to attain, through the power of the Spirit, and we are enabled from time to time to do some appropriate assessment of how we have progressed.

Rulers are not only for measuring, however. They have often been used to rap naughty schoolboys on the knuckles, and we can so easily be in danger of using a rule in the same way. We make it legalistic. We look at our standards only to see that we have failed, and that makes us rather hopeless about the whole affair, as I was as a newly confirmed teenager. Let us try right at the beginning to rescue the idea of 'rule of life' from such deadening legalism. This can be done by looking at another translation of *regula* – as 'pattern'.

Regular patterns

'Pattern' is vital to all of us in our day-to-day living. Without it we would live higgledy-piggledy, disorganized and directionless lives. But we choose, for example, to get up at a certain time in the morning, to eat breakfast at a certain time, to go to work at 8.15, to have lunch at 1.00, our evening meal at 6.00, to put the kids to bed at 7.30 and to watch the news at 10.00. We are creatures of pattern and, indeed, even the most uncivilized animals live by some pattern or other. In the course of an ordinary day or week, we do most of these things without thinking; they are simply a natural part of civilized existence. Most of us, mind you, when we get an opportunity for a break from the routine, will welcome it with open arms, and perhaps go to the other extreme for a period of time. On holidays we often do this. We go to bed knowing that we can lie in to our heart's content in the morning, and we simply eat when we feel hungry. We do what we want, when we want and as we want. But I imagine all of us know the great relief of getting 'back to porridge' after the couple of weeks' vacation. The release of not having to decide whether to have chips or roast beef or rosé wine for breakfast – or indeed whether to have breakfast at all! There is great freedom in being back in our own home with its known and freeing timetable. It is a despiritualized version of 'Make me a captive, Lord, and then I shall be free'!

Pattern is therefore normal in our everyday lives, and the same is true of our spiritual lives. We grow up with it. I was brought up in the kind of spirituality where we were encouraged to have a certain type of 'quiet time' first thing in the morning, majoring on devotional reading of Scripture and extempore prayer. We knew that all good Christians go to a Bible study once a week and to church twice on Sundays, and give at least a tenth of their income to the Lord's work. For many evangelicals this is a pattern which usually goes on unnoticed and causes (for the most part) no problems. It is simply, for us, normal Christianity and normal routine. We live by rule without even knowing it – just because rule is basic to being human.

Living by rule then, is a way of life, a pattern. It is, as Martin Thornton puts it,[3] like being a 'regular' soldier rather than a volunteer who only fights when he feels like it. Rule is not a series of little laws; it is rather our orderly way of existence which has as its opposite not liberty but chaos. This means that we 'embrace rule' (or pattern) rather than 'keeping rules'. I think the concept of embracing says it all. It warms up the cold feeling of the word 'rule' and points towards a loving and wholehearted acceptance of the Lord's pattern and discipline for us as individuals, born of grace and freedom and not of punishment and law.

Indeed, to put it at an extreme (but a true extreme), rule is not only not legalistic, but actually opposed to legalism. Martin Thornton is again of tremendous help here. He gives an example of a man who gives up smoking for Lent – a very good idea. His purpose is to deepen his walk with God, to renounce cigarettes, to offer this habit to God and to donate what he would have spent on smoking to those in need. But, like many of us, on Ash Wednesday he falls. He gives in and smokes one cigarette. What does this mean? The Pharisee would immediately leap in and say that he has 'broken' his rule, and that is that – very shocking. Having failed, he may as well give the whole thing up. The person who lives by grace, however, will accept his weakness and reinstate him in his rule. It may be that, by the end of Lent, he will have smoked 10 or 20 cigarettes, but he will also have begun to master his own habits and given some money to those in need rather than spending it on himself. And, hopefully, he will have grown closer to the Lord. On Easter Day, the Pharisee will look for perfection and if he has kept his Lenten discipline he will be over the moon. The Christian will not be too concerned about that, but will ask, 'How has my spiritual life deepened or expanded? How have I grown in love for God?' Rule without fault is of no importance whatsoever. Rule is merely the means to an end, which is that we might walk closely with God and live more effectively for him.

THE PURPOSE OF RULE

We move on to find out some of the ways in which the embracing of rule can be a help towards this overall aim.

Rule enables us to assess spiritual growth

There are problems in taking the metaphor of growth as the central or controlling metaphor for the Christian life – not least because Scripture itself uses it very rarely. Of course, our Lord did grow in stature and favour with both God and people (see Luke 2:52), and Peter enjoins us to 'grow in the grace and knowledge of our Lord and Saviour Jesus Christ' (2 Peter 3:18), but the dynamic and moving metaphors seem to me to be secondary to the static and given. Our being *en Christo* (in Christ), our being grounded in the saving work of our Lord, is much more focal. Nevertheless, there is a striving, a seeking for holiness, a growing in God which takes place in the 'normal' Christian life.

One of the things I have noticed is that Christian people find it very difficult to assess what, if any, growth has taken place, and this is not simply due to a false humility. Often it requires other people to tell us how we have changed over a period of time, and the whole concept of spiritual growth is so nebulous that it would be practically impossible to assess whether or not it was happening. Rule enables us to begin to focus on different areas where change and growth are necessary, and to begin to assess what is actually taking place. True, many concepts of rule focus essentially on 'acts of piety', but others are more life-orientated, and we need to be careful to look for spiritual growth not only in a super-abundance of religious exercises but also in lives which are different ethically and in love for other people. If we focus only on 'acts of piety', then surely the Pharisee goes away justified.

The other measure of spiritual growth often used by people today (perhaps especially those who have been influenced by charismatic renewal) is feeling – 'I feel closer to the Lord than I did a year ago.' For people like that, objective measures are both appropriate and important. Of course, we should from time to time 'feel' good about God, and it is often the case that we feel nothing because of sinfulness. Yet the history of Christian spirituality has enough to say about the 'dark night of the soul' to assure us that some lack of feeling or even negative emotions may be allowed by God so that we can grow in faith and deepen our dependence on him. Rule, then, is one of the things which enables us to measure spiritual growth.

Rule enables us to set objectives and goals

You do not run a race or fight a battle without objectives and goals. Runners and soldiers train and work towards new heights of achievement. Yet so many of us get nowhere in Christian terms because we have never decided what our goals are. Those living by rule will want to stand back from time to time (but not too often – too much navel-gazing is destructive) and ask not only, 'Where have I got to?' but also, 'Where am I going, and what are my objectives and goals in the spiritual life for the coming year?' We must remember all the time that the overall aim of walking closely with God is the vital thing, and objectives and goals are only means towards that end.

One of the chief pitfalls in this is the temptation of many Christians to want to achieve everything in one go – to become angels overnight. We read, for example, of John Wesley spending three or four hours in prayer each day and see his wonderful, exemplary life, and we think, 'Wouldn't it be great if I could do that?' We see how hours in prayer could put us in the place where we could get to know the Lord so much better. In a fit of impractical enthusiasm, we decide that one of our goals for the coming year will be to spend two hours in prayer each morning. We have not, however, considered the fact that at the moment we only spend two minutes in prayer, and that such a leap is unrealistic. We need to build up the length of our prayer time piece by piece, in a realistic but believing way. Rule enables us to set objectives and goals, but we must not burden ourselves with too many or too unrealistic ideals.

Rule enables us to find patterns suited to us

The title of this chapter, 'Finding a Personal Rule of Life', declares its overall purpose. At the end you should be able to set out on a pattern which is suited to you. The danger of this, of course, is excessive individualism, but the danger of imposing everything from outside is greater. You will naturally choose to develop to a large degree what is already part of you as a Christian, although you may actively choose to change some things which seem unhelpful, inappropriate or too binding. There is also a limit to what can and should be included in a rule, and most of us will and should have at the centre of our pattern the traditional disciplines. But God sees us as different individual people, each precious in his sight, and each with particular needs and at a particular point in spiritual development. You will find your own pattern, appropriate to your lifestyle and context, as you progress through this chapter.

Rule is efficient

This is one of Martin Thornton's main points in *Christian Proficiency*, but both 'efficient' and 'proficient' are cold, clinical words. We do not always like efficient people, but we are instructed in Ephesians 5:16 and Colossians 4:5 to 'make the most of the time' (NRSV), or, in the lovely phrase from the Authorized Version, to 'redeem the time'. We are at least expected not to be totally inefficient as Christians with regard to our spiritual development. The whole concept of efficiency shows up in a new light when we are reminded that the purpose of being efficient is that we might be effective for God. The purpose of rule is not only that we might walk more closely with God, but also that we might live more effectively for him. The truth is that, without a growing and deepening spirituality, without prayer, without knowing his word, without the means of grace, we cease to live effectively in God's service.

Rule is intended to encourage

One of the most encouraging things of all may be to write down something of your already existent pattern of spiritual life. Include as much as possible. Do not forget grace before meals, or those little times of prayer with which life is peppered, or your meditation on God's word, or the choruses you sing as you go about your work. A few years ago, we adopted the 'common discipline' of the Community of the Cross of Nails[4] for use in St John's College. One person noted that she was already living in a subconscious way by something very like it, and yet still had a lot to learn from it. So be encouraged by those aspects of the spiritual life which are already part of the warp and weft of your living. You might also like to consider how a common rule, or at least a partly common rule which you agree to use along with a group of other Christians, can give support and strengthening to you as an individual as you seek to grow more like Jesus. God has given us other members of the body to enable and uphold us.

THE CONTENTS OF RULE

Roots

The contents of any particular rule will be determined to a large degree by what the purpose of the rule is. Indeed, the area covered by the contents can vary a great deal from one rule to another. Illustrations are not hard to find if we look back for a moment to the roots of the concept, which are undoubtedly monastic. Joseph T. Lienhard defines 'rule' as follows:

> A rule is a document, usually composed by the founder of a monastery or religious order, that determines the particular ends of the foundation and the principal means by which these ends are to be attained, and contains vows and regulations that guide the life of the community.[5]

He rightly goes on to note that, although monasticism popularized the idea, there was also a prehistory. The first Christian hermits, called anchorites and anchoresses, separated themselves off from the world so that they could devote everything to God. Very naturally (especially if they were young and immature), they sought the advice and help of older Christians as to how they might organize and develop their spiritual lives. This led to personal, made-to-measure 'rules'. The first monastic rule was that of Pachomius (d. 346), the founder of cenobitism,[6] but the most famous and easily available rule is that of St Benedict (*c*.480-*c*.547).[7]

The Rule of St Benedict makes great reading because it covers every aspect of a monk's life. It is, of course, a rule whose content is predetermined and simply accepted *en bloc* by the members of the monastery. One passage which I find particularly amusing – and which I should not imagine any readers would want to include in their own rule – is Chapter 22:

How the Monks Are to Sleep

Let them sleep each one in a separate bed. Let their beds be assigned to them in accordance with the date of their conversion ... If it be possible, let them all sleep in one place; but if their numbers do not allow of this, let them sleep by tens or twenties, with seniors to supervise them. There shall be a light burning in the dormitory throughout the night. Let them sleep clothed and girt with girdles or cords, but not with their belts, so that they may not have their knives at their sides while they are sleeping, and be cut by them in their sleep . . .

The chapter concludes:

When they rise for the Work of God, let them gently encourage one another, on account of the excess to which the sleepy are addicted.

Perhaps this last sentence still has some relevance today! But the point of all this is to show that this type of monastic rule covered almost all possible eventualities. Every aspect of life for the monk was included.

Little or large?

When we decide on our own personal rule, one of the questions we need to ask is this: what are the appropriate areas to contain in it? There are certain dangers in seeking to include everything. It can become unfocused and too lengthy, and can end up being a long series of little regulations rather than something coherent and whole. Martin Thornton notes the danger of this in *Christian Proficiency*, and outlines what he reckons to be the essence of the rule of the Church through the ages – the factors by which a rule is seen to be 'catholic'. This essence is simply the following:

1 Office (daily liturgy)
2 Mass (Holy Communion)
3 Private prayer[8]

There is a great benefit in thus reducing or concentrating the contents of a rule. It avoids an unprincipled eclecticism; it includes every aspect of prayer (intercession, confession, praise, meditation, petition, thanksgiving); it includes regular reading of the word of God; it is both corporate and personal; it is in line with Christian history and tradition – and it highlights the essentials.

It is interesting to compare such an approach to the feel of Richard Foster's *Celebration of Discipline*, where he spends a large chunk of the book looking at more 'outward' disciplines which are very earthed and practical (granted, he is talking more generally about discipline and less specifically about rule). Some of the things he says nevertheless reverberate with the feel of the Rule of St Benedict:

> Consider your clothes. Most people have no need for more clothes. They buy more not because they need clothes, but because they want to keep up with the fashions. Hang the fashions. Buy only what you need. Wear your clothes until they are worn out. Stop trying to impress people with your clothes, and impress them with your life . . . [9]

He goes on to list other outward disciplines, with regard to the overall 'discipline of simplicity':

> Reject anything which is an addiction . . .
> Develop a habit of giving things away . . .
> Learn to enjoy things without owning them . . .
> Reject anything that will breed the oppression of others . . .

We need to decide whether our rule will be a more life-orientated one, embracing the whole of our experience, or a more strictly prayer-orientated one. In doing this, it may be important to assess whether we are temperamentally 'desert' or 'marketplace' Christians. I have often asked groups of people to put up their hands to say which of these two they veer towards, and the thing which has surprised me is that most people do not know. So let me ask you at this point to spend a few moments contemplating this in relation to yourself.

The desert and the marketplace

The desert Christian sees separation from the world as of the essence of true spirituality – setting time aside for God, getting away from the rush and bustle to quietness and being alone with God. Such a person will probably be drawn to 'religious' things, will spend much time at Bible studies, prayer meetings, Holy Communion on saints' days, and doing more religious exercises more intensely (or perhaps more 'passively' if inclined towards quietism[10]).

The marketplace Christian is quite the opposite. I remember a quotation from my student days which sums it all up: 'Eating spaghetti is prayer.' For this kind of person the whole of life is a

Christian experience, and the Christian is required to be light and salt in the world. Separation from the world is much less important, indeed sometimes anathema. This person will say, for example, 'The whole of life is prayer,' or, 'The whole of life is worship,' thus emphasizing a crucially important point, but being in danger of evacuating such words of all their meaning. For such a person, actual 'time set aside' will not be nearly so important.

Depending on whether you are inclined towards the desert or the marketplace, you will be likely to see the concept of rule from a particular angle. The desert Christian will be inclined to want more acts of piety, while the marketplace Christian will want something much more life-centred. Of course, it may well be the case that the one needs the balance of the other. Indeed, Jesus, our model, lived his life in a rhythm between the two – at times going aside to be alone with his Father, and at other times going out and about, living out the spiritual life in both ordinary and extraordinary situations. The problem with being at the desert extreme is that it so easily becomes just religion, and the problem at the marketplace extreme is that very little prayer or worship (in the traditional Christian sense) takes place. So you must decide on the content of your rule – unless, of course, you choose to embrace a 'given' rule.

Embracing a given rule

This may be done if you choose to become a member of a tertiary order, or if your church or Christian community has a rule of its own – for example, the 'common discipline' of the Community of the Cross of Nails mentioned earlier, or the Taizé Rule. It may be important to point up the benefits of such a given rule at this point, as most of the rest of the chapter is geared towards finding a personal pattern.

- A given rule may well have a balance which our own personal devisings (even in conjunction with others) will not have. It may also be much more obviously in line with Christian tradition.
- A given rule may be particularly useful for those who are indecisive.
- There are some people who find it preferable to be required to adjust themselves rather than to have the freedom to adjust the rule.

Conclusion

Assuming that most of you have decided on the purpose of your rule, and on what kind of spirituality (desert or marketplace) you are inclined towards, and that you are not embracing a fully given rule, where do we go from here in terms of content?

First of all, may I suggest that you note down what is already part of your rule? Include prayer, Bible reading, other reading, churchgoing, giving, fasting and so on. Try to think as widely as possible at this stage; you may like to get someone to help you with this. Then note down the areas in which you feel the need to progress and develop. Add any specific things which you feel may be helpful towards this. Remember, you will have the whole of your life in which to become more like Jesus. You will be choosing from these things what God wants you to pursue now, and you will be leaving to the side many other things which are not for the present.

Then set the paper aside. We will come back to it later, having looked at the various contexts in which rule functions.

THE CONTEXTS OF RULE

Looking for balance

We have already thought about balance in so far as it relates to the contents of rule. Now we go on to look at it in relation to the contexts of rule. Balance does have both negative and positive interpretations. Positively, it can be a very healthful thing to be a balanced person, to have a balanced diet, to avoid unhelpful extremes, but that is only part of the picture. As a college tutor I used a little chart which offered the student various continua on which to place him- or herself – such as 'introvert/extrovert', 'legalist/free thinker', 'lazy/activist'. Overall, I did not really mind what the answers were, but I dreaded the person who said, 'Oh, somewhere in the middle,' to every single question. Anyone who is really balanced on everything – and this is the negative side – must be an incredible bore!

The other introductory thing I would like to say about balance is that so often an overall equilibrium is achieved over a period of time rather than at every specific moment. Let me give a personal example. At St John's we had a very hectic life during term-time, with endless chapel services, group prayer times, prayer partnerships and so on. This could very easily lead one (that is, me) to being so spiritually 'full' that personal prayer went out of the window. However, at the time of my first writing this, I was on three months' sabbatical leave with no college duties. My approach then was to avoid college corporate and group worship at all costs and spend time building up personal prayer and prayer with my wife and family. If you were to examine my lifestyle either only during term-time or only during my sabbatical, it could be very unbalanced, but overall I hope an equilibrium was achieved.

Contexts

'Contexts' is the word I use for the different areas in which spirituality functions. These contexts will become an axis on a chart which you may fill in towards the end of this chapter. I have mentioned three or four already: personal, group, corporate, family. We could add to that two other things: the daily office, and life. Although for our purposes I am designating these as separate categories, they do in fact very much flow into one another. To take an obvious example, our corporate gatherings will be so much more effective and productive if everyone is personally close to the Lord, learning from him, getting to know him better, and bringing to the *ecclesia* a lively and rich personal faith. Equally, our personal prayer life will be so much richer if we bring to it our learning from other Christians, an understanding of their needs, and the solidarity and assurance which we can find in believing in and worshipping God together. Let us look briefly at each one.

Personal

I really believe that any spirituality worth its salt will have a strong emphasis on the individual's personal relationship with the Lord. It is a truism to say that what we are like on our own is what we are really like. I fear that Christians at the beginning of the twenty-first century are worse than ever at developing an intimate personal spirituality with their God. Given time on our own with no one looking, so many of us will choose anything other than the activity of prayer.

Group

Groups have been highlighted within and without the traditional churches more than ever over the last 15 or 20 years. For many people, a group spirituality has developed, encouraged more recently with the growth in interest in cell churches. It may be a prayer group, a fellowship group, or whatever, but it has added something spiritually which can only be achieved in that kind of setting. For many it brings a sense of warmth, a place where we can be ourselves and get to know other Christians in more depth, a place where we can discuss, try out ideas and learn, a place where we can ask others to pray for us, and find that agreement of two or three that helps us to discern and know the will of God. And of course it is a place of belonging.

Corporate

Within this context (the assembled people of God) we find what is for many of us a central point in our rule, Holy Communion. Without this we could not conceive of living as Christians. This corporate context also brings us into the sphere where our personal whims are laid open to, and tempered by, the preaching of the word, the liturgy of the Church, and the historical faith into which we have come. Some call this the 'congregation' or 'celebration' aspect of the Christian life.

Family

Just as there have been times in the history of the Church when group spirituality or personal spirituality have been particularly emphasized, so there have been times when the focus has been on family spirituality. During the commonwealth (when the Book of Common Prayer was outlawed) there was a liturgical family spirituality which carried on. Perhaps the Victorian era in particular was the one of family prayers, family teaching, even the family altar. Our day is not one in which this has been a particular emphasis, but we might very fairly ask (with our Judaic background) whether we are not unbalanced here. I suppose the last remaining vestige of it is grace before meals.

Also under this heading, but as a separate point, let me mention the subject of the spirituality of married couples together. I think many of us find this balance hard to get right. It is very easy when married to make all times of prayer joint times at first, or else simply to go on as you were before marriage, never praying together. My experience has been that it is not good always to pray together, and my wife and I seek to have a time of prayer together once a week. I know many others have found the saying of Compline last thing at night to be helpful. I simply mention the area here as one you will have to consider if you are married. Rules of life have implications for others, and the others may well need to be consulted and to agree on the way forward.

The daily office

I have written extensively on this elsewhere,[11] and will therefore be brief at this point. The office is one of the three elements in a traditional catholic rule, but the elements in it may of course be covered in different ways. I separate out the office because it has normally been considered not to fall into one particular category. It may be private, but it still has a public dimension, in that the reader is united with others reading the same service on the same day. It may be a group activity, or it may be pursued at home, on the bus, in church or in a cathedral, or even on the radio. It is worth considering how much it has to offer in the process of building your spiritual world.

Life

What do you want for your Christianity in the marketplace? Is that to be part of your rule? It is crucially important for many Christians (perhaps especially Christian leaders) to plan times of refreshment and relaxation – times to participate in the ordinary things in life, from which the busyness of their occupation may normally keep them. Other things which may be included are care for those in need, interest in what is going on in the world, even political or social involvement.

We move on now from the axis of contexts to the axis of time, and then will return to put it all together.

THE FLOW OF TIME

Rhythm is, as we noted earlier, absolutely natural to human beings, as natural as our heartbeat itself, and a comfortable (in the positive sense of the word) spirituality will be rhythmical. It is therefore quite usual for us to seek to develop our spiritual being on a timed basis. We live out our Christian lives in days, weeks, months and years, and these temporal units can be of tremendous benefit to us if used to the full.

Days

Some of us are good in the morning; others, like owls, come out and are at their best at night. Traditional evangelical spirituality has not been very good at taking account of this and, over the years, most of us have been made to feel pretty lousy as Christians if we do not make time early in the morning to pray and read the Bible, to begin the day with God. All of us have responsibility to account for our time before the Lord, and no doubt some of us who prefer to snuggle down under the covers rather than get up to pray need to find new ways of disciplining ourselves. Undoubtedly, for many people early in the morning is the only time when quietness can be found, and temperaments have to be changed so that we learn to be awake. The beat of the day, however, is crucial.

For those who are ordained (and for some who are not), the daily office may well surround our work by providing us with fixed points at the beginning and end of each day. Otherwise we may punctuate our time with particular points at which we remember what God has done for us, seeking from that to establish the pattern of habitual recollection of God in everything we do. When visiting the Republic of Ireland, I have often been very impressed with the concept of the Angelus in relation to this. Even the television stops for a minute at 6 p.m. to ring the Angelus, as a reminder of God in the midst of all our busyness. You may know that famous painting of the reapers ceasing from their work just for a minute as the bell rings. This is not to be frowned upon as mere superstition. It makes particular times in the day 'punctuation marks' in the midst of bustle.

Weeks

Days are 'given'. The sun rises and sets, and there is not much we can do about it. Weeks are different. There have been all sorts of experiments (for example during the French Revolution) in making a week a different length – for example, 10 days with only one day's rest. The Jewish and Christian traditions have usually, following the God who rested on the Sabbath day, held to six days' work and one day's rest. This is expressed in a modern way in the discipline of the Community of the Cross of Nails (adapted for St John's):

> Members should try to follow the rule of the Sabbath, and to respect the need for a day off a week, or should arrange their week that normal pressures of work and household duties are varied by the enjoyment of a hobby or other relaxing recreation.

The last thing we want to fall back into is Sabbatarianism, but it is important to ask the question when writing a rule: how do I seek to use the Lord's Day? Clearly many of the early Christians developed a weekly pattern of assembling on the first day of the week (see Acts 20:7), for teaching, prayer, the breaking of bread and fellowship, as well as a weekly pattern of giving. 'On the first day of every week, each one of you should set aside a sum of money in keeping with his income, saving it up, so that when I come no collections will have to be made' (1 Corinthians 16:2). We will need to develop our own weekly pattern in the light of our circumstances.

We will presumably have worship right at the centre of this pattern, perhaps the weekly Communion, and many of us will be involved in a weekly fellowship group, or will have time which we can set aside for proper Bible study. This may often be much better done for an hour at a stretch once a week, rather than in tiny bits each day. A life-orientated rule will not forget time for the family as well.

Months

I reinterpret the weekly injunction from 1 Corinthians 16:2 and make it a part of my monthly pattern. On the first Sunday in the month I seek to give – because I am paid at the end of each month, and this principle of giving to God's work first as a percentage of earnings is thereby worked out in my particular case. There are many other ways of using the natural pattern of months. I know of people who set aside one day a month as a day of fasting or abstinence – a reminder of the needs of the Third World, or an opportunity for specific prayer through missing a meal. Many of our churches are organized on a monthly basis. I remember attending a prayer meeting for healing on the second Thursday each month and that was, at that time, an important part of my spiritual rhythm.

Years

Finally, there is the annual round – the round of seasons which is so important for us in variety and direction, growth, death and life. There is something very powerful indeed about seasons. Most of us experience something of the reawakening of life and vitality, hope and joy, in spring, simply because that is what is happening in nature all around us. We experience winter with its mixture of coldness and warmth – the security of being inside when it is freezing outside. We experience autumn with its sense of maturing, harvesting and dying. I imagine most of us have one or two seasons which we prefer, but we also value the routine and variety of the natural year. It may well be that the seasons affect us more profoundly than we ever imagine.

Of course, it would be impossible to speak of years without mentioning the Christian year. Easter and spring, Christmas and winter are so tied together that they are inseparable for most of us, in the northern hemisphere at least. I imagine that very few of us are deep-dyed puritans who would prefer to be rid of the Christian festivals, and, while some will find that the use of the Church year is spiritually helpful and others not (Colossians 2:16 says, 'Do not let anyone judge you by what you eat or drink, or with regard to a religious festival ... or a Sabbath day'), I think it is important at least to look at how the Church year can be used in a positive and worthwhile way. Here are some of the possible values of keeping in line with the Christian year in one's own personal spirituality.

- *It is a given, recognized and agreed structure, which can offer a framework in which to develop.* Your personal spirituality will be in line with what is happening in the corporate gatherings of the Church. Some churches use official calendars and lectionaries in a thoroughgoing way and others do not, but it is valuable for you to be reading about the Ascension (for example) in your own quiet times at the same point at which the Church is celebrating the feast.

- *It provides a focus at different times in the year.* Most of us need this. The danger of being without a given focus is that we simply stick to our own 'theme songs' and read our favourite parts of Scripture over and over again. In some churches which denigrate the concept of a Church year, the focus is always on the cross or on personal salvation. One of the things I find valuable about the Church year is that it enables me to understand Communion from a different angle, according to the theme. When I go to Communion on Advent Sunday, I am reminded of the banquet to which we look forward. When I receive on Christmas Day, I am reminded that my God, 'contracted to a span', comes to me in the most earthly of forms, and continues to do so in simple bread and wine. When I receive on Maundy Thursday, I am transported back to the Upper Room and the Last Supper. A different focus gives a fresh angle and offers new spiritual insights.
- *It should provide a basis for reliving the events and applying them to ourselves.* We cannot apply the gospel to ourselves all in one go! The Church year reminds us that Scripture is essentially a story – not just a story in the past, but rather a story which still lives, in the sense that it has repercussions for today and is relevant to our world here and now. So the Epiphany (the visit of the wise men) becomes not just a story but a reminder that Christ is for all people of all nations; Ash Wednesday becomes not just a historical record of Jesus fasting in the wilderness, but a realization that his victory over temptation can also be ours, and that his setting time aside specifically to be with God can be an example for us and an encouragement to holiness of life.
- *It provides us with a balance*, not just thematically, but in terms of feeling. It includes festival days, ferial[12] days, fast days – times of joy, times of repentance, times of specific

prayer,[13] times of preparation and looking forward. The whole tenor of worship will vary much from season to season – perhaps the best example is the dullness and dereliction of a bare, colourless church on Good Friday compared with the blaze of colour, flowers, light and beauty of Easter Day. It might also be worth asking which part of that balance you find particularly hard. In the parish context it always seemed to me that people enjoyed festivals and avoided the more solemn times of the year, such as Ash Wednesday and Holy Week. It is equally likely that some of us can 'get into' the feel and reality of repentance and fasting, but cannot be free within ourselves simply to enjoy God, or praise him, or thank him in the joy of festival.

What, then, are the aspects of spirituality which might be organized on an annual basis? Let me list some:

- *Retreat.* This is something which I seek to do for a few days each year. It may not be part of your spirituality, and it may indeed be impossible at different stages in your life. Nonetheless, there are many retreat bases available, and more and more people are finding that extended time alone with God is necessary.
- *Confession.* Auricular confession[14] has not been part of the Protestant tradition, although it was always allowed by the Book of Common Prayer as a help to those who needed to talk things out in order to quieten their conscience. Many, again, do this annually at a certain time of year (see Chapter 12 for further guidance).
- *Assessment.* Spiritual direction is important for anyone taking on board a 'rule of life', and again it is good to write in a specific time (or specific times) at a certain point in the year. Otherwise it may well be forgotten. See further on this in Chapter 5.
- *Review of rule.* Again, specific dates are helpful.
- *Abstinence.* Disciplining yourself in relation to bodily appetites for a period of time (usually Lent) is again very helpful to many people as a declaration of the purity of God and as a determined discipline of other desires.

Cyclic and directional time

All the preceding could suggest that Christianity is essentially a cyclic religion in which we relive the same events over and over again, year by year. There is a sense in which the story should be told over and over again, but there is also a danger that, in our churches or in our individual spiritual lives, we become stuck. The Christian story itself is a directional one. God does things in history which move in a certain direction and are for a purpose. If our spirituality is to be a developing one, we will need to seek to ensure that we are moving in God's direction, so that we look back over the years and see that God's purposes have been fulfilled in our lives.

PUTTING IT TOGETHER

At this point it is important to bring together contents, contexts and the time factor, and I offer you a chart on which to do some diagnosis and some looking forward. From this, you will hopefully be able to draw up your personal rule of life for the next period of time.

First of all, please approach the chart (given towards the end of this chapter) in terms of what is. You have at an earlier stage noted those things which are already elements of your spiritual life. Now you might like to begin to categorize them. For examples, see the filled-in chart. This is not my own personal chart, nor is it intended as something by which to judge yourself. It is, rather, an example to show you the kind of thing you might be thinking about.

Having done that, you might wish to look forward to where you would like to be. This may mean subtracting things from your present 'rule' and adding new things. Please note, no one has endless time and resources, and subtracting what have become dead or lifeless customs may be crucial in clearing the decks for the future.

Adding new elements

The number of possible 'ingredients' to put into this menu is almost infinite. Let me list a few as reminders for you, so that you go about the exercise with the widest possible perspective: Bible reading; meditation; use of the lectionary; spiritual reading; prayer (adoration and worship, thanksgiving, intercession, confession); tongues; singing; giving; services; sacraments; grace before meals; family prayers; fasting, abstinence, feasting; the Church year; Sunday; retreat; silence. Other chapters in this book may give you further ideas and resources.

The important thing is that you add only those things which you believe to be right for you at this stage, in the sight of God. Do not try too much too soon. And do not feel that every space in the chart needs to be filled in! But do be open to new elements and new ways. It is so easy to become trapped in one's own particular tradition, and to miss the wealth of things available from other Christian traditions or backgrounds.

Writing your rule

This, if at all possible, should be done with someone else – not so that they can judge you, but so that they can provide a sounding board and a support. First, I suggest that you be as simple as possible. For example, you may wish to leave many things unsaid, areas which are so much part of you that they are and will be there anyway. You have noted these, drawn encouragement from them, and may wish simply to leave them in the background. Second, be specific but not legalistic. It does no harm to set a time on your prayers – try to aim at 20 minutes or half an hour – or to say, 'I will seek to set aside 9-10 o'clock on a Saturday morning to do Bible study.' Many of us need specifics, and have worked for far too long with vaguenesses. There is something businesslike about being definite, but there will be something crucial missing if our relationship with God becomes *only* businesslike. Third, be careful how you phrase your rule. In the end, how you state things affects how you think about things. Avoid the language of legalism: 'I must do this and that.' Let me give you some good examples from our 'common discipline'.

Let us not be ashamed to show our appreciation of one another.

Let us always be hospitable and offer our leisure.

Try each day to set aside time for the renewal of your personal discipleship of Jesus Christ . . . Let us not forget to pray for each other ... If you find it hard to pray, remember that our Lord himself found it hard too, even in Gethsemane; and his friends found it impossible. If you are not a religious person, do not forget that they were not either.

Unless prevented by illness or other good cause, members may abstain from one meal each week, and give the money thus saved to those in need.

This is, of course, written as a corporate rule, but the feel of the language may help you to write your personal rule in a less rigid and legalistic way.

Dealing with failure

This will be the most difficult thing you will have to face in your life as a 'regular'. Failure is something all of us have to face as fallen human beings, and it is something which either drives us into ourselves and our fallenness in a hopeless and pitiful way, or else drives us to our God who is able to deal with it constructively. Right at the beginning of the chapter we saw the danger of failure leading to legalistic thinking, leading in turn to the overthrow of our rule. The positive approach is to admit it, repent of any sin connected with it (if there is any, and there may not be), accept it and move on from it. But failure may also suggest not just that we are frail, but also that our 'pattern' does not fit, and that is where adaptability comes in. Changing mid-stream is not always wise. We are sometimes better to keep to our rule for its allocated period of time and then, in reviewing it, come up with something more productive. If it is really incompatible, however, there may well be times when we are left with no option but to review mid-stream. That can be an adult and appropriate choice to make.

'RULE OF LIFE' CHART

	Personal	Group	Corporate	Family	Office	Life
Daily						
Weekly						
Monthly						
Annually						

AN EXAMPLE

	Personal	Group	Corporate	Family	Office	Life
Daily	15 mins meditatory private prayer			Grace, prayers with children	Say Morning Prayer Mon-Fri	
Weekly	Half an hour's Bible study on Saturday	House group	Holy Communion Church a.m., p.m. on Sunday	Pray with wife each Sunday evening		Visit person in need. Sunday afternoon – relaxation
Monthly	Give 10% to church and other Christian work at start of month	Healing prayer group				Work for Christian Aid
Annually	3 days retreat abstinence and review during Lent					

THE FREEDOM OF RULE

So we come full circle. The title which I had originally intended to give to this chapter was 'The Freedom of Rule', but it was felt that such a title would not be immediately self-explanatory. Nevertheless, this is what it is all about in my mind: the discovery of that remarkable balance – that in the very thing which appears at first to be deadening law, we can discover our freedom; that indeed the serious, devoted and disciplined service of the Lord is 'perfect freedom'; that the Lord created us to take responsibility for the pattern of our lives, in the power of his Spirit, and that he himself strengthens us as we seek to make Jesus our example as well as our Saviour. But beware – there is within the human condition an incessant tendency to revert to law and 'will-worship',[15] and that is the first thing which will destroy both our rule and our trust in the Lord.

Finally, this chapter is not just something to be read, it is something to be done and something which will take a long time to work out. Your rule will need ongoing revision and review. It will change according to circumstances and needs – it may even come and go – but it is only in so far as this introduction has helped you to find a suitable pattern for your Christian life that it has succeeded in its objective.

Notes

1 See, for example, Galatians 6:16: 'Peace and mercy to all who follow this rule'; Philippians 3:17: 'Brothers ... live according to the pattern we gave you'.

2 The two words are brought together in the title given to clergy (especially in the twelfth century) who lived very strictly according to rule. They were called 'canons regular'.

3 Martin Thornton, *Christian Proficiency* (SPCK, 1969). I have found this book a great help in focusing my own thinking around the concept of rule. See especially Chapter 5. Many of my reflections here have their roots in that chapter.

4 This was developed by Coventry Cathedral after the war and is essentially based on the Taizé Rule.

5 Joseph T. Lienhard, article in Gordon S. Wakefield (ed.), *A Dictionary of Christian Spirituality* (SCM, 1983), p. 340.

6 Monks and other 'religious' living in community.

7 Justin McCann (trans.), *The Rule of St Benedict* (Sheed and Ward, 1976).

8 Thornton, *Christian Proficiency*, p. 20ff.

9 Richard Foster, *Celebration of Discipline* (Hodder and Stoughton, 1980), p. 79.

10 Quietism has a strong emphasis on the doctrine of internal quiet, with a surrender of the soul to God. The soul loses itself in passive contemplation of the divine.

11 David Cutts and Harold Miller, *Whose Office? Daily Prayer for the People of God* (Grove Liturgical Study 32, 1982).

12 Ordinary days, that is, days not appointed for festival or fast.

13 For instance, Ember days, when specific prayers are offered for the ministry of the Church, and Rogation days, when prayer is offered that God might provide the food we need.

14 Confession to a priest or minister 'into the ear', that is, in total confidentiality.

15 Richard Foster draws attention to this phrase from Colossians 2:20-23 (AV) in *Celebration of Discipline*, p. 4.

Approaches to
Spiritual Direction

Anne Long

Some readers may get no further than the title of this chapter –
suggesting, as it seems to, something austere, authoritarian,
Catholic and far removed from their own experience. But for those
who have read this far at least, let me say what this chapter is all
about.

First, I hope to clarify what spiritual direction is – and what it
is not – for it represents a tremendously rich tradition in the
Church's history which, by its very nature, has been both a hidden
and a profound influence in the lives of many. Some will have associated direction with Catholic rather than evangelical tradition, and
for that reason will not know much about it. If this study does no
more than whet your appetite, the bibliography given at the end
will take you further.

Second, I hope to encourage readers to consider spiritual direction as a personal resource, whether in the traditional one-to-one
way or in the context of a support group. All of us, leaders and laypeople, need regular opportunity for stocktaking and replenish-
ment if we are to minister effectively. A clergyman in his late
thirties recently said, 'No one has asked me about my praying since
I was ordained!' Whether he wanted anyone to ask him was not
clear, but the implication was that he needed it. Our clerical structures do not necessarily make it easy for pastors to be pastored.
Simon Barrington-Ward has commented, 'We certainly have an

experience all over the world of church leaders in loneliness need-ing to submit themselves to others, and this is a crying need that is just not being met.' Spiritual direction can also provide a resource for laypeople wanting to grow in Christian discipleship. I hope to encourage some to seek and find.

One of my excitements has been to learn about prayer and dis-cipleship from Christians of other traditions. It was in the context of direction that I first came across Julian of Norwich, and subse-quently a wealth of other spiritual classics. An Anglo-Catholic priest helped me to accept the desert experiences of prayer – no one had ever told me, after an experience of personal renewal, to expect the stripping and refining that was not a falling from grace but a growth in it. It was through direction from an Anglican monk that I learned more about spiritual warfare and the mysteries of pain in intercession. For all his enclosure, he seemed remarkably in touch with the world. More recently, at a Roman Catholic retreat, where we were asked to use no book other than the Bible, the personal daily direction became a memorable means of the Holy Spirit's teaching, healing and guiding. A cell group of col-leagues in my days at St John's College also proved an important means of personal review and direction. I mention these examples thankfully. They are all to do with spiritual direction and have brought learning that I might never have received within one tra-dition alone.

Third, I hope to indicate ways in which spiritual direction might be developed as a means of nurture within the Church. As Christians are taught, so they must be enabled to teach others also. This need not be just the prerogative (and burden) of leaders, but should develop into a healthy mutuality between laypeople, as is already happening in various parts of the Church.

THE SEARCH FOR DIRECTION

In society

A wide variety of experience and direction is on offer. Throughout the 1960s and 1970s there was an upsurge of move-ments and groups aiming to raise the level of consciousness and to offer religious and spiritual experience to those seeking personal meaning and direction, and this continues today. To guide people there is no lack of gurus, exotic or otherwise. Some psychologists are now investigating, with greater interest than previously, phenomenological and transpersonal experience. Carl Rogers, after 45 years as a humanist clinical psychologist, has challenged fellow psychologists to consider 'the possibility of another reality (or realities), operating on rules quite different from our own well-known common sense empirical reality, the only one known to most psychologists'.[1] Furthermore, is the turning to fantasy worlds, which has seen a remarkable upsurge in the last year or so, also a longing for 'another reality'? In a variety of ways, many are seeking meaning and direction in secular society today.

In the Church

There is also a hunger for spiritual experience and direction among Christians. Recent years have seen a boom in the retreat movement, especially directed retreats. Jesuits, with their strong tradition of teaching, now offer updated and biblically based Ignatian retreats with personal direction as well as training in directing others. Monasteries and convents – Catholic, Anglican and Orthodox – welcome many seeking help in spirituality and prayer, as do communities like Taizé. The shepherding within the house church movement has also met a need in people seeking direction, albeit often given in an over-paternalized way. Courses on prayer get booked up quickly. Nor is the search for direction narrowly pietistic. Many young people are asking hard questions about spirituality and war, spirituality and sex, spirituality and politics – and Christian spokesmen such as Thomas Merton, Kenneth Leech and David Sheppard have encouraged such links. A spirituality which is not earthed is not biblical.

Although we shall be looking at spiritual direction in its narrower Christian connotation, we need to see that it is also relevant to the wider contemporary scene, where people are seeking both spirituality and direction.

WHAT IS SPIRITUAL DIRECTION?

'Direction' implies making a journey, movement, finding the way, directed living – and directed rather than aimless living is at the heart of Christian discipleship. We are, as pilgrims, to pursue and live out the values and priorities of the kingdom of God. How? Certainly by walking in the steps of Jesus, who is the Way, and through the leadings of the Holy Spirit, who indwells God's people. The Spirit is the director *par excellence*. Yet such direction rarely happens in a vacuum. We were created for relationship and most of our learning happens in a context of relationship, whether through talking, questioning, discussing, telling, offloading, or through listening, watching, considering, receiving, taking in. Relationship is vital to personal learning. Many times good teaching in churches is wasted because its hearers never engage with it in a context of personal relationship, be that a one-to-one or a group relationship. Where there are good house groups, personal learning is more likely, although groups are not conducive places for everyone.

Spiritual direction originated in monasticism. Whereas in the Early Church believers were discipled through the teaching and corporate life of the Christian community, the third and fourth centuries saw many of the devout withdrawing to the Egyptian and Syrian deserts to pray and give themselves to spiritual warfare. One safeguard to counter the excesses of individualism was to find a spiritual 'abba' or director for guidance and support. The *Apothegmata*, or 'Sayings of the Fathers', remain a witness to the simplicity and depth of much of this guidance. This was not simply a feature of desert spirituality. Basil of Caesarea (*c*.330-79), bishop, monk and social reformer, also directed many to self-renouncing service in the marketplace, for 'God the Creator arranged things so that we need each other', as the Longer Rule VII says. Thus through the centuries spiritual direction became a resource for personal formation and teaching, either in a one-to-one relationship or in a group. Men and women of God gifted with spiritual discernment and wisdom found that, often in quiet and hidden ways, they were being sought out to help direct Christians of different traditions.

How does this ministry apply to today's Church? Some leaders (and laypeople) are already doing it regularly – guiding individuals in their praying, Bible reading and daily living. Others, already over-busy, might well groan at the thought of the faithful queuing up for individual direction. Others again might welcome the very possibility.

At this point we need to say what spiritual direction is not. A spiritual director is not a problem-solver to whom we run for infallible answers. We are to work out our own salvation, and Christian discipleship is not a collecting of recipes from others for instant sanctification. Some temperaments hanker after blueprints – 'If only I could find the right formula, I would triumph.' Discovery there might be, but Augustine said that 'we come to God by love and not by navigation'. Nor is a spiritual director a guru to whom we turn to satisfy our needs for dependence, even though we may recognize the hand of God providing this particular person at this particular time.[2] Spiritual direction is not an invitation to prolonged introspection, even though personal reflection will be necessary. Nor is it to do with rarefied ascetical exercises, a 'feet off the ground' spirituality. It is not, as some seem to think, necessarily linked with making confession; this may be included, but certainly does not have to be.

Spiritual direction is not the same as pastoral counselling or therapy, although there may well be areas of overlap. Brian Hawker, both a spiritual director and a pastoral counsellor, says, 'Spiritual direction is dealing with eternal realities, pastoral counselling is dealing with problems in the here and now which are blocking me from looking at eternal realities.' Martin Thornton insists that spiritual direction is not need-orientated (helping those in trouble, counselling the disturbed, solving human problems – the 'ambulance syndrome', as he calls it), but 'the positive development of the man-God relation, which is prayer'.[3] He clarifies the difference by comparing the humanistic pastoral counsellor's attitude to suffering as 'something to be relieved', with the spiritual director's 'which might at least suggest the counterclaim that it was rather something to be interpreted and creatively redeemed'.[4] Kenneth Leech makes a similar point: 'Spiritual guidance is not crisis intervention but a continuous process, the movement to God and in God.'[5]

Growing together

Even so, there are clear links between psychological and spiritual progress if mature integration is to happen. Self-knowledge is close to knowledge of God. Discerning directors will want to learn from counselling insights and skills (disciplined listening, empathy, genuineness, appropriate confrontation), together with an understanding of human personality, its development and needs. But they will not accept these uncritically or become imprisoned within them. Likewise, Christian pastoral counsellors might well be helping to nurture and direct individuals' relationships with God through the recognition and healing of blocked or problem areas. The important thing for pastors who sometimes direct and sometimes counsel is to know what they are doing and when.

The basic premise of spiritual direction is that in order to grow we need each other. Through reflecting on and articulating aspects of my Christian life and discipleship – my hopes and fears, my successes and failures – with someone who will help me look for the Spirit's direction, my private world becomes shared, I can make more sense of my pilgrimage and continue in it supported. So Thornton says,

> Spiritual direction is the way forward. It is the positive nurture of man's relationship with God, the creative cultivation of charismata; the gifts and graces that all have received.[6]

And for this ministry,

> the director needs, or might need, the total picture ... because all aspects of life might impinge on the development of prayer.[7]

Merton describes a spiritual director as,

> ... concerned with the whole person, for the spiritual life is not just the life of the mind, or of the affections, or of the 'summit of the soul' – it is the life of the whole person.[8]

Gratton, too, recognizes that,

> Spiritual direction is not concerned only about the spiritual dimension of the person. It is concerned with the whole person, body, soul and spirit combined ... Spiritual direction that ignores the structures of human emergence and its implied limitations as well as its possibilities will not be helpful to real human beings who are called to respond to God's initiative in a truly human and whole manner.[9]

Spiritual direction, then, fully includes our humanity, but is far more than personal adjustment or social adaptation. It is about a mutual seeking in which one person (the director), mature and skilled in his or her ministry, is alongside another (the directee) in his or her pilgrimage towards Christian maturity and that integration in which the inner and outer person become united. But if it is to do with relationship, it needs witnesses. Here are some people's comments on what they have gained from direction:

> He helped mostly by just being there. He gave me few specific directions, but I could pour out my hopes and fears and failures and be reassured and restored. Knowing this was a great support. If I wrote, his answer might well be on a postcard, but I knew he understood and cared. (A retired bishop)

> Just the knowledge of each other's being there is great even though we are scattered. I know we have the Lord but actual flesh and blood is really good too, and clergy so need not to be alone. (An ordained minister belonging to a cell group)

> She gives new insights, new ways of looking at things ... she helped me begin to see pain as gift and grace. (A Christian counsellor)

> A chance for the clergy wife to share in her own right. (A minister's wife)

In his *Genesee Diary*, Henri Nouwen wrote of his first encounter with John Eudes, head of the Trappist Abbey of Gethsemani, who was to become his director:

> He gave me much time and attention but did not allow me to waste a minute; he left me fully free to express my feelings and thoughts but did not hesitate to present his own; he offered me space to deliberate about choices and to make decisions but did not withhold his opinion that some choices and decisions were better than others; he let me find my own way but did not hide the map that showed the right direction. In our conversation, John Eudes emerged not only as a listener but also as a guide, not only as a counsellor but also as a director. It did not take me long to realize that this was the man I had needed so badly.[10]

The title 'spiritual director' inevitably smacks of something authoritarian and paternalistic and might deter some from seeking such a relationship. Leech's use of 'soul friend' sounds gentler. Others would prefer 'guide' or 'spiritual companion'. Essentially, though, we are talking about a man or woman of experience, knowledge and skills; one who sits alongside, rather than above, another. In spiritual direction the focus of control is in God rather than people. This is the very reason why good spiritual directors do not mind the title because they, more than anyone, recognize that the prime director is the Holy Spirit.

DIRECTION AND THE BIBLE

In Scripture there are certain recurring themes which support the concept of spiritual direction, and to these we now turn.

Journey

The story of God's people is one of journeying. As pilgrims the children of Israel journeyed, led by the guiding hand of God. 'Leave your country, your people and your father's household and go to the land I will show you' (Genesis 12:1). So Abram set out on a journey where faith rather than sight would be the guiding light, seeking a home, a city, a country. Through desert and warfare, grumblings and fightings, God continued to lead them. Kings led them into battle for the land (see 2 Kings 8) and prophets pointed them to a righteousness that would bring them to a new highway, a land where mountains would be levelled, rough places smoothed (see Isaiah 40:4) and the Prince of Peace would establish his kingdom (see Isaiah 9:6).

Jesus taught that discipleship was a journey and that following him meant taking a narrow path (see Mark 8:34). Hebrews describes Christians as 'aliens and strangers ... looking for a country' (Hebrews 11:13; cf. 1 Peter 2:11), and John's Revelation gives glimpses of the final destination, a heavenly city with ever-open gates and a clear flowing stream lined by fruitful trees (see Revelation 22:1-2). No wonder the theme of journey and pilgrimage has inspired Christian writers ever since. 'With the drawing of this Love and the voice of this Calling we shall not cease from exploration.'[11]

Spiritual direction is essentially about a journey where God is guide, Jesus is the Way and the Spirit is the Paraclete. As we journey we make our own story, which, like the story of God's people, includes creation, pilgrimage, wilderness, covenant, deliverance, passion, death and resurrection. Personal reflection helps me to discover my whereabouts, and articulating this with another encourages me on.

Together, not alone

If we need each other in order to grow, then the Christian pilgrimage is not about footing it alone. Of course we shall sometimes feel lonely, but we were never meant, grim-faced and tight-lipped, to slog on alone. Mutuality is at the heart of the Godhead, 'the divine litany, the Father to Son to Spirit communication that is going on in the life of God himself'.[12] Rublev's fifteenth-century icon of the Trinity shows three angels seated around a table on which is a chalice. The basic form of composition is a circle, symbol of unity, embracing all three angels. They look at each other in mutual love and self-giving, a trinity yet together revealing the unity of the Godhead.

In both Testaments we see men of God discipling others – Moses and Joshua, Elijah and Elisha, Eli and Samuel, Paul and Timothy. Supremely we see it in Jesus' ministry as he came alongside others. Conversation with Zacchaeus led to a radical change of heart and consequently of direction (see Luke 19:8-9). With the Samaritan woman he directed discerning answers to her questions and discerning questions to her statements. Again there was a radical change of heart and direction (see John 4:1-26). Particularly he spent time directing a group, his 12 disciples, living, eating, travelling with them and teaching about prayer (see Luke 11:1-13; 18:9-14), about worry (see Luke 12:22-31), about watchfulness (see Luke 12:35-48) and about true greatness (see Luke 9:46-50). Much of Paul's ministry was spent in directing individuals and groups. Timothy was his 'true son in the faith' (1 Timothy 1:2) whom he instructed (see 1 Timothy 1:18; 4:6). He was to 'set an example' (1 Timothy 4:12) and to be 'diligent . . . and . . . persevere' (1 Timothy 4:15-16). As a son he was to learn from his father (see 2 Timothy 2:1-2). Paul did the same for the churches he founded, handing down the Christian tradition, not impersonally but as inherited truth within the context of relationship. Letter-writing has often been an effective means of direction, and Paul made the most of it.

Some Christians know such mutuality in fellowships and house groups. Spiritual direction is not an elite alternative, for a guiding relationship is no substitute either for corporate life and learning within the body of Christ, or for everyday relationships. Yet there will also be times when we sit down with someone we trust to open our lives and share our pilgrimage:

> Therefore, a Christian needs another Christian who speaks God's word to him. He needs him again and again when he becomes uncertain and discouraged, for by himself he cannot help himself without belying the truth. He needs his brother man as a bearer and proclaimer of the divine word of salvation.[13]

Another aspect of mutuality is that of spiritual gifts given for mutual building up. Encouragement or exhortation (*paraklesis*, Romans 12:8) was often used by Paul. Discernment (*diakrisis*, 1 Corinthians 12:10) has always been a key element in spiritual direction, especially in the understanding of spiritual warfare. 'Discernment involves clarity of vision ... discerning, discriminating, judging between truth and falsehood.'[14] Gifts of wisdom and knowledge (see 1 Corinthians 12:8) are also listed and are important to direction. Pause for a moment and think of someone (or more than one) whom God has used for your own teaching, encouragement and guidance, perhaps in your youth or young adulthood or marriage, or at a crisis point in your life, or very recently. It may have brought much comfort (or discomfort), it may have been continuing or a once-only meeting, but nevertheless it was important in that another Christian was alongside to listen and share in such a way that you travelled on encouraged. This is something of what spiritual direction is about.

Changing direction

Jesus taught a way and called himself 'the Way' (John 14:6). The challenge of his person and teaching involves a turnabout, a change of direction involving heart and action – repentance (*metanoia*). This is not a once-only experience, but a continuing one. We cannot do it for ourselves; it is gift and grace – God acting on and in us to create a new willingness to see with his eyes, think with his mind, adopt his values and attitudes (see 1 Corinthians 2:16; Philippians 2:5). *Metanoia* is about transformation and God is agent and goal.[15] 'It is grace that transforms and not human effort, and that applies to every aspect of the Christian life from the beginning to the very end.'[16] But our 'yes' is necessary, the 'yes' of faith which is 'the empty hand that we hold out to Christ and that he fills with himself, and the impulse and strength to stretch out the hand comes from the Spirit'.[17] 'Yes' is for each day as God seeks to implement in us changes of thinking, choosing and feeling. Spiritual direction makes opportunity for self-examination 'in order to uncover the sins, failures and inconsistencies which contradict the following of Christ and the love of God and neighbour'.[18] If self-examination is not to deteriorate into introspection or be ignored, we need wise guides with whom to articulate the inner movement of our spirits and the outer movement of our lives.

Progress

If the grace of God is all gift, there is also consequent human effort needed and Paul uses some strenuous metaphors for this. The Christian is like an athlete in training (see 1 Corinthians 9:24-27). *Askeo* means to train, exercise, endeavour,[19] and Paul exhorts the Corinthian Christians to 'run in such a way as to get the prize' (v. 24). He says of himself, 'I press on towards the goal to win the prize for which God has called me heavenwards in Christ Jesus' (Philippians 3:14).

Coaching involves knowledge which can be either taught or practically applied. Thornton looks helpfully at the role of the director as spiritual coach:

> The coach is not necessarily the better player ... It is satisfying to play a game well but there can be greater satisfaction in coaching another to higher standards ... One of the supreme blessings for the spiritual director is to watch his client surpass him ... which frequently happens.[20]

Paul also uses battle language. The Christian is a soldier in training needing to learn how to get equipped for battle.[21] Another concept

Paul uses that speaks of progress is growth into maturity (see Ephesians 4:14-15). We are to 'put off' the old self and 'put on' the new (Ephesians 4:22-24), which will involve moral, mental, emotional and behavioural changes. Moral change is also part of his metaphor of fruitfulness – a picture of growth and progress (see Galatians 5:22-23).

These pictures speak of the kind of movement that implies progress and therefore appeals to us, but what about movement that feels backwards rather than forwards, down rather than up? Metaphors of growth must be used with care, and 'Which way is forwards?' can be a right question to ask. Bewildering reversals will sometimes be part of the journey.

> In order to arrive at what you are not
> You must go through the way in which you
>   are not.[22]

Darkness can be necessary to progress, whether it be the cloud hiding the sun (as, for example, in Exodus 13:21), or the earth covering the seed (see John 12:24), or the deep pit without foothold (see Psalm 88:4).

Chaos may sometimes be an important condition of growth, the chaos leading to new integration. Pruning precedes fruitfulness (see John 15:2), dryness can increase our longing for water,[23] and emptiness our capacity for God. Comforts and consolations may appear to wean us from the gifts to the Giver. Staretz Sophrony, an Orthodox priest, said, 'In following Christ's commands a person will feel less and less capable. "Progress" is to do with death itself, an increasingly profound death.'

Lest we settle for limited models of productivity, we must see the cross as the ruling principle of the Christian life, for there can be no true reflection of Christ that does not consist of bearing his cross. It is through suffering that we learn obedience and trust, and God, in his wisdom, will lead us through stages of growth that feel like anything but growth to bring us to Christlikeness – 'a condition of complete simplicity (costing not less than everything)'.[24]

It is in the darkest, most unprogressive times that I return to base and say *baptizatus sum*, 'I am a baptized person' – and that is sheer gift and grace.

SPIRITUAL DIRECTION IN THE HISTORY OF THE CHURCH

From a wealth of historical material we shall look briefly at examples illustrating three working models.

One-to-one direction

Many towns in the Middle Ages sought to have as part of their local welfare services a Christian recluse whose chief work was prayer and availability to people as a spiritual adviser. Julian of Norwich was much sought after for her wisdom in the fourteenth century. She regarded herself as a woman 'unlettered, feeble and frail', yet comes across with sanity, strength and tenderness. After receiving a series of visions, she wrote down her *Revelations of Divine Love* and, 20 years later, a longer version including meditative material. Her intention in writing was chiefly pastoral. Captivated by Christ and his love, she 'was greatly moved with love for my fellow Christians that they might know and see what I was seeing, for I wanted to cheer them too'. She describes Christ's dying love on the cross in graphic detail, teaches about love's triumph over sin, and gives practical advice about prayer. The images she uses – the hazelnut, the herring scales, the seabed, the clothes blown in the wind – show how she reflected on life in East Anglia and on God at work in his world. One can imagine how ordinary people coming to her for help would have gone away cheered and instructed by this sane visionary.

> Our Lord says, 'pray inwardly, even if you do not enjoy it. It does good, though you feel nothing, see nothing, yes, even though you are doing nothing. For when you are dry, empty, sick, or weak, at such a time is your prayer most pleasing to me though you find little enough to enjoy in it.'[25]

> Flee to the Lord and we shall be strengthened. Touch him, and we shall be cleansed. Cling to him, and we shall be safe and sound from every danger. For it is the will of our courteous Lord that we should be as much at home with him as heart may think or soul desire.[26]

Julian's writing is explored more fully in Chapter 10 below.

Direction through letters

Personal correspondence has been a significant means of direction down the years. Probably many of us have treasured letters containing gems of spiritual guidance which have come to us when the writer could not, or during times of personal need or crisis. The length of that sort of letter hardly matters – one sentence might give six months' nourishment, or a paragraph may become food for reflection.

Samuel Rutherford (*c*.1600-61), during nine years of pastoral ministry in the small parish of Anwoth, Galloway, believed passionately that the gospel of Christ should shape the character and life of his people, and the 'cure of souls' was central to his spirituality and ministry. His letters, published within three years of his death, were widely read in Scottish homes. To Marion McKnaught, whose husband appears to have been falsely accused in the local town council, he wrote:

> Sister, remember how many thousands of talents of sins your Master hath forgiven you: forgive ye therefore your fellow-servants one talent ... Be not cast down: if ye saw Him, who is standing on the shore holding out His arms to welcome you to land, you would not only wade through a sea of wrongs, but through hell itself, to be at Him.[27]

C. S. Lewis would probably have laughed at being called a spiritual director, yet many of his letters contain such insights. In reply to a letter from Sheldon Vanauken, who, after his wife's death, wrote to Lewis about their love which had remained for him an end in itself, Lewis wrote:

> One way or another the thing had to die. Perpetual spring-time is not allowed. You are not cutting the wood of life according to the grain ... You have been treated with a severe mercy. You have been brought to see (how true and very frequent this is!) that you were jealous of God. So from US you have been led back to US AND GOD; it remains to go on to GOD AND US.

Vanauken comments, 'After this severe and splendid letter I loved Lewis like a brother. A brother and father combined.'[28]

Direction in groups

Spiritual direction need not be limited to a twosome. Church history offers many examples of how it can happen in a group context. Richard Baxter (1615-91), during 14 years of pastoral ministry at Kidderminster, gave himself to the pastoral care of some 800 families. He was concerned that preachers of the word should also take it into homes and minister it at closer quarters. He set aside every Monday and Tuesday for personal ministry of the Scriptures to whole families, listening to them, pastoring them and teaching them. The Clapham Circle, functioning at the turn of the eighteenth and nineteenth centuries, was a means of mutual direction for Charles Simeon, William Wilberforce and others.

The early days of Methodism saw a similar concern for group direction. From 1742 Methodist societies were organized into 'classes' of 8-10 people, each with a leader, based on Wesley's conviction that spiritual oversight needed to be intimate and personal. He wrote:

> It can scarce be conceived what advantages have been reaped from this little prudential regulation. Many now happily experienced that Christian fellowship of which they had not so much as an idea before. They began to 'bear one another's burdens', and naturally to 'care for each other'. As they had daily a more intimate acquaintance with, so they had a more endeared affection for, each other. And 'speaking the truth in love, they grew up into Him, in all things, who is the Head, even Christ'.[29]

The duties of class leaders (women as well as men in 1847) were to 'ask each member in turn to speak of their experience in the Christian life, after which he (she) would give a word of encouragement, advice or reproof, as was necessary'.[30] No wonder leaders 'found their highest joy in the cure of souls committed to them, and they accepted the responsibility of their office as a most sacred trust'.[31]

So far we have sought to define spiritual direction, provide some biblical undergirding, and give some examples. In this next part we shall look at what is required of a spiritual director and suggest some ways of exploring it as a personal resource.

WHAT SORT OF PERSON?

Good directors are neither numerous nor ready-made. Their ministry tends to be a background rather than a foreground one. There are probably more of them quietly getting on with it than is apparent, although they may not call themselves 'spiritual directors' – clergy, religious, laypeople, tutors in jobs where Christian formation is important. They should not be self-appointed. What then should they be? Someone who finds people turning to him or her for spiritual counsel or direction might start by considering the importance of four kinds of knowledge – of God, of the tools of the trade, of others, and of self.

Knowing God

If I am attempting to guide others in their pilgrimage I too must be a traveller, perhaps further on but still travelling, seeking, discovering. If the journey to God is the agenda of our meeting, then I too will be continuing to pray, meditate, think, and will have both a prayer discipline and a living theology of prayer. I shall be open to the prayer of listening to God.[32] 'In prayer we are gradually hollowed out to become more *"capax Dei"* [capacious for God],' said Maria Boulding, and someone pastoring others will be only too aware of the need to receive even at the price of felt (and often uncomfortable) emptiness. Father Sophrony says of his ministry as spiritual director, 'The way is to pray every day with a flaming heart. "Do not permit me to be wrong in my work for this service transcends my capacity." It is not *human* capacity that will do it. "Without me you can do nothing!" [John 15:5]'

The director will also pray for the gifts necessary for his or her ministry – discernment (1 Corinthians 12:10; cf. Luke 7:39-47; John 4:1-26; Acts 5:1-11), to be able to listen with compassion and truth through the layers of a person; encouragement (Romans 12:8), to help people on their way; wisdom (1 Corinthians 12:8), often given when the director is least aware of it. Barsanuphius, a sixth-century director, wrote, 'I said nothing from myself, but I prayed, and then said whatever God gave me the confidence to say ... when the need arose, God opened even the ass's mouth.'[33]

Michael Ramsey says more pithily, 'Rely on your consecrated hunch!'

Those guiding others should themselves be being guided, for, as Bernard said, 'He who is a spiritual director to himself is counsellor to a fool.' It is all too easy for Christian leaders to become increasingly cut off. If they are to guide others, they too must know the resource of guidance.

Think of some who have influenced you through their knowledge of God. Sanctity has little to do with a pietistic otherworldliness and much to do with ordinariness and simplicity – being oneself in God, accepted by the Father, met by the Son, and indwelt by the living Spirit.

Knowing the tools of the trade

St Teresa put learning as a high priority in spiritual guides, but what kind of learning? Directors need to know and use the tools of their trade. First, they need to know the Bible. Clement of Alexandria said that the true seeker after God would be 'in and out of the Scriptures every day'. Those directing others need to know the Bible as their own resource of study and meditation, to know its teaching about our relationship with God in covenant, encounter and incorporation, to know about its teaching on prayer and about those who, in its pages, are seen at prayer. Second, they need an ever-deepening understanding of Christian doctrine. To see why someone relates more to the transcendent Father, or to the incarnate Son, or to the indwelling Spirit, they need a growing understanding of the Trinity. To help someone develop his or her individual gifts, directors need an understanding of the complementarity of the individual and the corporate within the Church, the body of Christ. To help someone see the nature of his or her justification (and live by it), they need an ever-deepening understanding of grace. Third, they need knowledge and experience of different sorts of prayer and of those in history who have explored them. If someone is finding words burdensome, he or she may need an introduction to the prayer of quiet or the Jesus Prayer.[34] If that person needs to use his or her body in prayer, encourage this.[35] If he or she wants greater unity between work and prayer, introduce the teaching of Brother Lawrence.[36] If he or she needs a more imaginative approach to biblical meditation, explain about the Ignatian method.[37] For some, a new way of praying will be a welcome release from the straitjacket of past patterns.[38]

Knowing another

Essentially, a director must believe in the person he or she is guiding. It was said of the Curé D'Ars that he believed in those who came to him more than they believed in themselves. One feels vulnerable in baring one's soul to another, so respect, compassion and commitment are essential. So is disciplined listening, and those guiding others should learn some of the skills of pastoral counselling.[39] The director will discover what is significant in the other person's life. A Russian director, criticized for spending time advising an old peasant woman about the care of her turkeys, replied, 'Not at all. Her whole life is in those turkeys.'[40]

Appropriate confrontation is also necessary. The director needs freedom to offer it and the other person needs freedom to receive it, and this very much depends on the trustful quality of the relationship already built. Spiritual direction is not simply a cosy chat, and being straight may be one of the most important contributions you make. After one such painful confrontation, someone wrote, 'Thank you for being straight with me – I needed it.' Likewise, we shall sometimes need to challenge a person's values – there are sins before God which are not necessarily sins before society. Our concern to hold that person into God's truth will be greater than our concern for him or her to become adjusted to society.

Very clearly, we are not in the business of directing people into modes of prayer that are unsuitable for them. It is all too easy to do this, especially if we know no other ways of praying than our own. To encourage the basically extrovert person to develop his or her praying in a way more suited to the introvert is to do that person a disservice, and since many books on prayer are written by introverts we can quickly fall into this trap. The world-affirming person should not be forced into a world-renouncing spirituality, nor someone who is basically a thinker into an affective spirituality. A person's own spiritual propensity is to be encouraged, whether it is similar to or different from one's own.[41]

Knowing oneself

Spiritual directors' own life experience is one of their greatest assets. They know they have not arrived – they are still travelling – but they have learnt through the experiences of life and there is a maturity about them.

What will characterize growing maturity? An integration of my own life experience through reflection, self-examination and help from others. 'A guide who has not encountered his own passions, his own inner conflicts, who does not truly know his darkness and his light,' will be of no value in the spiritual battle.'[42] As our life experience, including suffering, becomes integrated, so we can put it at the disposal of others, explicitly and implicitly. It is only as we become at ease with the condition of our own humanity that we can accept another person's. This will give birth to humility in us, and humility will help us resist the temptation to play God to people.

Maturing through self-knowledge will lead us truly to put self aside for the sake of another. Particularly, this will show itself in the gift of availability to another – a conducive meeting place, the courtesy of taking the phone off the hook, keeping confidences and having grace to forget as well as remember things people tell us. We shall not feel obliged to fill silences with words, but learn to speak out of silence. Someone told me how her director always says at the end of her outpourings, 'Let us keep silent and wait on the Holy Spirit.' And they do, for 5-10 minutes, then he speaks out of the silence, 'and I know what he is saying is of the Holy Spirit – it resonates so clearly in me and rings true'. Spiritual direction can sometimes be a lonely ministry, and one can encounter resistance and blocks, both in oneself and in the other person. These can helpfully be looked at with a supervisor or 'senior partner'.

Self-knowledge is vital, yes – but humour is too. Richard Rolle wrote in the fourteenth century of spiritual direction as 'full merry counsel with his ghostly Father'. It would be a pity if our spirituality did not increase in us the ability sometimes to laugh, especially at ourselves!

PATTERNS FOR TODAY

Reflection

Before looking at one-to-one and group direction, it is worth thinking about the place and content of reflection in our lives. Socrates said that the unexamined life is not worth living. If life is nothing more than a moving from one activity to the next, it is not surprising if we become restless, cluttered and superficial. 'Superficiality is the curse of our age ... The desperate need today is ...

for deep people.'[43] Depth is acquired partly by learning to be reflective, taking time to reflect on the world around us and how we spend our lives. Its end is not introspection, which, taken to extremes, can become an opting out of life, but integration, a gathering up of the fragments to find, under the hand of God, a wholeness in living.

One way to begin is to keep a daily journal. It can be a simple one, or much fuller if you wish. Whether short or long, however, the important thing is to make it serve you so that it becomes not a burden but a means of personal reflection and integration.[44] A simple way is to use a notebook, dating each day and following these headings:

1 Insights, thoughts, questions emerging from my Bible reading and prayer.
2 Notes about my spiritual journey – things that are currently concerning me, challenging me, strengthening me.
3 Something I am reading or thinking about at present that I would like to remember.
4 A current event or relationship on which I need to reflect.

For a fuller version, the following headings might be useful:

1 My personal salvation history. It can be both encouraging and revealing to review one's life journey and trace the different stages within it. Each of us has a Bethlehem, a wilderness, a Good Friday, an Easter Sunday, a Pentecost, although they do not necessarily occur chronologically or even once only. Roger Pooley writes on this at greater length in Chapter 7.
2 My vocation – the work, ministry or roles to which I am called and the gifts I have been given for these.
3 My ongoing journey and significant events in it.
4 My path in prayer.
5 The place of the Bible in my life.
6 Other kinds of reading and study and their influence on me.
7 Things that cause me blocking, bondage, fear, sin or shortcoming. (For this I will sometimes need another's help, especially if they involve my past. 'There is no healing of the memory until the memory itself is exposed ... the word

of forgiveness is not audible for the one who has not "turned" to his or her past.'[45])

8 Lifestyle.
9 Recreation (i.e. re-creation).
10 Relationships in my life (e.g. family, friends, work colleagues, neighbours).
11 My place within the people of God (in the local church, house group, etc.).
12 Use of money and giving.
13 Solitude and retreat.

The idea is not to attempt all these at once – they could be used as sections in a loose-leaf file and added to at intervals. It is helpful to date entries. Out of this material will emerge some of the items you may want to discuss with a spiritual director.[46]

Some find it helpful to reflect last thing at night as a prayerful self-examination. Such reflection might take the following form:

1 Ask for God's light on the past day. This is not your own analysis, but what the Holy Spirit wants to show you.
2 Review the day and see where you need to give thanks. (It will not necessarily be through feeling thankful.) Express your gratitude to God.
3 Ask God to show you how he has been present in your life today, in you and others. How have you responded to his leadings? Think of your moods and see what stands out – joy, pain, turmoil, love, anger, anxiety, the presence of God, isolation, etc. Is there any one area on which you are being asked to focus for prayer or action?
4 Confess to God those times when you sinned and ask for the gift of an ever-deepening sorrow for not co-operating with him.
5 Ask God for your need for tomorrow.

One-to-one direction

By now some may well be asking, 'Where can I look for a spiritual director? And if I find someone, what shall I say?'

Spiritual direction may well develop within a context of friendship. There are both advantages and disadvantages to this. To be already known and understood gives an obvious head start, but since this is a particular sort of meeting, disciplined boundaries and clear objectives need to be set by both parties. One might prefer a priest or minister, and sometimes retired clergy have both the experience and time for this sort of ministry. Spiritual direction is not, however, just the domain of clergy. Some dioceses are now running training courses in spiritual direction, and a diocesan education officer might know someone suitable. If you have a monastery or convent nearby, it is worth enquiring there too, for those who have spent years in a ministry of prayer can have much to offer. If there is no one nearby, it is well worth spending time and money to travel to a good director, perhaps with visits twice or three times a year. Another possibility is to attend an individually conducted retreat. An increasing number of monasteries and convents offer Ignatian retreats, where the focus is on personal Bible meditation. Each day the retreatant has a few suggested passages given by the director, and they meet once a day for sharing and reflection. Above all, if you need someone, pray. You will eventually be shown where to turn. It may turn out to be one or two meetings only, or a much longer period of time. (Richard Foster used Dallas Willard as his director for over four years and reckons his life to be 'the embodiment' of the teaching in *Celebration of Discipline*).

The kind of person for whom you are looking has been indicated above, but other questions to ask yourself might be the following:

- Is this someone I can respect and trust?
- Is this someone with whom I can be really honest?
- Is this someone with whom I can learn?

In making initial contact with someone, write or speak to him or her about what you are looking for – that is, someone with whom to discuss your Christian life and pilgrimage. If the person concerned is not used to the concept you may need to do some initial explaining, but once your expectations are understood, he or she may turn out far better than either of you imagined!

It is important to attend your first meeting prepared to do the following things:

- To talk about yourself, including information that will show your background, present life circumstances, and your Christian pilgrimage. Think this through beforehand.

- To share your present pattern of prayer and how this relates to patterns of corporate worship in your own church. You have nothing to lose and everything to gain by being completely honest, even if you feel your devotional life is in a mess. That is one reason why you are seeking help.
- To tell of any particular practical things that could be of importance (for example, you spend a long time travelling to and from work each day; you have recently had a bereavement in your family; you have to get up each night for the children, and so on).
- To open up any particular areas where you are seeking guidance, or new learning, or particular goals (see the previous section on reflection).
- To ask if any financial payment is required.

You may need help with self-discipline, praying for others, spiritual gifts, suitable reading, dryness, or even finding that your own praying is very different from others in your house group. Direction is not simply for times of crisis, but for ongoing growth.

The items on my own agenda for spiritual direction over the past two or three years have included the following: lifestyle – being over-busy and needing to rediscover a rhythm where prayer finds its right place alongside a full teaching and pastoral ministry; bereavement and particular aspects of my mother's death; reading; pain in prayer; spiritual warfare; a major decision. Some of the learning and insights gained come back to me with great clarity as I write. Our sessions together (usually about one hour each) included talking, listening, crying, laughing and praying, and I continue to be thankful for the encouragement, challenge, prayer, assurance of forgiveness and support which they provided.

Would there ever be reason to stop such a relationship? Sometimes. If you feel the 'fit' is wrong, and that the relationship is not working well, you might need to consider ending it, for there should be a growing sense of ease as you get to know each other. Occasionally a director gives bad direction. We are clearly never obliged to follow any human direction contrary to what we know to be scriptural or morally right. On the other hand, running to a succession of people for direction may well indicate our own immaturity and instability. We rarely find one person who provides answers to all our questions, meets all our expectations and generally measures up to perfection. Moreover, the relationship is never an end in itself. A director is only 'God's usher' to lead us to our real Director. For this reason alone directors need our prayers as they seek, all too aware of their own fallibility, to fulfil their ministry responsibly.

Group direction

Aware as we are these days of groups and their many uses, little exploration has been made until recently of the group as a context for spiritual direction. In this final section we look at some examples.

Previously we considered one person as director and one as directed, but direction can also be mutual, each in turn directing the other. In his *Life Together*, Bonhoeffer told how he tried this in his experimental community before the Second World War. Based on the teaching of Jesus about confessing faults one to the other, each brother chose another and they confessed to and directed each other. This kind of mutuality can certainly happen between friends, although there must be a clear understanding by each as to the nature of the exercise, a proper respect for confidences and for each other's judgement.

The cell group of three or more people who pray together and discuss their growth and life in God also has its place. This happens in the Kimbanguist Church in Zaire, where they have small cells for mutual confession. This has also been a feature of the East African revival and was probably also present in Watchman Nee's church. In the UK there has been some experimenting with different sorts of cell groups.

Some clergy belong to 'Jesus Caritas' groups. At each meeting one person lays before the others some current situation requiring guidance and wisdom. After that person has spoken, the group members wait in silence, praying, listening to God, open to receive. Then they speak out of the silence, bringing their insights to that individual's situation.

Interest was awakened for some when a television programme about the late Robert Runcie, formerly Archbishop of Canterbury, showed him with his cell group. A few weeks later, while visiting St John's College, he shared with us about the mutual support within the group and the high priority given to it by its members. Some of our final-year students who were soon to be ordained, feeling the need for some kind of support system, especially during the first few years of ministry, decided to create their own cells. There are now several in existence, some of which I have monitored, and, with their permission, I note certain findings below.

Cell A comprises a group of six (men and women, married and single), all in full-time church ministry. They chose each other carefully before leaving college on the basis of previously existing friendship. They decided to meet for 24 hours every nine months, with an initial commitment of three years. They make time to share their situations, discuss, pray and relax together. If anyone wants specific spiritual direction, they seek to give it. They also pray for each other at a distance and give each other freedom to phone at any hour of the day or night if necessary for personal support. (One has taken advantage of a night call.) So far they list the advantages of the group as getting away together, mutual support, time to reflect, being straight with each other, and mutual prayer.

Cell B comprises a group of seven (three married clergy couples and one single woman minister). They also chose each other before leaving college on the basis of friendship. They meet for 48 hours every eight months and have a rotating leadership for group sessions. Some of their agreed objectives are as follows:

- To provide an opportunity for each member to share the joys and sorrows of the past months, with the opportunity to receive prayer and/or ministry.
- To provide a forum where we can review the content and balance of our lives as far as work, personal spirituality, family time, leisure and outside interests go. Each of us will be open to the counsel of the rest of the group as to possible areas of change.
- To provide consistent prayer support for each other and our families and to be open to receive prayer requests for each other at any time of the day or night.
- To provide meetings which have about them a sense of mental, spiritual and emotional homecoming.

Each person in this cell has personal time allotted to use as he or she wants, and this requires preparation and reflection beforehand. So far, advantages include listening to each other, the opportunity to defuse strong feelings, and mutual trust. One member of the cell wrote, 'We trust and appreciate each other's discernment given by the Lord and recognize his authority in each other. The bond between us enables us to pray into each other's situations – it is different from friends simply getting together.'

Cell C comprises four people (one married couple and two single ministers). Their mutual commitment is strong and their sharing deep. 'We have "permission" to share and question on a deep and challenging level without fear of losing friends . . . We are prepared to travel the length of the country to meet . . . There has to be a willingness among all the members of such a group to be prepared to give and take, to offer criticism and receive it, to encourage and to be encouraged.'

Could there be pointers here as to how some clergy and their spouses could find more resources in mutuality for their heavy ministerial demands?

The superior of an Anglican convent, writing about the cell to which she belonged (which included members from outside her community), considered the following to be essential factors in such cells:

- They should meet in a neutral situation.
- They should be a 'peer' group in so far as the relationship within the group is on an equal footing.
- They should come together at regular intervals and meetings should, if possible, be reckoned as sacrosanct engagements.
- Meetings should be long enough to provide opportunity for fun and relaxation as well as worship and discussion.

Her cell met every nine months, each person giving an account of him- or herself and others responding, commenting, advising, suggesting. She spoke of it as a tremendously rich and enlarging experience: 'Friendship expressed at its very best, I think.'

Is there anything in this for church house groups? David Prior believes there would be real value in a house group seeing the provision of such spiritual direction and help as latent within the group itself. While this is expecting a great deal for such groups, a measure of personal ministry to the individual plus group ministry to one another would seem to preserve the right balance. One church's house groups did this as they made a study, chapter by chapter, of Richard Foster's *Celebration of Discipline*. Another house group looks together, from time to time, at personal affairs of group members (such as job interviews, family sickness, finance). Many groups have not yet discovered that degree of mutual trust. There are clearly possibilities to explore here, so that members of such groups come to see group guidance as normal rather than exceptional.[47] Obviously there can be abuses of any group – authoritarian leadership, group pressure, collusion, loss of individual responsibility. Nonetheless, the possibilities can greatly outweigh such things if groups are well taught, and some of these expressions of mutual direction could well offer ways forward out of the isolated, anxious states of modern living and into the fellowship of God's people.

> We all need someone who will carry us through our nights and days, our winters and summers, and our times of darkness and clarity. We all need someone who knows the secret of our hearts.[48]

> Speaking the truth in love, we will in all things grow up into him who is the Head, that is, Christ. From him the whole body, joined and held together by every supporting ligament, grows and builds itself up in love, as each part does its work. (Ephesians 4:15-16)

You may find it helpful, having read this chapter, to ask yourself the following questions:

- What experiences of spiritual direction or companionship have I found helpful in my own life?
- Would some kind of spiritual direction or companionship be an enrichment to me currently?
- If so, how could I go about finding it?

FURTHER READING

William Barry, *Spiritual Direction and the Encounter with God* (Paulist Press)
Walter Conn, *The Desiring Self* (Paulist Press)
Barry Connolly, *The Practice of Spiritual Direction* (Seabury Press)

Margaret Guenther, *Holy Listening* (Darton, Longman and Todd)
Gerard Hughes, *God of Surprises* (Darton, Longman and Todd)
Kenneth Leech, *Soul Friend* (Darton, Longman and Todd)
Richard Foster, *Celebration of Discipline* (Hodder and Stoughton)
Richard Foster, *Study Guide to Celebration of Discipline* (Hodder and Stoughton)
C. S. Lewis, *Letters to an American Lady* (Hodder and Stoughton); *Letters to Malcolm* (Hodder and Stoughton)
Gordon Jeff, *Spiritual Direction for Every Christian* (SPCK)
Gerald May, *Care of Mind, Care of Spirit* (Harper and Row)
Francis Kelly Nemeek and Marie Theresa Coombes, *The Way of Spiritual Direction* (Liturgical Press)
Brother Ramon SSF, *Deeper into God* (Marshall Pickering)
Martin Thornton, *Spiritual Direction* (SPCK)

Notes

1 Carl Rogers, *Some New Challenges*, p. 385, quoted by Kevin Culligan OCD, *Towards a Contemporary Model of Spiritual Direction: A Comparative Study of St John of the Cross and Carl Rogers, Carmelite Studies Volume 2* (ICS Public, 1982), p. 149.
2 Compare some Eastern models of spiritual direction where the authority of the guru is absolute.
3 Martin Thornton, *Spiritual Direction* (SPCK, 1984), p. 10.
4 Ibid., p. 12.
5 Kenneth Leech, *Soul Friend* (Darton, Longman and Todd, 1994), p. 96.
6 Thornton, *Spiritual Direction*, p. 10.
7 Ibid., p. 29.
8 Thomas Merton, *Spiritual Direction and Meditation* (Anthony Clarke, 1975), p. 15.
9 Carolyn Gratton, *Guidelines for Spiritual Direction* (Dimension Books, 1980), p. 158.
10 Henri Nouwen, *The Genesee Diary* (Image Books, 1981), p. 15.
11 T. S. Eliot, 'Little Gidding'; see also hymns such as 'Guide me, O thou great Redeemer', and John Bunyan's *Pilgrim's Progress*.
12 T. A. Smail, *The Forgotten Father* (Hodder and Stoughton, 1980), p. 144.
13 Dietrich Bonhoeffer, *Life Together* (SCM, 1949), p. 12.
14 Leech, *Soul Friend*, p. 131.

15 See 2 Corinthians 3:18. Note the passive mood, *metamorphoumetha*.

16 T. A. Smail, *Reflected Glory* (Hodder and Stoughton, 1975), p. 28.

17 Ibid., p. 30.

18 Christopher Bryant, *Jung and the Christian Way* (Darton, Longman and Todd, 1983), p. 78.

19 Thus *askesis*, 'ascetical'.

20 Thornton, *Spiritual Direction*, p. 28.

21 *Askeo* can also have a military connotation: see 2 Timothy 2:3 and Ephesians 6:10-17.

22 T. S. Eliot, 'East Coker'.

23 See T. H. Green, *When the Well Runs Dry* (Ave Maria Press, 1979).

24 T. S. Eliot, 'Little Gidding'.

25 Julian of Norwich (ed. Clifton Wolters), *Revelations of Divine Love* (Penguin Classics), p. 124.

26 Ibid., p. 200.

27 'The Loveliness of Christ', from *The Letters of Samuel Rutherford 1600-1661*, selected by E. S. Lister (Samuel Bagster, 1958), pp. 115-16.

28 Sheldon Vanauken, *A Severe Mercy* (Hodder and Stoughton, 1977), pp. 209-10.

29 Thomas Jackson (ed.), *The Works of John Wesley* (John Mason, 1829-31), Vol. VIII, p. 253.

30 R. C. Swift, *Lively People* (Department of Adult Education, University of Nottingham, 1982), p. 142.

31 Jackson (ed.), *The Works of John Wesley*, p. 253.

32 See Michael Mitton, *The Wisdom to Listen* (Grove Books, 1981).

33 Source unknown.

34 See Simon Tugwell, *Prayer: Volume 2. Prayer in Practice* (Veritas Publications, 1974); R. M. French (trans.), *The Way of a Pilgrim* (SPCK, 1930).

35 See Tugwell, *Prayer*, Chapter 4.

36 Brother Lawrence, *The Practice of the Presence of God* (Epworth, 1959).

37 See, for example, Richard Foster, *Celebration of Discipline* (Hodder and Stoughton, 1980), pp. 22-23, 26.

38 For a thorough and helpful study of these 'tools', see Thornton, *Spiritual Direction*. See also Foster, *Celebration of Discipline*.

39 This might well apply to other aspects of personality development and needs, such as projection and transference, distinguishing between a 'dark night' and a clinical depression, and being aware of when help other than, or as well as, ours is needed.

40 Merton, *Spiritual Direction and Meditation*, p. 16.

41 See Ruth Fowke, *Personality and Prayer* (Eagle, n.d.).

42 Leech, *Soul Friend*, p. 89.

43 Foster, *Celebration of Discipline*, p. 1.

44 For more on the process of reflection, see Michael Williams, *Learning through Experience* (Grove Pastoral Series No. 8). See also Roger Pooley's chapter on 'Spiritual Autobiography' later in this book (Chapter 7).

45 Rowan Williams, *Resurrection* (Darton, Longman and Todd, 1982), p. 21.

46 See Chapter 4, 'Finding a Personal Rule of Life', by Harold Miller.

47 See David Prior, *Sharing Pastoral Care in the Parish* (Grove Pastoral Series No. 3).

48 Jean Vanier, *Community and Growth* (Darton, Longman and Todd, 1979), p. 178.

PILGRIMAGE

David Osborne

THE EXPERIENCE

The road across Mull to the Iona ferry climbs up through Glen Mor and then drops down to wind along the Ross. Finally, a mile from the Sound of Iona, the road crests a hill and on a clear day the island can be seen ahead. This first sight of the destination is an exciting moment in any pilgrimage. The pilgrims with whom Jesus walked would have burst into one of the 'songs of ascents' when, after several days' journey, they came over a hill and Jerusalem lay before them.[1]

Pilgrimages do not just happen; they involve preparation and effort. When the end is in sight, it might be months or years of planning and travel which are reaching a culmination. The effort and rigours of the journey are now behind them as pilgrims to Taizé or Lourdes approach their destination. Similarly, with people approaching Minehead for Spring Harvest, where Christians in their thousands gather to holiday, worship and learn together, when they see other cars with fish stickers there might be a sense of fellowship with those who are making a pilgrimage to the same place.

Each year millions of people make pilgrimages. Buddhists and Ba'hais, Hindus, Muslims and Sikhs, all travel to shrines and holy places. Australian Aborigines go on 'walkabout'. Southern Baptists organize trips to the Holy Land. Catholics walk up Croagh Patrick, and Orthodox travel to Mount Athos. In much of their religious practice these people may appear to have little in common, but they all share the desire and decision to go on pilgrimage.

Definition and description

The word 'pilgrim' could be applied to any traveller, although such a general meaning is now uncommon. The word derives from 'peregrine', a *peregrinatus* being one who travelled abroad – literally, 'across fields'. It has come to mean a person whose journey is made for God, or at least for some deep purpose.

A person might speak, not quite facetiously, of making a pilgrimage to the place where they were born, to their father's grave in Normandy, or to the city from which their grandparents emigrated. This journey is being undertaken for some purpose beyond entertainment that has something to do with the person's identity or life story. The destination of the journey is a place of significance for the individual, or for a group or movement of which they are a part.

The pilgrimage will involve a period of preparation. This may involve extensive planning, gathering equipment, saving money and booking tickets. The journey may not be particularly complicated, but there will still be a period of thought, of mulling over the reasons and hopes for the journey.

The preparation will have begun with an idea which got hold of the person until it became something he or she was determined to do. A spontaneous decision to jump on a bus and go to the local cathedral could hardly be called a pilgrimage. One would expect that before the journey actually began there would be a period of anticipation. A journey which is going to be a significant time will be approached with care and thought, possibly with prayer.

The journey itself is important. One is going on a pilgrimage, not just getting to a certain destination. This may mean that the journey is not by the most direct or simple route, nor by the easiest means of travel. A pilgrim is one who makes a certain kind of journey, not one who arrives at a certain place.

This means it is also possible for a person to make an open pilgrimage, travelling as a pilgrim but to an unknown or undecided destination, like Abram leaving Haran (see Genesis 12:1) or St Brendan setting sail with his companions.[2]

Often the pilgrimage may also involve more than one individual. The pilgrim may have fellow travellers and meet others arriving at the same place. Even the lone traveller will have left people behind and may well return to them, and these people are also affected by the pilgrimage.

This study

We will later consider the practice of making a pilgrimage in more detail – thinking about the preparation, the departure, the journey, the arrival and the return as five stages in the process. First, however, we will consider the theological and historical background to the activity of pilgrimage and some aspects of its spirituality.

As a widespread phenomenon, pilgrimage takes many forms. We will take as a basic model of pilgrimage a journey made, perhaps on foot, to a particular place. Historically this has been the most common form of pilgrimage until recent years, although there have been other forms, including open pilgrimages to no known destination and short pilgrimages around churches, cathedrals and other special places.

We will also be considering it from within the Protestant Christian tradition. While recognizing that pilgrimage is an almost universal religious practice, we will look at what pilgrimage might mean for someone who is at home in that part of the Christian movement. We must therefore note that Protestant Christianity is one religious tradition which has not, on the whole, looked favourably on the practice of pilgrimage. We will look at why that is, although first we will turn to the Bible.

THE BIBLE

The Old Testament

Old Testament worship principally took place at shrines. In the later monarchy the multitude of local shrines was suppressed in favour of the one central shrine, be it Jerusalem in Judah or Shechem in Israel. Worship therefore involved travelling to a special place. The festivals, when all males would be required to 'appear before the Lord' (see Exodus 23:17; 34:23), would be times of great pilgrimage – long journeys for some, and a large number of people gathered together. Worship involved gathering together at the place where the Lord was, literally, 'entering his gates with thanksgiving and his courts with praise' (Psalm 100:4). The exception to this was the Passover, which was celebrated at home, although it was the celebration of a journey. In time even the Passover came to include pilgrimage.

The exodus is perhaps the supreme journey, but the Bible is full of people travelling. Before the settlement in Egypt the patriarchs moved from place to place, often led or prompted by God. From the very beginning journeying had spiritual significance. The first man and woman were cast out of the garden, and Cain was condemned to wander the land following the murder of his brother. With archetypal images the storyteller here addresses, among other things, the tension between the nomadic existence of his own ancestors and their continual longing for a place of their own. In Deuteronomy the celebrant at the harvest thanksgiving is bidden to remember his nomadic origins: 'My father was a wandering Aramean...' (Deuteronomy 26:5). In Judges, Samuel and Kings both warriors and prophets are frequently on the move.

From the exile onwards, a key feature of the Jewish experience was *diaspora* (dispersion). Among the exiles there was a longing to return, but when the opportunity came a majority did not take it and, among those who did, the leaders Nehemiah and Ezra had to work hard to get the people to act on the dream of re-establishing the holy city.

In exile Israel had learnt how to worship without shrines and pilgrimages, gathering instead in meeting houses to pray and study the law. By the time of Jesus there were the two distinct foci for worship: the synagogue and the temple in Jerusalem. For some, like the Pharisees, the synagogue was of more importance, because it was the study and carrying out of the law which mattered most in a person's life. To others, like the Sadducees, the temple was the place of worship *par excellence* and the foundation of their identity. It was they who would have encouraged, and sometimes exploited, the whole practice of pilgrimage.

The New Testament

Despite the development of synagogue worship, pilgrimage was important in Jewish life and worship at the time of Jesus. Tens of thousands travelled, sometimes great distances, to be at Jerusalem for one of the great festivals – Jesus among them. In the beginnings of the Christian movement the Hebrew believers still worshipped at the temple. For Gentile believers it mattered less. Then the temple was destroyed, Judaism consolidated around the 'Books of the Law', and Hebrew Christianity diminished and faded. Jerusalem became a leading church among Gentile Christians, but as a place it mattered little. For them the focus was the risen Christ, and the energizing power of the Spirit. In John's Gospel, although Jesus goes frequently to Jerusalem for festivals, he also says to the Samaritan woman, 'The hour is coming when you will worship the Father neither on this mountain nor in Jerusalem ... true worshippers will worship the Father in spirit and truth' (John 4:21, 23 NRSV). Generally, for the early Christians, the particular place of worship mattered little (see Acts 7; 1 Corinthians 3:10-17; Hebrews 8-10).

Nevertheless, at another level travelling remained a significant feature of the Gospel story and the Christian life. In the Gospel narratives, even from before his birth Jesus is on the move. Jesus' messianic activity involves him travelling around Galilee, north to Tyre and Sidon and Caesarea Philippi, east to the Decapolis, and south to Jerusalem. In Matthew's Gospel the risen Christ then commands the disciples literally to go out and make other disciples from all nations. In Luke he meets two disciples on the road to Emmaus. From Pentecost onwards the apostles travel, impelled or drawn by the Holy Spirit. Jerusalem remains a centre, but the dynamic of Acts is that the holy city is becoming one of a number of centres. Antioch is Paul's base, but he is headed for Rome. Beyond the narrative of the book the Church was spreading in all directions, east as well as west, south into Africa and, within a short while, north as well.

Given that throughout the Bible people are on the move, it is remarkable that in that mainstay of Anglican liturgy and doctrine, the Book of Common Prayer, there is no mention anywhere of travel. There are no prayers for travellers, no provision for pilgrims or missionaries. The only journeys mentioned are those which crop up in the biblical texts. Travelling is not assumed to be a feature of the lives of Christians, and we need to consider why that is.

CHRISTIAN PILGRIMAGE: THE EARLY CHURCH AND THE MIDDLE AGES

The Early Church

The Early Church did not appear to give importance to particular special places. It gathered in houses, halls, synagogues, beside rivers – anywhere suitable. The Church of the first century was also a mobile one. The movement grew among people of all walks of life, not least slaves and the urban poor, whose freedom of movement was minimal. But it also grew among the merchant classes, and much of the spreading of the Gospel was done not by people who travelled specially to preach in strange places, but by those who travelled or migrated with their work.[3]

Christians would also have travelled to worship with others if they were able to. For isolated Christians that might have meant a considerable journey. As early as the mid-second century there were commemorations of martyrs taking place at their tombs.[4] For these meetings people travelled not only to be with others, but to be at a particular place.

With the Constantinian settlement the whole business of religious journeys took a leap forward. People began to travel to Palestine specifically to visit the places where Jesus had done various things and, especially, the place where he had been crucified. Churches were built at these alleged sites, some of them determined by Constantine's pious mother Helen. This was not, however, just an establishment exercise. Some of the radical critics of the established Church who took to the desert made journeying to the Gospel sites in Palestine a part of their ascetic discipline. The practice grew, and continued beyond the collapse of the Empire in the West and the coming of the Arabs to Palestine in the seventh century.

The Middle Ages

This practice of pilgrimage was not always viewed entirely positively. Jerome saw a definite value to the believer of visiting and worshipping at the places where Jesus had stood, but this was not to deny God's omnipresence: 'I do not presume to limit God's omnipotence or restrict to a narrow strip of earth him whom the heavens cannot contain,' he commented. 'Access to the court of heaven is as easy from Britain as it is from Jerusalem.'[5] Even Britain!

Gregory of Nyssa argued that 'the places which witnessed the crucifixion and the resurrection profit only those who bear their several crosses, who day by day rise again with Christ.'[6] And an ancient Celtic saying had it: 'To go to Rome is much trouble, little profit. The king whom you seek there you will not find, unless you take him with you.'[7]

Despite these qualifications, pilgrimage was generally encouraged until it became a major feature of church life – and revenue. A number of religious forces led to this development.

There was a desire to be for a while in the actual places where the great things had happened. Much as Christians from Missouri might feel moved having a bread and fish supper by the Sea of Galilee today, a medieval pilgrim could feel in touch with the Lord by walking the streets of Jerusalem that Jesus himself had walked. They would not be the same streets, since the city had been destroyed and rebuilt, but the pilgrim might not know that, and if he did he might not care. The Sea of Galilee is not the same water by or on which Jesus walked. That evaporated long ago (and some of it will be in the Missouri river by now). Neither is the grass the same. Yet many people are not deterred. The place is food for the imagination, and a sense of contact develops through being in the place, hearing the story and engaging the imagination.

There were other, less laudable reasons for the development of pilgrimage. The growth of the cult of saints and an associated interest in their relics drew many to the places of birth, ministry or death of these people. A pilgrim might return with a mark of his pilgrimage, a palm from the Holy Land or a shell from Compostella, and so the pilgrimage industry grew. No doubt the importance of the saints was related to popular perceptions of the nature of God. Without widespread access to Scripture prior to the Reformation, it was easy to see the spiritual world as a reflection of medieval feudal society, and God as the ultimate feudal lord who had to be placated. Then there was the ever-present threat of hell and purgatory. To pay for some of one's sins now, rather than later, one could undertake a pilgrimage, a voluntary banishment. Time undergoing the privations of the road would be time not spent later in purgatory.[8] Giving generously to the custodians of the shrine, handing over the result of one's labour perhaps over many years, could also secure more time free of punishment in the terrible hereafter.

Thus pilgrimage became big business in the Middle Ages. There was competition for relics. Income was invested in fine buildings to attract more pilgrims. Stories of the saints' miracles multiplied. There was opportunity for the strange and the bizarre to attract the faithful or the gullible. These practices, however, were not without their critics.

The experience and regulation of medieval pilgrimage

Four other points should be borne in mind concerning medieval pilgrimage. First, pilgrimage was the only opportunity or excuse many people had for getting away from their home parish and manor. Some pilgrims may have wanted to get away from obligations or bad marriages. Others would simply have been bored stiff with local life. Pilgrimage was also possibly a way of exercising a universal unconscious drive to move occasionally from one place to another. For many pilgrims, like Chaucer's company, it would have had the character of an adventurous holiday.

Second, pilgrimage was often a hard and dangerous practice. The pilgrim had to contend with the weather, epidemics, thieves, con men, pimps, rapists, cheating sailors, leaking boats, wild animals. It was hardly a Cook's Tour. Even the most well used pilgrim trails were not without their dangers and risks.

Third, not all pilgrimage in the Middle Ages was to holy shrines or to earn merit for the afterlife. In the early Middle Ages people travelled to bring the Gospel to others, or for a period of intense spiritual exercise. Following the invasions which came after the collapse of the Roman Empire, Western Europe was evangelized by organized missions from the Roman Church, as well as the rather more haphazard missions of the Celts. Celtic Christians talked of 'red' martyrdom and 'white' martyrdom. Red martyrdom meant getting killed for Christ. White martyrdom meant leaving one's home for the sake of Christ.[9] Some did this out of love for Christ, others to work out a sense of guilt or grief. Columba is said to have left Ireland for Iona after the death of several hundred people in a battle that he had started. The semi-legendary St Brendan set off in a boat to see where the wind of God would take him.

Fourth, the image of the journey became a significant motif in the spirituality of the Middle Ages. Amongst a people who were very restricted in their freedom of movement, the universal drive for travel took on a mythical character. The journey was seen as an image of the spiritual life. *The Quest of the Holy Grail* and *The Voyage of St Brendan* were among the most popular books of the period. It is possible that some pilgrims setting off on a journey were acting out a myth, their motive being not to pay off God for their sins but to grow in holiness and to become more as God intended. Their stimulus might not have been a feeling of guilt, but rather a sense of being called by God.

Criticism of pilgrimage continued, and there were attempts to regulate the practice. The Council of Chalon in 813 condemned various groups of so-called pilgrims: clergy trying to escape their pastoral duties; laity who thought they could sin with impunity by regularly going on pilgrimage; powerful people who demanded payment to protect fellow travellers; poor people who were simply looking for a better place to beg; and full-time pilgrims who thought they would purge their sins simply by seeing holy places.[10]

Pilgrimage was also criticized because the practice gave opportunity for sins which would not arise in the stable home situation. There was a medieval proverb: 'Go a pilgrim, return a whore.' Wyclif criticized the practice because it did nothing to help the poor. The Lollards criticized the veneration of images which was associated with pilgrimage, and saw the only true pilgrimage as the living out of a life of faith and charity. These criticisms were reiterated with wit and force by Erasmus. As with other criticisms of the religion of the time, significant changes came when the Reformers not only levelled against bad practice but also created a paradigm shift in people's understanding of their whole relationship with God.

PROTESTANT PILGRIMAGE SINCE THE REFORMATION

The Reformers

Luther weighed into the whole practice of pilgrimage. The fact that it was not commanded by Christ was just one of his criticisms. He made a full-blooded attack on the cult of the saints and indulgences, condemning the latter because they were based on a false understanding of the grace of God. There was, and needed to be, no mediator but Christ. Christ was the one who was alongside humanity and pleaded for sinners to the Father. The grace of God was to be received by faith, by trust in God's forgiveness and love, not earned by arduous journeys to holy places, nor paid for with penances or money. The practice of pilgrimage was based on a misunderstanding, Luther argued, and it encouraged the notion of earning God's forgiveness and gave unscrupulous churchmen an opportunity to deceive and cheat their people. It should, he said, be abolished.

For Calvin, pilgrimage was less of an issue, but he condemned all the practices associated with the cult of the saints, and particularly the use of images. Within his style of Christianity the church building was a place of learning, like the synagogue. It was not the place that was holy, it was the book that contained the word of God. If one travelled, one travelled to learn and to meet with fellow believers, the saints of the present time. One did not travel to make contact with the saints of past ages, let alone to try to earn favour with God.

Nonetheless, among many of those who studied the Bible with vigour and enthusiasm, the recurrent image of the journey became significant. Bunyan's Christian was a pilgrim, and his book joins *The Grail* and *Brendan* among the foremost of Christian fantasy writing, employing the same primary image of the journey. Those who left England for a new life in America were known as 'the Pilgrim Fathers', travelling with a sense of God's call to a new life in a place that he would give them. In the spirituality of the Presbyterian Church in Scotland there was a strong sense of identification with the Israelites leaving their slavery to be led by God into freedom. Although widely sung in Anglican churches, the hymns 'O God of Bethel' and 'Guide me, O thou great Jehovah' are both from Nonconformist writers.

The Church of England

In the Church of England the 'Romish Doctrine concerning Purgatory, pardons, worshipping and adoration, as well of images as of reliques, and also invocation of the saints' was condemned as being 'repugnant to the Word of God' (Article XXII). Pilgrimage was seen as part of all this, and the Anglican liturgy settled into a domestic annual cycle through the Christian year with baptisms, confirmations, marriages and funerals. It assumed a stable society in which people stayed in their home parish throughout their lives. The collects and lectionary readings exhorted people to holy living in the grace of God. It left little room for a sense of mobility in society, be that for financial, social or even spiritual reasons.

The missionary movement was another thing it gave little space for. Mission became an interest and activity of voluntary organizations within the Church – yet, while the need for social reform and the drive for increased franchise, protection of workers and better living conditions for the poor was foremost in the hearts and minds of some Anglicans, such motivation found little support in the liturgy and ethos of the Anglican Church. In the eighteenth and nineteenth centuries, however, the idea that people would live all their lives in one parish became even more unrealistic than it had been in Cranmer's day. Even in the countryside in the Tudor period, people had moved from place to place. With the land enclosures and the development of the industrial cities, this tendency simply increased.

Scots Presbyterians on board ship to America might have been able to identify themselves in some way with the children of Israel on their way to a promised land. David Livingstone pushing through the forest towards the Zambesi could sing 'O God of Bethel', his favourite hymn. By contrast, Anglicans with their carts heading towards Manchester to look for work, or on board ship to India, had little from their Prayer Book with which to make spiritual sense of their journey.

Developments

Nineteenth-century Protestantism developed new forms of pilgrimage. In America there were the camp meetings, large gatherings for teaching, praise and encouragement, with accompanying signs of the Holy Spirit's work. In Britain these had their parallels in Bible conventions and holiday gatherings. They have their successors today, such as Spring Harvest, New Wine and Greenbelt, all holiday events incorporating teaching, worship and fellowship.

Among those with money and the freedom to travel there developed quite naturally the idea of the Holy Land tour. Many of those who studied their Bibles had come to know their way round Palestine better than they knew their way round their own country, so there was nothing more natural than to want to go and look at it. The British middle classes had taken in Palestine on the 'Grand Tour'; now evangelical Christians with money to spend developed the religious version. Once there, however, they became unhappy with the traditional holy places, dominated by Catholics and Orthodox, and so sometimes set up their own centres, more conducive to their own style of prayer and worship. The evidence for the Garden Tomb at Jerusalem being the actual site of Jesus' burial is even weaker than that for the site of the Church of the Holy Sepulchre, but that will not persuade hundreds of evangelicals to transfer their focus. As with the medieval pilgrim, what feeds the spirit through the imagination matters more than brute facts.

By the time of the Industrial Revolution the Church of England needed to respond to the requirements of a mobile society, uprooted from rural life to the cities – and it failed. This movement of people has continued into the present time, but there are now other dimensions to social mobility. People no longer only travel to find work or a better place to live. They travel for the fun of it. They go on holiday, to the extent that a holiday spent at home is often not thought of as a 'real' holiday. In some sections of society there is also a kind of 'myth of the traveller'. People at the end of their tether, or grieving the death or departure of a partner, have a strong urge to go somewhere else. Desperate homeless people sometimes get themselves an old bus or van to drive off and join other travellers, dreaming of being able to move from one piece of common land to another, feeling the fresh air of the countryside rather than the fumes of the pavement. Other people travel to festivals – rock festivals, folk festivals, beer festivals, and numerous other gatherings of people with common interests which form a high spot in what might otherwise be a humdrum year. These people are perhaps secular pilgrims, or followers of alternative and experimental religions. There are also those who set off to find 'the Truth' on the trail to Nepal or Ladakh or among Native Americans. The Church in the present time needs to respond to the needs of a highly mobile society, a society which by and large *expects* to travel.

The desire to roam

It has been suggested that travelling is a primeval urge among human beings, that it is not an aberration from the 'normal' settled human life, but that it is settlement that is the abnormality.[11] History would seem to point that way. *Homo sapiens* was a hunter-gatherer or a nomad for many thousands of years before settlement and agriculture were developed. If this is the case, then a Church that develops practices which help faith to grow and develop within the context of travel is tapping into something that is deep in the human subconscious.

Alongside the desire to travel, however, there is clearly also another human aspiration – to find a place to settle. Images of the settled existence – such as 'Ambridge', the archetypal village made famous through the radio programme *The Archers* – continue to appeal to people. While the Bible is full of people travelling, there is also the continual hope for a place to stay and to rest. This will be the promised land, although, for the writer to the Hebrews, the promised land is not here; the better country is a heavenly one, where God has prepared a city for those who trust him (see Hebrews 11:16).

The practice of pilgrimage is one way in which the Church can respond to a deep-seated desire in people both to travel and to have in their mobile lives a few fixed points. Places of pilgrimage can be special places of meeting, places where the spiritual and the material come together, places where people might have a sense of home more significant than the neighbourhood of their present house or flat. In pilgrimage the journey and the arrival become parts of one activity and can be a means to spiritual growth.

Before we turn to think about the practice of pilgrimage, we must first consider the theological framework in which it might be creatively developed.

THEOLOGICAL APPRAISAL

Reformation criticisms

Anyone who lives within the Protestant Christian tradition is going to want to listen to the voices of the Reformers. Their condemnations of the practice of pilgrimage do not need to be held as condemnations for all time, since circumstances change, but they can still be heard as warnings of possible abuse and misunderstanding.

First, there is no justification by works. We are justified by grace through faith (see Romans 3:21f.). So a pilgrimage, however arduous, cannot put one into a right relationship with God. Having said that, however, few would argue that there is therefore no need to pray, to meet with other Christians, to go to church, or to study the Bible. These are not things the Christian does in order to earn God's favour, but they are ways in which the faith of the Christian can become more deeply rooted and developed in the struggles and challenges of life with God. It is in this context that pilgrimage must be seen, as an activity which might help faith to grow.

Second, God is equally present to be known in every place. God is not somehow located in some places and absent from others. He is not more present in Jerusalem than in Neasden, nor more present between the covers of a Bible than in the pages of the *TV Times*. Nonetheless, there are some places that are more helpful to be than others, and some things that might be more helpful to read than others.

In the Bible the two images of the journey and the place of rest are in tension with each other. The journey leads to the promised land. The hope of the promised land draws the traveller on. On the way, however, there are periods of rest, oases in the desert, places of retreat from the pressing crowds. Jesus travelled from place to place, teaching and healing. He also withdrew into the hills or to Gentile territory where he thought he might remain unrecognized. And sometimes on his journeys he was surprised or challenged. A Syro-Phoenician woman made him think again about his mission (Matthew 15:21ff.). A centurion demonstrated a faith beyond any Jesus had met among his own people (Matthew 8:10). It was the same with the apostles. Time and again in their travels they were surprised by God. The Holy Spirit came visibly on Gentiles, even before they were baptized (Acts 10:44ff.). A council of leaders at Jerusalem had to decide how to respond to the mission of the Church, not how to plan it (Acts 15:1ff.).

This means that any pilgrimage is not a journey to meet with God, as if such a meeting could be generated by careful planning. Any journey to a particular place will certainly be one in which the traveller hopes to meet with God, to be surprised, perhaps, and to learn and grow in the process. But the traveller might also be disappointed, and the meeting with God might take a form the pilgrim does not expect.

Sacraments

The Reformation was in some respects a movement to interiorize religion. The activities of prayer and worship became in

Protestant churches much more activities of the mind and the emotions. There was not a great deal of sympathy for moving the body in bowing, genuflecting or crossing oneself, let alone in dancing. There was less lighting of candles and moving things around. In some churches the congregation remained sitting and the minister simply stood before them in the pulpit. Apart from the extremely radical Quakers, however, they all retained the practices of baptism and Holy Communion. The justification for these was that Christ had commanded them. In keeping these practices, they did continue to allow for some movement in worship, with the intention of helping the congregation while obeying the Lord.

This obedience involved remembering and imitation. It was also reckoned to be a participation in the activity of God in Christ. In baptism one was buried with Christ. In Communion one was in table fellowship with the Lord, and in sharing the broken bread and poured wine one was also involved in the suffering, death and resurrection of Christ. However that process is understood, the existence of sacramental acts opens up the possibility that what can happen in baptism or Communion could also happen in another context, perhaps on a journey. A journey undertaken for the Lord is not something commanded in the Gospels, but it could be open to the same process – participation in the work of God through an imitative activity. Jesus travelled, through Galilee to Jerusalem, to the cross, and through death to resurrection. In a dramatic re-enactment participants might be drawn into this process.

This was the origin of the 'stations of the cross'. It began in Jerusalem, when pilgrims walked round the city stopping at the alleged sites of the different events in the great drama. This practice of re-enactment was then brought back to Europe and became a small pilgrimage round the 'stations' set out within the church or cathedral.[12]

In a real pilgrimage, by contrast, the script is not set. The pilgrim sets out towards a destination, but with a path unknown. Even if the pilgrim knows the route and the places on the way, the encounters with others, the thoughts, the challenges, the worries, the imaginings all remain unknown, as yet uncreated. Even the destination remains something of a mystery, because even though the pilgrim may have been there before, that was another time, with different company, and the thoughts and feelings generated on arrival will be unique to each occasion.

In Holy Communion the participants are praying with their bodies as well as their minds. Their senses are being used to bring them into closer harmony with the life and ways of God. In pilgrimage the same process occurs. A pilgrimage is fundamentally an activity, something one does with one's body and not just with the mind. Like Communion, a pilgrimage can be a way of prayer.

The cloud of witnesses

The Reformers criticized the veneration of the saints which went with the practice of pilgrimage, yet there continues to be a recognition that certain people have been (and still are) used specially by God. Travelling to a place associated with such people, to reflect on their life and example, to meet them if still living, is part of appreciating the 'cloud of witnesses' (Hebrews 12:1). To visit a place that has particular associations with a great exemplar of Christian living, or even with Jesus himself, could be of benefit to a Christian. If the visit also involves fellowship with other believers of like purpose, then there may be other opportunities for encouragement in the life of faith.

It is along these lines that pilgrimage has slowly crept back into Protestant thinking and spirituality. Different practices have had a different focus. Sometimes the pilgrimage might be to places associated with Jesus or one of his exemplary followers. Some large gatherings of Christians have taken on the character of a pilgrimage as they have acquired a reputation as places where the Spirit of God is active, and so people go away to conventions, conferences and weeks of teaching and spiritual refreshment.

New frameworks

The criticisms of the medieval teachers are also worth hearing in this regard. The Council of Chalon, were it to sit today, might issue a warning against clergy who are so busy making pilgrimages and attending conferences that they have little time for their pastoral duties; or against Christians who think that discipleship involves clocking up a regular number of conventions and weeks of renewal, but who ignore God's demands for justice worked out with love; or against people who make themselves rich by providing services to pilgrims who lack the experience or the wherewithal to arrange their own journey; or against those using their Christian devotions as an excuse for not pulling their weight in the community; or against those who think they will become better Christians simply by going to the right places.

The warning that pilgrimage could give rise to sins which might not occur in the stable home situation is also pertinent, and points to a significant feature of the experience of pilgrimage. Pilgrimage does take people out of their normal frameworks of relationship, with all the expectations, checks and constraints those involve. In a different context people behave differently. While in the medieval situation pilgrimage was one of the few occasions when people were out of the constraints of their home life, in our society the holiday away from home is thought of as a normal occurrence. People do behave differently on holiday from the way they do at home. They talk with strangers about things they would never share with someone who knew them well. Conservative and upstanding community members go shopping in bikinis and play cricket on the sand. People drink more, eat more and fall into affairs. Families on holiday are sometimes under greater stress than when they are at home, although equally they can discover new ways of relating and appreciating one another.

The other side of this is that a self-aware person can learn through the experience. Time spent in a different situation, particularly a situation where normal life is put on hold and the boundaries are moved, can be a time of self-discovery.[13] Sometimes people discover things about themselves they would rather not know. They may also discover strengths they did not think they had. Together with the opportunities for making new friends and acquaintances, for broadening experience of life, prayer and worship, for unloading some of the mental clutter and baggage from the home situation, and for looking at the normal context of one's life from a distance, the experience can be an effective means of personal and spiritual growth and discovery.

Travelling in God's creation

Allowing such growth to happen involves seeing the journey as a response to God or as something undertaken as part of one's living by faith. A sense that God is neither left at home nor only waiting at the destination, but is to be encountered on the journey, may open a person to new insights and possibilities. This sense might be described as an attitude of openness, getting on with the journey but at the same time waiting to see what happens. Such openness involves letting sights and sounds, words, ideas and dreams connect with each other to form new patterns, and allowing fear, anxiety, sadness, deep joy and pleasure to arise, acknowledging them when they do.

Speaking of life itself as a journey is a well-worn image. Many people write books or sing songs about 'the journey of life'. Reflection on a real journey with all its blended difficulties and pleasures, struggle, hardship, tedium and satisfaction can give insight into the nature of our relationship with God in the whole of life. Making a pilgrimage might increase our sense that the rest of our life is also, in a way, a pilgrimage – even a continuation of that one significant journey. God is not only on the pilgrimage but also on the bus to work.

This points towards one final theological theme seemingly ignored by the medieval writers and the Reformers, and that is creation. The world is God's world. It is called into being by God, permeated with God's glory, resonant with life, and appreciated by its Creator as good. To travel through new parts of that world, and to appreciate it and enjoy it, is a faithful response to God. The fact that a pilgrimage can also be enjoyable is not something to be decried, and it could perhaps be justified on those grounds alone.

MAKING A PILGRIMAGE

Preparation

A conference begins when people arrive, and the Communion service begins with a greeting and preparatory prayer. A pilgrimage begins when a person first starts to consider the possibility and the prospect of such a journey. Before the pilgrim leaves there is a time of preparation, an exploration of ideas and possibilities, and these are all part of the journey.

A long pilgrimage might take a person on a journey of several days or weeks to a particular destination. The means of travel will make a considerable difference to the character of the journey. A walker is in touch with the elements, feels the wind, the rain, the sunshine and the slope of the ground. Walking from one place to another gives a sense of continuity. A journey by bicycle still gives something of this sense. With public transport the traveller is moving at a pace set by other people, and it is possible to sit back and let it all happen, to let one's thoughts wander as one is carried towards the destination. Decisions about means of transport are likely to be very personal. For some, travelling by bicycle is the next thing to heaven.[14] I prefer to walk. For other people buses and trains do great things for their spirit. Such decisions will all be part of the preparation for the journey.

A pilgrimage with a group will be very different from a pilgrimage made alone. When travelling with others one can develop a strong sense of fellowship, but one might also find them hard to get on with. This is an opportunity for self-discovery and growth, and one might not want the challenge of difficult relationships on this particular pilgrimage. Nonetheless, travelling alone might involve long periods of loneliness, as well as the freedom of travelling at one's own pace and by a route one chooses for oneself. Both have their good points and their challenges, and such decisions need to be weighed carefully.

The pilgrimage may also include places which are of personal significance to the pilgrim, places of significant meeting or prior religious experience, places associated with a grief or with family roots. Returning to such places can stir up powerful memories which might then be dealt with creatively, but which could also create further problems if they cannot be faced constructively. This is another factor for careful consideration.

It is possible to make an open pilgrimage – a journey to an unknown destination. In a sense any pilgrimage will have a degree of openness, as the pilgrim never knows what will happen on the journey, but a long, totally open pilgrimage would involve setting off for a period of time and seeing what opens up in terms of ideas, opportunities, invitations and possibilities. It is generally young people filling time around college courses, or people with severe emotional or practical problems whom one meets undertaking this kind of journey, but it has a long history within various religions. Traditionally, a Hindu man at the age of 50 would leave on what might be an open pilgrimage as he moved into the next phase of his life. The open journeys of some of the Celtic saints have already been mentioned. One might see Paul's missionary journeys in this way, too. He and his colleagues did not set out with a clear itinerary, but responded to the opportunities given by the Holy Spirit. As they approached Antioch on their return, the character of the journey would have changed and become more like a pilgrimage to a destination.

Some pilgrimages are short – perhaps a walk between the churches in a deanery or to a cathedral. On Iona there is a pilgrimage around the island every Wednesday, stopping at significant places for meditation.[15] A contemplative walk, going slowly and quietly around an area, open and alert to signs of the kingdom of God, might be thought of as a short open pilgrimage. There are many other similar possibilities. Simon Bailey's book *Stations* gives suggestions for a pilgrimage in one's own home.[16] It is a matter of definition at what point a meditative exercise ceases to be a real pilgrimage and becomes a pilgrimage by imagination.

Every pilgrimage involves some preparation, however. For a long pilgrimage this will involve decisions about destination, route, means of travel, company, support, and when the journey will be undertaken. For a very short pilgrimage it will be more a question of opportunity and mental preparation. The basic decisions for a journey which is deliberately undertaken as a part of one's spiritual life will need to be made carefully. This does not mean that they should be made solemnly. It might be that it is a sense of pleasurable excitement which draws a prospective pilgrim into deciding on a particular kind of pilgrimage.

Departure

After what might have been a long period of preparation, the moment comes to leave. The medieval pilgrim left with the blessing of the local priest, and prayers by the congregation and masses were offered for travellers.[17] The moment of departure is significant and will normally be marked with prayer. The form this takes will depend on the tradition and spirituality of the pilgrim and the group to which the pilgrim belongs. It may be that congregational prayers are appropriate. As well as being supportive of the pilgrim, this enables others to participate in the whole undertaking. The pilgrim will usually return, and those at home will then want to know what happened on the journey. This is appropriate, as gifts are usually given to be shared. The way that others can participate in the pilgrimage needs careful consideration. Prayer at the point of departure is just one obvious way.

Another way that might be worth considering is sponsorship. In a society where vast sums of money are raised by people sponsoring others to do absurd and dangerous things, there is perhaps something challenging about going off on a long journey and *not* being sponsored. 'If you're not being sponsored, why are you doing it?' The struggle for an answer to such a question is good for the pilgrim and for those asking the question. Nevertheless, sponsorship might give people a chance to be involved in the pilgrimage. They would literally have some investment in it, and that might benefit both pilgrim and sponsors.

Nevertheless, it is important to remember that the journey is the pilgrimage. It has been said many times of the Pennine Way that the only good thing about it is getting to the end, and the sense of achievement one has gained. The point about a pilgrimage, however, is the journey and not just the destination – let alone the sense of achievement at the end. On a long journey there is a pressure to focus one's mind on how far one has come, how much distance is left and when one will arrive, but God is in the present moment, not only at the destination. Part of the spiritual discipline of the journey will involve developing an openness to God along the way. An awareness that another mile done means several more pounds for the good cause may distract from this openness.

It is also possible that the pilgrimage is a very personal affair, and so an appropriate rite of departure might simply be a period of quietness, or a conversation with a soul friend. This cannot be prescribed. Like the preparatory decisions, plans for the departure can only be made carefully by the pilgrim.

The journey

The pilgrimage is a response to God. God was involved in the promptings which led to the decision to go on pilgrimage, God is in the thousand meetings and encounters of the journey itself, in the lives of people and the glory of the whole creation, and he is at the destination. It is difficult to prepare for surprises, but there are activities which can help a person develop an attitude of openness to encounters with God on the journey, and a number of writers describe some of these.[18] The pilgrim, however, is not going to carry a pile of books. These techniques and practices really need to be a part of the pilgrim's spiritual toolkit, to be used on the journey: helping the pilgrim to attend to the present moment and not just be pulled to thinking about the arrival; maintaining a sense of expectation about the journey itself; being open to learning from or making new discoveries in meetings with other people; letting go of concerns from back home, about the work that is left behind. As well as books by spiritual writers, the work of other reflective travellers may well be helpful.[19]

If the pilgrim has a framework of prayer which is helpful in everyday life, it might well be good to maintain this on the journey. A New Testament and a small, familiar book of prayers can be helpful, particularly if the journey extends over several days. Keeping a journal or diary can also be useful, not just for the sake of memory but also as an aid to reflection and to making objective any emotions, thoughts, anxieties and fears which might otherwise overwhelm the pilgrim, especially if the journey is a solitary one.

Arrival

As the destination approaches, it is easy to be caught up in the rush and excitement and to lose touch with what has been learnt or encountered on the journey. If the destination is a place of great activity, the pilgrim might need to make space to reflect on the journey as well as on the feelings and thoughts triggered by the arrival. Here again a journal is helpful. One also needs to be open to the possibility of feeling different from how one expected to feel. If the pilgrimage is made to a place which is well known but not previously visited, there is always the possibility that it will not fit in with expectations. It is important to take the place for what it is. The practice of taking things as they are, which the pilgrim might have developed on the journey, needs to be extended into the arrival. God, who was on the journey, is also in the destination.

The return

God is also back home. The typical pilgrimage story finishes when the pilgrim arrives, but the pilgrim must usually return to his or her home base. The means of travel home needs some thought. If the journey has been a very slow one, it might not be helpful to return at high speed. If the return journey is too fast, the whole pilgrimage can seem unreal once one is back in the normal home routine. As careful thought has been given to the question of leaving on the journey, so equally careful thought needs to be given to the process of departing from the destination and returning home.

The pilgrimage may have been a time of great insight. It could well have been a significant time, perhaps even the journey of a lifetime. Everyone back home, however, has carried on with life in the usual way. They have probably not seen anything much happen that is different from the usual, and somehow the pilgrim has to join back in with their lives. Getting back into the normal business of life can be difficult and might involve feelings of sadness or frustration, or a sense of depression – Monday morning feeling with attitude! It helps to be ready for this, and if it does not happen that is a pleasant bonus.

Anthony de Mello has an exercise which can be helpful. It involves stilling and centring oneself and then intensively remembering a place of peacefulness.[20] Moments or episodes on the pilgrimage can possibly become material for this kind of prayer, whether they be times of peace or of insight and excitement. Words of a poem or a particular prayer might also help to recall such times. In the same way that medieval pilgrims returned with their palm or shell to remind them of the encounters of the journey and the destination, so too our photographs and souvenirs might be of help in our praying in the life to which we return.

A pilgrimage can be a time of insight and a deepening sense of God, or a building up of fellowship. It is important that these gifts are not dissipated when the pilgrim returns to the routines and different struggles of more ordinary life. If the pilgrimage has led to a renewed commitment to the way of Christ, it is vital that this experience is absorbed into the rest of the pilgrim's life. It is in the ordinary rather than the special that the commitment must be worked out.

Nonetheless, the ordinary and the special are part of one life, and the home and the journey of pilgrimage are part of one world. Although a pilgrimage is a very different activity from the stuff of most people's everyday lives, it takes place in a similar context. The buildings in which we worship are often very different from people's homes and workplaces. What we feel or think there can easily evaporate once we return from the place of stone walls and pews to the sitting room with its television and magazines, or to the desk with its files and papers. On a pilgrimage, however, we are deliberately setting out hoping to meet with God on footpaths, sitting on buses or trains, in hostels or pubs, looking at the clouds and the trees, and feeling the rain. It might therefore be that the experiences of the journey and the skills developed on the pilgrimage can translate without great difficulty into many people's ordinary lives.

Pilgrimage can thus be seen not simply as an esoteric practice to be undertaken by a few enthusiasts, but as something to be encouraged that will help people to deepen their sense of God in the ordinary business of life. Most people travel to work, or to shops, colleges or day centres. These journeys are so easily seen as wasted time. Developing the practice of pilgrimage can help people to make these journeys into a part of the spiritual pattern of their lives.

If that can be done with the small journeys, it can also be done with the big ones: the move to another area, the first journey to university, the flight to visit relatives abroad. These journeys are a significant feature of life in our society. In encouraging and developing the practice of pilgrimage, the Church can help people to become aware of God in both the mundane and the special journeys of their lives, on the way as well as at the destination.

Notes

1 'A song of ascents' is the title given in the text to each of Psalms 120-34.

2 See 'The Voyage of St Brendan', in *Lives of the Saints* (Penguin, 1965).

3 Stephen Neill, *A History of Christian Missions* (Penguin, 1964), p. 24f.

4 J. G. Davies (ed.), *A New Dictionary of Liturgy and Worship* (SCM, 1986), p. 433.

5 J. G. Davies, *Pilgrimage Yesterday and Today* (SCM, 1988), p. 80f.

6 Ibid.

7 A. M. Allchin and Esther de Waal, *Threshold of Light* (Darton, Longman and Todd, 1986), p. 56.

8 Alan Kednall, *Medieval Pilgrims* (Wayland, 1970), p. 17.

9 See Shirley Toulson, *The Celtic Alternative* (Rider, 1987), p. 80f.

10 See Davies, *Pilgrimage Yesterday and Today*, p. 82ff., on the pre-Reformation and Reformation criticism of pilgrimage.

11 See Bruce Chatwin, *The Songlines* (Pan, 1988), p. 180ff.

12 See Davies (ed.), *A New Dictionary of Liturgy and Worship*, p. 498.

13 See Victor Turner and Edith Turner, *Image and Pilgrimage in Christian Culture* (Blackwell, 1978), Chapter 1.

14 See, for example, Tom Davies, *Merlyn the Magician and the Pacific Coast Highway* (NEL, 1982).

15 See *The Iona Community Worship Book*, 3rd edition (Wild Goose Publications, 1991), p. 60.

16 Simon Bailey, *Stations* (Cairns Publications, 1991).

17 See F. Cabrol, *Liturgical Prayer, its History and Spirit* (Burns, Oates and Washbourne, 1922), p. 267f.

18 See, for example, David Adam, *The Cry of the Deer* (SPCK, 1987); Bailey, *Stations*; Anthony de Mello, *Sadhana* (Doubleday, 1984).

19 See, for example, John Hillaby, *Journey through Britain* (Constable, 1968); Gerard Hughes, *In Search of a Way* (Darton, Longman and Todd, 1986); Peter Matthiessen, *The Snow Leopard* (Chatto & Windus, 1979).

20 De Mello, *Sadhana*, p. 68.

SPIRITUAL AUTOBIOGRAPHY

Roger Pooley

On many Sunday evenings, hunched in prayer at the end of the service in the little Methodist Mission where I had first been led to faith, it struck me that what was demanded of the young Christian was a constant intensity of inwardness. My friends at school were bright, questioning, self-defining, but how many of them were forced into the exercise of serious self-examination week after week? Are you saved? Are you really dedicating your life to God? How often do you witness to the gospel? Steamy as it seems in retrospect, I am very grateful for that intensity, because it brought out very clearly the either/or at the heart of the gospel, and gave me a habit of self-examination crucial to my life as a Christian. This chapter is, in many ways, a product of that kind of rather pietistic spirituality, but also an expansion and a critique of it.

SEEING THE SHAPE OF OUR LIVES

As with other chapters in this book, and some booklets in the Grove Spirituality series, the aim here is to introduce readers to some of the riches of our heritage as Christians, both from inside the evangelical tradition and from beyond it. There will be times when readers will recognize that this is the work of a Christian who is a literary critic by profession and no expert at biblical studies, history or theology. All these activities, however, are too important to be left to their guilds of professional practitioners, and in any case, what I am interested in is not so much a historical survey, with the odd devotional remark thrown in, but an encouragement to Christians to look back and see the shape of their lives in the context of God's providence. In attempting the exercise myself, I have been dogged by my own dishonesty, my inability to see life whole rather than in 'religious' and 'secular' compartments, and by certain other kinds of short-sightedness which, I fear, are encouraged by the state of the Christian Church at the moment. In the final section I make a number of suggestions for 'exercises' in self-examination and personal story-telling which attempt to circumvent some of these personal and collective shortcomings.

The perspective of time

The distinctive feature of spiritual autobiography, as opposed to other forms of self-examination and self-revelation, is the perspective of time. Autobiography is the survey of one's own life from the perspective of one point in time, which is what distinguishes it from journals and memoirs; spiritual autobiography is that survey perceived as the story of a relationship with God. The definition marks a real problem: what should be excluded from a spiritual autobiography? I will try to deal with that more systematically in the historical section, but here I want to draw on the experience of writing a short spiritual autobiography, which was perhaps my most instructive preparation for writing this chapter.

One distorting temptation was to write simply about 'religious' things – so my account of my childhood became an account of being a choirboy, being taught the Lord's Prayer and 'Gentle Jesus, meek and mild' by my parents, and so on. That is not to be dismissed, but is it enough? It gets dangerously close to cutting God down to size. But, of course, mundane details like falling down the back steps and knocking a tooth out, while a vivid childhood memory, would sit uneasily in a spiritual autobiography, less for their triviality than for their irrelevance, I think. It is because one cannot fit it into a pattern – and all autobiography is a search for a pattern, a metaphor, as James Olney puts it, 'which will express the unknown in terms of the known'.[1] A second, non-religious, example, which I had forgotten but was reminded of by an old family friend, concerns the death of my budgerigar when I was eight or nine. 'Never mind, Roger,' she had said, 'you can always get another one.' 'No,' I had blubbered, 'what's the use? You only learn to love them and then they die.' I will leave aside the interest of my internal censor having excised the memory – but that incident still reverberates in my mind like a clue, and I get different readings when I see it as a clue to my relationships with my family (my father died four years later), girlfriends, other friends and God. It is part of my spiritual autobiography, without a doubt, because it helps to show how God's story and my story intertwine. It needs mediating through other stories, most notably my experiences of warm Christian fellowship after I became a real Christian.

The turning point

For most Christians, the time of conversion or something like it becomes the axis of understanding, the crucial turning point in the story. Paul talks about putting on 'the new self' (Colossians 3:10), and the radical nature of the change cannot be denied. One purpose of spiritual autobiography is to see that change clearly. It is usually the main feature of the 'testimony' model, as practised in services, evangelistic meetings and publications. Should we be happy with that model?

It has the disadvantages of all formulae – the jargon which is impenetrable to all but the initiates (and one suspects that some of the initiates are not too sure of it either), reducing an individual's experiences to some cramped template of what conversion ought to be like, and discouraging proper thought and reflection by a closing-off cliché. 'I was brought up in a Christian home...' still produces an inward groan. Does the Holy Spirit work on the principle of the tape-loop, rather than with a variety of his work in the old creation? Do we not induce a premature disappointing sense of having 'arrived' in thus encouraging the new convert to witness (another word from the jargon basement) to his or her new faith?

Formulae do have their advantages. A conversion which did not include some conviction of sin and the sense of the need for God's grace would be very curious; and one which produced no change in the subject's behaviour or orientation would be suspect. To the extent that the model encourages people to look for such biblically expected evidence, it is useful. The recital of the formulae can also be a reassuring way of saying that the converted individual is part of his or her new Christian family. It is just that we cannot afford to stop there.

Are we not encouraging an excess of subjectivity just when a stress on the objective work of Christ is most needed? Not really. The danger of subjectivity is the danger of a short-sighted, short-term inwardness; the habit of spiritual autobiography encourages the long view, the proper perspective. It is also a way of linking what might be remote and abstract to the here and now, a mode of 'incarnation', metaphysically speaking.

The theology of story

This kind of argument is characteristic of the 'theology of story', as it has been called, an investigation mostly carried on in the USA.[2] This argues that understanding of God is to be found, not in propositions, doctrines or commands, but in the action of God among his people as it has been recounted within a narrative framework. The motives are partly those of an anti-systematic, anti-dogmatic theology which has many parallels with liberation theology. Its strengths and weaknesses are similar, too: a strong commitment to the here and now in an attempt to identify the story of Christ with the story of his people, and a suspicion of knowledge which does not relate to action, somewhat blunted by a reluctance to listen to those parts of biblical discourse, like simple ethical commands, which do not easily fit into a narrative model.

The Christian considering his or her own story will need to take this into account. There will be bits that do not fit – not just the experiences that I mentioned earlier as not necessarily 'religious', but sins to which the proper attitude is revulsion rather than stoical acceptance. Different Christian viewpoints tend to generate their own classifications of sinful activity. The liberation theologians tend to major on greed and exploitation (both individual and corporate); many evangelicals (apart from those testimonies of God's rescue from a life of spectacularly criminal behaviour) on sexual misdemeanour as the main temptation facing Christians. There are any number of ways of ignoring sins by focusing on those we have not committed, but the story model does have an advantage here, because it encourages a vision of process and progress as well as a sharp eye on falling back. One criticism trained against Christian autobiographers is that they tend to exaggerate their sinfulness before conversion. It may be that non-Christians are inclined to underestimate the revulsion of Christians towards their sinful pasts, something that increases with time, but it is a danger when linked to the pride which an injudicious encouragement of 'testimony' might foster.

An unfinished symphony

It has to be remembered that a Christian autobiography should never be 'finished', in the sense that it has a beginning, a middle and an end. What is so striking about Paul's autobiographical remarks in 2 Timothy 4 is that, right at the end of his life, he retains a future tense – 'there is in store for me the crown of righteousness' (v. 8). The final act is still to take place. Euphoria or uneasy tension may be the state of mind at the time of writing or speaking, but the 'finished' quality of the Christian's story stems from the resurrection of Christ and thus the eschatological hope. Premature attempts to 'finish' the story – at conversion, at some other watershed experience (of assurance, for example, as in Wesley's pattern), or even at death – should be resisted. A disappointing and discouraging sense of having 'arrived' is no help to a young Christian; imagination and hope need to be stimulated.

In Dostoevsky's *Notes from Underground* the hero argues that 'consciousness is a disease', and in our consumer culture a certain kind of selfish inwardness is being encouraged, even prized. Yet inwardness as a preparation for action is the characteristic rhythm of the Christian life, as practised by Jesus and Paul. We need to understand the most fruitful way of self-examination, which is part of that inwardness. Wrongly done, it can be a hindrance to Christian action, a stunting of growth, even a path to despair – but to ignore it completely is to risk spiritual stupidity, and to do it well could lead to a personal growth in grace and to the edification and encouragement of others. Getting it right, I think, involves at least three steps: reading the Bible, reading some of the classic spiritual autobiographies, and doing some exercises.

SPIRITUAL AUTOBIOGRAPHY IN THE BIBLE

First-person narratives in the Old Testament reflect the central characteristics of the spirituality which runs through all its books. It derives from a strong sense of God in history; such a formula as 'the God of Abraham, of Isaac, and of Jacob' points at once to his transcendence, and to the specific nature of his action in time. He is a God with whom people have relationships which can be paralleled with human friendship (a difficult concept for most of the world religions), and he also sustains a relationship with a whole race of people over many generations. Old Testament spirituality is also often visionary. Visions of God's grandeur, of the situation of the world, of God's particular people, of the future – all these are expressed through a vividly pictorial prophecy.

It is clear that the God of the Old Testament cultivates a metaphoric imagination in his people, but perhaps most central to Old Testament spirituality is the idea and cultic observance of holiness, a feature of God which is to be the distinguishing feature of his people. While that is often expressed in law, the creation of it is seen as a historical process, whether through the great collective movement of the exodus, or through the stories of individuals like David and Isaiah.

The Psalms

The Old Testament's most important treasury of spiritual autobiography is the book of Psalms. For Christians, too, it has provided a hymn book, a pattern of approach to God, confession and praise, and, on equal footing with that, a surprisingly indecorous 'nagging'. True spiritual experience can be unsettling in its honesty and intensity. The 'problem of pain', discussed in a rather abstract way in Christian apologetics, appears in the Psalms as a direct accusation of God and a direct experience of his solidarity with human suffering. John Goldingay has explored this in some depth in Chapter 2 of this book.

For our purposes it is important to consider those psalms where story has a crucial role. For the psalmist, his story is contiguous with that of Israel as a whole. Even when the individual feels isolated, he can see himself as part of a larger human – and divine – history.

Psalm 22 is one such, opening with the words, 'My God, my God, why have you forsaken me?' In his feeling of abandonment, David appeals to the sense of God that he has through his fathers' experience (meaning, presumably, that of the patriarchs like Abraham and Jacob), as well as his own past experience of rewarded trust.

> In you our fathers put their trust;
>> they trusted you and you delivered them.   (v. 4)

> Yet you brought me out of the womb;
>> you made me trust in you
>> even at my mother's breast   (v. 9)

The personal or group story becomes a guarantee of God's basic faithfulness, even when present perception of it is dim or problematic. This psalm is one of a number of instances in the Old Testament when looking back on past experience, in the spiritual autobiography framework, is undertaken in a spirit of something less than euphoria. Our use of it, either in the book or the evangelistic meeting, tends to encourage the thought that it is best done on a 'high', a plateau of achievement or experience that looks back down on a previous reprobate or unfruitful life. A biblical model like Psalm 22 indicates that we ought to attempt it at the low points as well.

Psalm 89 gives a similar picture, although here the psalmist sees his past history as a history of God's promises (actually a very perceptive way of viewing Old Testament history generally), except that at the moment God seems to be breaking them. In the crisis, the feeling of abandonment, look to God and, at any rate in part, look to him by looking back.

There is much debate in the churches about the dangers of 'triumphalism', dangers which occur at all sorts of levels. A personal autobiographical triumphalism can be discouraging, even unreal at times, and perhaps is not to be perceived as the norm if we are to take the Bible seriously on the matter. Yet there is triumph in the gospel. Jesus said, 'I have overcome the world' (John 16:33), as well as, 'Blessed are the meek' (Matthew 5:5). We can find the psalmist in an ecstasy of triumph as well as in the pits of despair. The important thing is that we find him being real in both places. The rhetoric helps too, with the majority of psalms being addressed directly to God and only secondarily to others. Not only is that an extra incentive to honesty – you can fool a human audience, but not God – but it also redirects the emotional charge in the most fruitful way.

My favourite of these, loosely speaking, autobiographical psalms is 139, not least because it has become part of my own story as a Christian.

> O LORD, you have searched me
>   and you know me.
> You know when I sit and when I rise;
>   you perceive my thoughts from afar.   (vv. 1-2)

It is that completeness and comprehensiveness of God's knowledge of me that eventually led me to trust him, though not without that note of near-reluctance, of huntedness, that runs through the first half of the psalm. That movement, from 'Where can I flee from your presence?' (v. 7) to 'How precious to me are your thoughts, O God' (v. 17), I see now as the main sign of my becoming a Christian. This is, I would argue, one of the values of spiritual autobiography: it provides a map for the new believer when dealing with, shall we say, the 'promised land' into which the Spirit takes him or her.

Ezekiel

The other piece of autobiographical writing in the Old Testament that I want to consider is the book of Ezekiel. As far as I know, it has not been adopted as a key text by the theologians of story, but it does demonstrate the unity of vision, thought and action that they value so much. It is also a useful starting point for dealing with those spiritual autobiographies which centre on a visionary experience of God.

As so often with the Old Testament narrative, there is a laconic directness of presentation which excludes much circumstantial, realistic detail. Ezekiel presents his material as a series of commands, visions and prophecies – many of them to be acted out, so that Ezekiel becomes a living symbol of God's message, as well as an expression of the fate of the people of God to whom he is sent. The gap between speech and action is thus removed; there is no sense that the visionary has a simply private experience, even if he has a special relationship with God. The focus of the book is on the direct presentation of the visions and prophecies, but it also shows us the process by which an individual becomes identified, in his whole life, with the message he has to proclaim. As a result, the often exotic visions are put over with a kind of innocence. For those with a public Christian ministry, as well as the visionary, Ezekiel is one important model – a life which, for a period at least, becomes an image of the messages that it has to proclaim.

The New Testament

We see a similar urgency in the New Testament. The disciples in the period of the Acts of the Apostles were under immediate pressure to give an account of their faith. For many occasions, the injunction of 1 Peter 3:15, 'Always be prepared to give an answer to everyone who asks you to give the reason for the hope that you have', will mean giving an account of the life, death and resurrection of Jesus Christ, and answering the kind of questions with which Christian apologetics is familiar. But the sentence that follows seems to indicate that Peter has in mind some form of personal account, as well as the kind of argument he gave in Acts 2: 'But do this with gentleness and respect, keeping a clear conscience, so that those who speak maliciously against your good behaviour in Christ may be ashamed of their slander' (1 Peter 3:15b-16).

Let us consider Paul's two testimonies in Acts 22 and 26. The dramatic clarity of his conversion experience hardly needs emphasizing. The difference between the two accounts is interesting and can be attributed largely to Paul's sensitivity to his audience. In Acts 22 he is addressing Jews in Jerusalem, a well informed, religious and hostile crowd. In Acts 26 he is addressing King Agrippa in a more relaxed atmosphere, but one where religious knowledge is much patchier. The starting points in both cases are attempts to gain the sympathy of his audience – in Acts 22 the strict Pharisaic Jewish upbringing, in Acts 26 the same point (he is still defending himself against Jewish accusation) but with footnotes for those who may not understand the religious language. Acts 22 is like Old Testament narrative, 'laconic but by no means in a uniform or mechanical fashion',[3] dealing with some matters with startling swiftness, with others quite fully. In Acts 26 the obsession with the persecution of Christians gets as much detailed treatment as the road to Damascus. Paul wants Agrippa to understand the man who was converted. This is not autobiography as a spiritual exercise; this is skilled, humanly sympathetic evangelism through the kind of self-understanding which Christians have received as a gift from God.

We also see Paul in a more intimate, self-revealing mood in some of his epistles, where he is writing to fellow Christians. For instance, in 1 Timothy 1:12-17, the autobiographical snippet is a personal version of a theological theme. The phrase 'I was shown mercy', which occurs twice, is an interpretation of those events which, in Acts 22 and 26, are told with the minimum of theological commentary. Writing for Christians, the emphasis can be different, and even an element of speculation – why should God have done it this way? – becomes admissible. The teaching stance, affection towards his addressee Timothy, and his growing self-understanding all contribute to this development in Paul's account of his conversion. A 'rote' testimony would hardly have fitted all three occasions. Story-telling always involves an element of interpretation, even in such basic matters as what to leave out and what to put in.

Thus we can see that the biblical material offers us a number of examples and modes of spiritual autobiography. The variety is in itself encouraging – different moods, different situations, different spiritual understanding can be seen even in the accounts of the same person at different times. There is a wide spectrum of what is admissible. What seems common to all of them, however, is that they spring from lives which have not simply chugged along but have been made by God. That is surely one of the central points of spiritual autobiography – the perception of God's activity in the human sphere.

SOME CLASSICS, AND SOME HISTORY

Augustine's Confessions *(397-98)*

Augustine was born in 354 in Numidia, a Roman province of North Africa. His *Confessions*, the first and perhaps the greatest of Christian spiritual autobiographies, traces his path from contempt of Christianity to a warm and wholehearted embracing of it. Augustine is important in all sorts of ways. Henry Bettenson calls him 'the greatest formulative influence in the shaping of the thought and life of the Western Church'.[4] I cannot begin to say why and how; all I want to do is to send my readers away intent on reading the *Confessions*, and then to indicate something of the importance of this foundation text for those who wish to describe the Christian life from the inside.

It is quite possible to read the *Confessions* 'cold', simply to pick up a translation (F. J. Sheed's is considered the best, although R. S. Pine-Coffin's is more easily available and also reliable) and find an immediate response in the opening paragraph. But some remarks on the context of the book may help.

First of all, the vantage point from which Augustine writes, 10 years after his conversion, is important to the flavour of the book. In part, he was impelled to write by criticisms of his early involvement with the Manichees, an influential religious group who were regarded as a kind of 'superspiritual' rival to the Christian Church within a province of Rome, which, while recently having become 'officially' Christian, was akin to modern California in its proliferation of religions and philosophies. The Manichees, like many thinkers of the time, were convinced of the dualism of spirit and matter and of the essential evil of material things. Augustine's stress on the importance of feelings seems to be partly the response of a Christian who is convinced of the incarnation, and thus of the idea that feelings, indeed the whole material of creation, are to be redeemed rather than rejected. He recognizes the rebellious pull of sensuality, even in his converted state, but it does not dissolve into bland, fashionable world-weariness. The need to combat Manicheism, and to transcend the neo-Platonist philosophy which appealed very much to Augustine, also explains why the *Confessions* conclude with an interpretation of the first chapter of Genesis – something which looks curious in the narrative framework.

The second point is about the fourth-century Church, in which Augustine was now a bishop. On the one hand, there was a great need for systematic intellectual defence of the faith against rivals outside and heretics inside the Church. Augustine started to fulfil that need in a number of works; indeed, his *City of God* contains some of the classic arguments still used by Christian apologists. This was also the era of the credal formulations of the great Church Councils. Yet, at the same time as this firming up of the public, systematic side of Christianity, there was an increasing stress on its inward, personal side. Augustine discusses the new monastic and ascetic drive among Christians in Book VIII,

Chapter 6 of the *Confessions*. Their straightforward dedication was a crucial challenge to him. Peter Brown also points out:

> By the time of Augustine, the Church had settled down in Roman society. The Christian's worst enemies could no longer be placed outside him: they were inside, his sins and his doubts; and the climax of a man's life would not be martyrdom, but conversion from the perils of his own past.[5]

The *Confessions*, then, are a response to a new situation among Christians as a whole, of whom Augustine was an unusually gifted but not unrepresentative example.

One reason why the *Confessions* has been found so attractive is its treatment of sin. Many know the young Augustine's prayer, 'Lord, make me chaste, but not yet,' and he does not let his subsequent disgust with his sensuality disguise the pull it had on him – and still has at the time of writing. One of the most telling moments of self-analysis is when he recognizes that he postponed exploring and submitting to Christianity properly because he wanted his lust for sex, beauty and success to be satisfied rather than cured. Even after his conversion he continues to wrestle with the problem; the human body needs food to sustain it, and yet he finds that satisfaction slipping into gluttonous pleasure.

Women play a crucial role in the *Confessions*. Augustine's frankness and tenderness are displayed most clearly in his treatment of his mother and his mistress. We may feel that his treatment of his mistress, with whom he lived for 15 years, was rather rough in the end, but the episode (described in Book VI, Chapter 15) serves to show the wreckage caused by a half-hearted attempt at moral improvement:

> The woman whom I had been living was torn from my side as an obstacle to my marriage, and this was a blow which crushed my heart to bleeding, because I loved her dearly. She went back to Africa, vowing never to give herself to any other man, and left me with the son she had borne me. But I was too unhappy and too weak to imitate this example set me by a woman. I was impatient at the delay of two years which had to pass before the girl whom I had asked to marry became my wife, and because I was

more a slave of lust than a true lover of marriage, I took another mistress, without the sanction of wedlock.

The pain of separation, though, gets worse, and there is little hope of cure – except that, looking back, Augustine can see that God got closer to him as his largely self-inflicted misery increased.

More important still to Augustine, and to the shape of the *Confessions*, is his mother Monica. His meditation on her death in Book IX, Chapter 12, brings to an end the narrative of the book. It is as if he can only see her clearly in the light of his conversion and her death, and can find a justifiable outlet for the emotion expressed earlier in the midst of his yearning and frustration:

> And if [any man] finds that I sinned by weeping for my mother, even if only for a fraction of an hour, let him not mock at me. For this was the mother, now dead and hidden awhile from my sight, who had wept over me for many years so that I might live in your sight. Let him not mock at me but weep himself, if his charity is great. Let him weep for my sins to you, the Father of all the brothers of your Christ.

Augustine reminds himself and others that death is not complete extinction for her, and so immoderate grief would not be appropriate. Her last days, however, are the climax of what Augustine is so often concerned with as a thinking Christian. The material, sensual delights of this world, even at their highest level, can only be shadows of spiritual delight. That is the conclusion to which Augustine and Monica come in her last days, that the life of the saints is higher than any bodily pleasure. The occasion is described in precise, alert detail – 'leaning from a window which overlooked the garden of the courtyard of the house where we were staying at Ostia' – and in a context which emphasizes that they knew what love was. Spiritual love is no abstract in the *Confessions*; it is not a substitute for those incapable of other sorts, fleeing from the world with no desire to save it.

This leads us to another feature of the attraction and the authenticity of Augustine's record of his search: the relationship between his intellectual questioning and the way in which he realized that it needed to be kept within bounds. On the brink of conversion he realized that his real objection to Christianity was not intellectual but moral, and yet his conversion was far from mindless. Augustine has the knack of spotting the potential collusion between intellectual and sensual curiosity, without losing sight of the fact that the God of truth demands intelligent worship and service. Here he is in Book III, Chapter 6, on his association with the Manichees:

> Truth! Truth! How the very marrow of my soul within me yearned for it as they dinned it into my ears over and over again. To them it was no more than a name . . . But I gulped down this food, because I thought it was you. I had no relish for it, because the taste of it left in my mouth was not the taste of truth – it could not be, for it was not you but an empty sham. And it did not nourish me, but starved me all the more. The food we dream of is very like the food we eat when we awake, but it does not nourish because it is only a dream.

As so often in the *Confessions*, it is the brilliant image – food in dreams – that encapsulates the situation and the argument.

Augustine was rather suspicious of his facility with images, partly because of their sensual appeal, partly because they were a tool of his trade as a professional rhetorician – 'the chair of lies', as he saw it. Yet his elaborate allegorical readings of the Bible, here and elsewhere in his work, are an attempt to demonstrate that every detail has some spiritual significance. In other words, the theory and practice are different, and in the end he recognizes that Christian language has to be symbolic, even if those symbols are only hints of the spiritual reality we find so difficult to apprehend.[6] The audience needs it; Augustine himself needs it. After all, the rhetoric of the *Confessions* is second person; they are addressed to God and only secondarily to us, and that makes them more like the Psalms, perhaps, than anything else in the Bible. From the Psalms Augustine plunders quotations in plenty, and they give him the sense we have noted above: honesty before God means that you have to tell him everything, the pain and the failure included, and a retrospective view tells you a lot about the way God works.

In trying to find the pattern of that way within his own life, Augustine comes to the view he expresses right at the beginning of the *Confessions*: 'You made us for yourself and our hearts find no peace until they rest in you.' Humanity has an often unacknowledged instinct for God – not so much a God-shaped blank as a lack of an integrating principle of significance – which false religions and sensuality cannot supply. Augustine's sense of his own story is, then, a discovery of wholeness, of doing what he was made to do. Everything else in his life had served a double purpose – as a false goal in itself, but nonetheless a pointer to what lies beyond, to the true goal of a search for God who is waiting for us and drawing us to himself.

THE REFORMATION PERIOD

For the historian of my sort of autobiography, the movements of Renaissance and Reformation all add up to one thing – a new consciousness of the self. While there was a tension between some of the Renaissance humanists and the reforming (and counter-reforming) Christians, there was no necessary conflict of purpose. So when we list the features of this self-consciousness – that the self is an important area of investigation, that the self has a protean, many-sided quality and an unwillingness to accept the given social role – we should not assume that any one of them has particular Christian or secular humanist roots to the exclusion of the other. Nor should we ignore the break-up of the feudal economic, social and religious consensus. The renewed Christian impulse to examine the individual's relationship with God did not arise independently of intellectual fashion. That should not worry us too much, however, when we consider how first-century Christianity appropriated and sanctified the intellectual and religious modes of its time.

I have chosen to look at two outstanding figures – St Teresa, from the Roman Catholic monastic tradition, and John Bunyan, from the Reformed, Puritan tradition – and, more briefly, at some less remarkable figures. It may seem odd to start with one of the instigators of the Counter-Reformation in the country of the Inquisition, but I go along with the argument of Eric Ives, that one must recognize both that God was reforming his Church in the sixteenth century and that 'the authentic note of Christian conviction' can be found on both sides of the Catholic/Protestant divide.[7]

ST TERESA

St Teresa wrote her *Life* in 1565, at the instigation of her confessor. It is the account of her spiritual adventures from childhood
until her founding of a reformed Carmelite priory at Avila, a picture of a lively, humorous and persuasive personality with a deep
desire for solitude, and a guide to the various stages of mystical
prayer from her own spectacular experience. The core of the book
is this guide, but it stays an autobiography rather than a treatise,
because the focus is not finally on the mystical experiences but on
their effects. If they produce a greater love and obedience towards
God, and refine the personality so that holiness becomes an attractive option to those outside, that is the sign of genuine ecstatic
encounters with God. She scolds those foolish nuns who regard
'raptures' as the goal of the spiritual life. Rather, she regards the
goal as obedience to the God who almost always appears in the text
as 'His Majesty'. His favours are not granted as rewards for a particular length of devotion to the life of prayer, or for achievement.
They are gracious gifts which only serve to underline that God
gives far more than we deserve.

How can one convey spiritual experience in words? St Teresa is
generally straightforward and brisk, but she does make use of some
key images, most notably the watered garden – one that is particularly striking if one looks at pictures of Avila, a fortress town in dry,
rocky terrain. The various ways that God waters the garden corre-
spond to the various stages (she distinguishes four) of prayer. Two
things about this, and her other images for the path of prayer, need
to be noted. First is the common factor of movement; she sees
prayer as a dynamic, rather than as a frozen moment, even if bodily
stillness is one of its symptoms.[8] Second, although they involve some
sense of ascent or progress towards greater union with God, that
goes with her feeling that one must also return to the beginning at
times – one of the lessons of many spiritual autobiographies. 'There
is no soul on this path who is such a giant that he does not often
need to turn back and be a child at the breast again.'[9]

Images are important to St Teresa. She notes that they help to
collect a wandering mind. They can come from pictures, books or
nature:

> I also found it helpful to look at fields, water, or flowers.
> These reminded me of the Creator. I mean that they woke

me, and brought me to a recollected state, and served me
as a book. They reminded me also of my ingratitude and
my sins. (p. 68)

St Teresa was a woman in an age which expected women to be
weak. She managed to transcend that stereotype by accepting it,
but not being it when it came to obeying God. Her reformed nuns
were unable to take part in the greater Counter-Reformation missions except as prayer supporters, and yet their practice of humility stood in telling contrast to the obsession of the rest of Spain with
'honour', pride and status.

The poet Richard Crashaw's 'Hymn' to St Teresa centres on
two incidents which have become symbolic of her life for many
readers. The first is the childhood incident when she ran away to be
a martyr but did not get far, being preserved for other achieve-
ments. The second is the most intense of her experiences of visionary union with God:

In an angel's hands I saw a great golden spear, and at the
iron tip there appeared to be a point of fire. This he
plunged into my heart several times so that it penetrated
to my entrails. When he pulled it out, I felt that he took
them with it, and left me utterly consumed with the great
love of God. The pain was so severe that it made me utter
several moans. The sweetness caused by this intense pain
is so extreme that one cannot possibly wish it to cease, nor
is one's soul then content with anything but God. This is
not a physical, but a spiritual pain, though the body has
some share in it – even a considerable share. So gentle is
this wooing which takes place between God and the soul
that if anyone thinks I am lying, I pray God, in his goodness, to grant him some experience of it. (p. 210)

The spiritual eroticism, derived by St Teresa from the Song of
Songs, is disturbing but compelling. Less easy to take for those outside the Roman Catholic fold are her visions of souls rising from
purgatory, and her total opposition to Reformation 'heretics'.
Nonetheless, the book remains a riveting account of a spiritual
journey, one which ends not on the high point of spiritual ecstasy,
but in settled obedience to God in considerable physical illness.
Crashaw's poem begins:

Love, thou art absolute sole Lord of life and death.

One is also reminded of that English woman mystic, Mother Julian of Norwich, who asked the Lord the meaning of all the visions that she had seen. 'Love was his meaning.'[10]

John Bunyan

Love has very little to do with Puritanism, at least in its caricature dress of black and white with attitudes to match. Yet one of the most important Puritan spiritual autobiographies, John Bunyan's *Grace Abounding to the Chief of Sinners* (1666), makes a great deal of sense if read as a search for love.

The book was written halfway through a 12-year imprisonment imposed on Bunyan for preaching without a licence after the Restoration. It describes his early life, his conversion during the period 1650-3, and the start of his preaching ministry. To that extent it is in a form common to many of the lives of the 'mechanick preachers' (Bunyan was a tinker) in the seventeenth century, evidence that Tyndale's ambition to have 'the meanest ploughboy' know more of Scripture than the average medieval priest had succeeded. But Bunyan's imagination – it is often uncertain whether imagination is a help or hindrance to a Christian – means that his story is far less straightforward than that of many of his contemporaries, and far more compelling.

After an early, almost romantic, reverence for priests and the apparatus of church religion, he is interrupted at a Sunday game:

> As I was in the midst of a game at Cat, and having struck it one blow from the hole; just as I was about to strike it the second time, a voice did suddenly dart from Heaven into my Soul, which said, Wilt thou leave thy sins, and go to Heaven or have thy sins, and go to Hell?[11]

His response is to plunge more hungrily and desperately into sin, but not for long. He focuses his longing on the poor Christian people of Bedford:

> About this time, the state and happiness of these poor people of Bedford was thus, in a kind of Vision, presented to me: I saw as if they were set on the Sunny side of some

high Mountain, there refreshing themselves with the pleasant beams of the Sun, while I was shivering and shrinking in the cold, afflicted with frost, snow, and dark clouds; methought also betwixt me and them I saw a wall that did compass about this Mountain; now, thorow this wall my Soul did greatly desire to pass, concluding that if I could, I would goe even into the very midst of them, and there also comfort myself with the heat of their Sun.

About this wall I thought myself to goe again and again, still prying as I went, to see if I could find some way or passage, by which I might enter therein, but none could I find for some time: at the last I saw as it were, a narrow gap, like a little door-way in the wall, thorow which I attempted to pass: but the passage being very straight, and narrow, I made many offers to get in, but all in vain, even untill I was well nigh quite beat out by striving to get in: at last, with great striving, methought I at first did get in my head, and after that, by a side-ling striving, my shoulders, and my whole body; then I was exceeding glad, and went and sat down in the midst of them, and so was comforted with the light and heat of their Sun. (pp. 19-20)

The image is a remarkable one, and Bunyan sustains our interest in it by the force of his own struggle. It is interesting, and characteristic of Bunyan's approach, to see that following this 'vision' he questions it for its significance, and finds a couple of Bible texts to substantiate the meaning. As we would expect of the author of *The Pilgrim's Progress*, he submits his religious imagination to the discipline of allegory. Intensity is not enough; it must have meaning, and it has to be authenticated.

If we compare this image with the garden of St Teresa, we will see certain differences which perhaps epitomize the difference between the two spiritualities. For Bunyan the central issue is an either/or, exclusion or inclusion, warmth or coldness. For St Teresa contemplative spirituality is a continuum, from childlike dependence to ecstatic union. For Bunyan, assurance becomes the target after conversion – but that is no unsubtle, smooth, easy-going process. His relapses and his periods of despair sometimes last a year. He is floored by fears of having committed the unforgivable sin; and then other biblical texts (which have an almost physical weight in this resolutely inward autobiography) will lift him again. He is afraid that church bells will fall on him, even bounce off the wall to catch him if he shelters under a beam – a neurotic's testimony, I suppose. But as Owen Watkins argues:

> He never surrendered: he constantly sought, and was ready to grasp, any vestige of hope, though even in his most miserable moments he wanted truth rather than comfort. To label him as a pathological case may not be medically unjustified, but far from discrediting his heroism this would underline it.[12]

Bunyan's heroism, as we can call it, is often isolating – from his family, from those whose spiritual experience turns out to be second-hand – but it cannot be accused of indulgence. He does not wish to escape from fear, but to discover the true nature of godly fear, 'a grace of God in the hearts of his children'.[13]

This single-minded intensity can make for some effects which a modern reader may find curious, even slightly repellent. For instance, we learn that his first wife brought two books of piety with her as a dowry, but her name, or her temperament, or even her husband's feelings for her, are absent from the account. It will be clear by now that Bunyan was not unfeeling; it was just that he dared not play about. A comment that is often cited in stylistic contexts makes the point implicit in the whole text:

> God did not play in convincing of me; the Devil did not play in tempting of me; neither did I play when I sunk as into a bottomless pit, when the pangs of hell caught hold upon me: wherefore I may not play in my relating of them, but be plain and simple, and lay down the thing as it was.
> (pp. 2-3)

The publication in the 1980s of the church records of the 'gathered' church in Westfield, Massachusetts, brought out again how important the relation of spiritual experience was in the Puritan tradition. The 'public relations' of the faith of the founder members is, by and large, evidence for the crucial role of sermons in the spiritual awakening of these people. Clearly, they were not in the habit of thanking their vicar for a nice sermon; 'like daggers in my heart' is a more usual compliment. The main role of these relations seems to have been to encourage the expression of personal faith among those for whom listening to sermons and living a largely respectable life was liable to make them 'insensible' spiritually. The danger is, of course, that these relations in turn become routine. The relation of John Ingerson stands out for two reasons. First is the striking way he calls up his father-in-law at midnight to get counsel about the unforgivable sin (a common worry, it would seem), and second, the way in which he specifies the Scripture that brought him through to faith, Isaiah 43:24:

> Thou hast brought me no Sweet Cane – but hast made me to serve with thy sins; yet I am he that blotteth out all thy sins for my name's sake. Whereupon I found myself willing.[14]

So often, the way to break out of the routines that trap us is to focus on a single, key issue; so often, it is the metaphors of Scripture that break through into our situation and speak to us the liberating word.

C. S. LEWIS

Forty years after his death, Lewis is still one of the most fruitful of Christian apologists and his children's books are a source of joy, and, dare one say it, Christian conditioning of the mind. Here I want to consider him as an autobiographer, although the qualities that make for clear apologetic and imaginative novels are part of the secret.

Surprised by Joy (1955) is the story of Lewis's conversion from atheism to Christianity. As the title (a quotation from Wordsworth) would lead one to suspect, it is the story of a man whose imagination needed to be 'baptized' as much as the rest of him – a process accomplished largely by reading George Macdonald. Instead of leading him away from this world, the holiness of Macdonald's imagination made him realize the joy of this world. In other words, it is incarnational.

> For I now perceived that while the air of the new region made all my erotic and magical perversions of Joy look like sordid trumpery, it had no such disenchanting power

over the bread upon the table or the coals in the grate ...
I saw the common things drawn into the bright shadow.[15]

Balancing Lewis's search for joy, defined variously as an unsatis-
fied desire almost like pain and the by-product of attention to something else, is his sense of God as a kind of chess-player, making a
series of moves which make Lewis a reluctant convert before the
joy comes: 'I gave in, and admitted that God was God, and knelt
and prayed: perhaps, that night, the most dejected and reluctant
convert in all England' (p. 215).

This has been preceded by the ironic advice: 'Really, a young
Atheist cannot guard his faith too carefully. Dangers lie in wait for
him on every side' (p. 213). *Surprised by Joy* is distinguished by its
shrewd appreciation of the attractions and derelictions of the alter-
natives to Christianity, and by its avoidance of the Shangri-La
approach to conversion narrative (once things were rotten, but
now they are wonderful).

Even more impressive in that respect is the brief but agonizing
journal *A Grief Observed*, about the death of Lewis's wife, and not
surprisingly only published under a pseudonym in his lifetime. In
his useful book *The Problem of Pain* Lewis had suggested some of
the answers. They come out differently, perhaps less clearly, but
utterly compellingly in this record of immediate grief. Perhaps this
is more of a journal than an autobiography in its closeness to the
event, but the ideas, as well as the coping, are important. Thus,
for instance, our faith is tested by adversity so that we can see how
strong it is – God must know. And God is his own iconoclast:

> My idea of God is not a divine idea. It has to be shattered
> time after time. He shatters it Himself. He is the great
> Iconoclast. Could we not almost say that this shattering is
> one of the marks of his presence? The Incarnation is the
> supreme example; it leaves all previous ideas of the Mes-
> siah in ruins. And most are 'offended' at the iconoclasm;
> and blessed are those who are not. But the same thing
> happens in our private prayers.[16]

Perhaps that is the key to the best spiritual autobiography – that
it changes our view of God, and ourselves. Where we had a partial, rather over-comfortable image, the living God places new
possibilities.

EXERCISES

The reading of the lives of the saints can produce an unhealthy 'gee-whiz' effect: 'That was great. What a boring worm I am, and likely to remain so.' Wrong. God's grace is no less available to you. These simple suggestions are made to help you recognize something of it, particularly in the group context.

First, the *post-conversion testimony*. The only rule is that you have to start the story *after* you became a Christian. When I was first invited to do this, I found it of enormous value. This whole chapter can be traced back to that time, in a way, because it was there that I learned the value of the metaphoric imagination to the Christian, not just for illustration, but for understanding. The night before I was due to deliver the testimony, I walked out from the camp to a beach where the moon was out and the tide coming in. As you know, these are connected, and the wonder of that impelled me to think of the way we as a fellowship were linked together, how prayer and action (often felt to be at a distance) were in fact held together by Christ (see Colossians 1:16-18). Try it, with another rule added to the one I was given: confession of failure is also allowed. Too many testimonies are given under the restraints of institutionalized dishonesty.

Second, the *psalm*. I have found older Sunday School pupils capable of this, and it is very creative. Introduce it by discussing the technique of the personal psalm, or perhaps by referring to some of the patterns of testimony highlighted in Chapter 2 of this book. Then invite people to write a psalm of confession, praise or thanksgiving, addressed to God. Parallelism or Augustinian rhetoric should not be required! You may even like to try writing a psalm on your own.

Third, the *group testimony*. It has often been the experience of closely knit fellowship groups, friends, even whole congregations, that their spiritual autobiography can be seen collectively over a particular period. Try mapping this out together one evening. The differences may turn out to be part of it.

Journals, prayer diaries and so on are also found to be of great value by some, but I have never really tried them. And what of the big one, the attempt to see the shape of the whole of your spiritual life? It may not be for publication, but just for you, addressed to your Saviour, or to your family as a bequest, or to your Christian friends whether scattered or closely linked. It will be worth trying. Most of all, it will help you to understand yourself, and to trust and praise God more. That much can be guaranteed.

Notes

1 James Olney, *Metaphors of Self: the Meaning of Autobiography* (Princeton University Press, 1972), p. 31.

2 For an introduction and bibliography, see John Navone, *Towards a Theology of Story* (St Paul Publications, 1977).

3 Robert Alter, *The Art of Biblical Narrative* (Allen and Unwin, 1981), p. 20.

4 Henry Bettenson, *The Later Christian Fathers* (Oxford University Press, 1970), p. 25.

5 Peter Brown, *Augustine of Hippo* (Faber, 1967), p. 159.

6 My argument here is indebted to Robert J. O'Connell, *Art and the Christian Intelligence in St Augustine* (Blackwell, 1978), Chapters 5 and 6.

7 E. W. Ives, *God in History* (Lion, 1979), Chapter 10.

8 See Robert T. Petersson, *The Art of Ecstasy: Teresa, Bernini and Crashaw* (Routledge and Kegan Paul, 1970), p. 27.

9 D. M. Cohen (trans.), *The Life of St Teresa* (Penguin, 1957), p. 94. Further page references in the text are to this edition.

10 Julian of Norwich, trans. Clifton Wolters, *Revelations of Divine Love* (Penguin, 1966), p. 211. For more on Julian, see Chapter 10 of this book.

11 Roger Sharrock (ed.), *Grace Abounding to the Chief of Sinners* (Oxford University Press, 1962), p. 10. Further references are to this edition. (Readers may find the *Everyman* paperback more immediately available.)

12 Owen C. Watkins, *The Puritan Experience* (Routledge, 1972), pp. 118-19.

13 John Bunyan, *Treatise on the Fear of God* (1679).

14 Edward Taylor, *Church Records and Related Sermons*, ed. Thomas M. and Virginia L. Davis (Twayne Publishers, 1981), p. 117.

15 C. S. Lewis, *Surprised by Joy* (Geoffrey Bles, 1955), pp. 170-71. Further page references are to this edition.

16 C. S. Lewis, *A Grief Observed* (Faber, 1966), p. 52.

SILENCE

David Runcorn

Somewhere in the tunnel between Victoria and Green Park, the tube train stops for no apparent reason. The noise of the engine dies abruptly and a harsh stillness descends on the passengers. Conversation that was being shouted moments before now becomes subdued and self-conscious. The silence is uncomfortable. We avoid each other's eyes. There is a need to be doing something. We cough, blow our noses, re-read the newspaper – anything to fill the emptiness of the moment. At last the train comes to life again. Noise fills the world and the relief is almost tangible.

Do you know the feeling? We have an awkward relationship with silence. It attracts us and repels us. We protest loudly that 'all I want is some peace and quiet', but, given an unexpected hour of space, we have to go looking for something to fill it. Even in our churches we speak more about silence than we allow it. How often the invitation to be 'quiet before the Lord' takes longer than the silence that follows!

We may be coming to a subject like this with the feeling that we are approaching something new. We may even feel that there is something about silence that is 'not natural'. It may help us to realize that silence is much more a part of our noisy world than we are generally aware. It surrounds and influences all aspects of our lives – however profound or ordinary.

We have all had times on holiday when a bend in the road surprises us with some quite spectacular scenery. All conversation stops. We gaze in silence. It is, literally, breathtaking. Times of grief and tragedy can leave us silent and numb. At such times it is the silent company of friends that we appreciate most, not their words.

Silence can be quite unpredictable in its moods, however. For example, I may enjoy a quiet evening by the fire, on my own and content to be so, thinking of little and doing nothing in particular. On another occasion, such an evening would be agonizing. It might feel overwhelmingly lonely and the silence of the room becomes unbearable.

Lovers lapse into silences without knowing it, completely absorbed in each other's company. For another relationship, however, silence is a deadlock and an awful inability to communicate. Silence may express positive involvement or passive (even negative) non-involvement. An angry silence is a withdrawal weapon in conflict. Some things, we say, are 'better left unsaid'. Police investigation can meet with a 'wall of silence' that is non-cooperation.

So what is this thing called silence that at either extreme of experience will complete our joys or confirm our dread? It speaks of solemn gratitude at the Cenotaph. It keeps those birthday secrets hidden until the day. It breaks the mind and will of the man in the solitary cell. It is the legendary choice of the British in the rush-hour train. But how well do we understand it?

THE INVITATION TO GO DEEPER

Perhaps the mistake we often make is to assume that silence is the possession of a particular mood or emotion. It is very easy, for example, for children to understand silence only as a rebuke (from parents) or as a punishment (at school). Yet in all the varied encounters of our lives, silence is part of an inner response that invites us to deepen the moment. It expresses the need to 'take it in'. It may accompany feelings of joy or grief, excitement or despair, but its gift will be to allow the moment to 'sink in' and go deep. If we refuse the gift, then we remain on the surface of it all.

All these 'accidental' or spontaneous brushes with silence are not enough. Spontaneity cannot be the foundation for mature spiritual growth any more than it can be for human relationships. If we are not to remain strangers to silence, we must choose what we seek – we must 'will' to be silent.

Having said all that, let me close this introduction by sharing my first encounter with silence. Some years ago I stayed at the Taizé community in France for a week. The thousands of young people who pack Taizé each summer are encouraged to participate in the daily round of worship and to choose, from a variety of different themes, a group for daily Bible study and discussion. Faced with crowds of strange people and feeling that I had really come for a holiday, I opted for the last one on the list – the *pays de silence* (field of silence). I cannot claim any higher motivation than that!

Between the church and the sprawling campsites, a small field was set apart with basic facilities for those who wished to spend time in silence. The day was unstructured, with the exception of a short Bible reading each morning from one of the brothers and an optional 'talking time' over tea in the afternoon. For all the impulsiveness of my initial choice, I felt a growing enthusiasm for the idea. I wanted to have a go at 'being silent'. In the warm afternoon sunshine I sat down on the grass with my Bible and tried to still myself for God.

I found I could not. I was almost immediately overwhelmed by a torrent of random thoughts and feelings. Rather than feeling peaceful and closer to God, I was drowning in a turbulent flood of inner clamour that made concentration quite impossible. I did not know such noise was in me! It was as if the act of being silent had lifted the lid from all kinds of inner voices that I did not know were there. They were powerful, too. Prayer and reading were hopeless. I soon felt completely desolate and worn out by the struggle. It was all so unexpected.

For three days I could only wander restlessly, attending the worship and wondering if it was not a mistake to have ever tried. After four days I became dimly aware that the flood was slowing down. At last there were moments of genuine stillness in which I began, very chastened, to pray.

THE ROOTS OF SILENCE

> Silence is of various depths and fertility, like soil. Now it is a Sahara where men perish of hunger and thirst, now a fertile bottom, or prairie, of the West.
>
> HENRY DAVID THOREAU

Yahweh is first and foremost a God of the Wilderness.

KENNETH LEECH

We begin by looking at the place of silence in the Scriptures.

If our culture struggles with silence for fear that it brings an 'absence', the Bible understands that silence is a wrestling with 'presence' – the presence of God. We have a tendency at this point to stay with familiar and comfortable texts on the subject – 'Be still, and know that I am God' (Psalm 46:10) – but silence is clearly more than just an aspect of the spiritual life. Kenneth Leech argues that in a profound sense the faith of God's people was born out of silence – the solitary, rugged silence of the wilderness.[1] It was here, too, that it had to grow and mature.

We are well accustomed to studying the words of the Scriptures. We neglect the silences. This may seem a strange suggestion at first, but in fact communication and language actually depend as much on silence as on the words between. The ability of actors or comedians to give power and humour to their lines comes out of their skill in using timing and silence. Someone once described language as a 'cord of silence' with the words as knots in it.

If there is a cord of silence linking the words of Scripture, it is found in the wilderness. We must learn to meditate on the silences of Scripture if we are to enter into the life and faith behind the words.

To understand the spiritual roots of God's people, then, we need to consider the influence of the desert in their living experience. It is those dry, solitary wastes that provide the Hebrew people with their most vivid imagery in prayer and worship.

> O God, you are my God,
>   earnestly I seek you;
> my soul thirsts for you,
>   my body longs for you,
> in a dry and weary land
>   where there is no water. PSALM 63:1

More fundamentally, we must look at the possibility that this desert silence says something about God himself. It may be that only with silence will we ever draw near to the Eternal Presence. What marked out this wilderness God of the Hebrews from other gods was that he could not be expressed. No art could express his likeness and no words could avoid falling short and so misrepresent him. Any attempt to do so became an idol. The true God is inexpressible in the mystery of his holiness. He is, and dwells in, silence. As Henri Nouwen says, 'Silence alone shares something of God's infinity.'[2] So the place of meeting must be the desert of loving silence. St John of the Cross wrote, 'One Word the Father spoke, which Word was his Son, and this Word he ever speaks in eternal silence and in silence it must be heard by the soul.'[3]

In a study entitled 'The God of the Desert', Kenneth Leech suggests four characteristics of desert spirituality in the Bible that lie at the heart of a Christian understanding of prayer.[4] We will use these to explore the place of silence a little more.

Simplicity

The desert is a place where we are simplified and stripped of all non-essentials of life. There is a scene in the film *Lawrence of Arabia* when a man finds himself alone in the middle of the desert and begins a desperate journey to safety. As the sun gets hotter, he casts off piece after piece of his possessions and clothing (his former securities) – his gun, his ammunition belt, his knife, his cloak – a proud warrior mercilessly stripped to nothing. He finally collapses on the desert sands and lies there helplessly, awaiting rescue or death.

The desert is the place where God's people learn hard lessons of life and faith. It is a place to learn the real priorities, and there are no margins for error. In the desert there is no room for luxuries and no respect for human status or strength. To contemplate the desert, then, is to understand the call to walk by faith in God alone. It is a place that simplifies us, down to our true selves, until we are ready to meet the God of life and death. René Voillaume puts it like this:

> The desert – the real desert – bears in its physical reality the sign of isolation, not only from people and human life, but from any semblance of man's activity and presence. Being something that man cannot put to use, it likewise bears the sign of aridity, and consequently the subduing of all the senses, including both sight and hearing. It also

bears the sign of poverty and austerity, and of most extreme simplicity. In short, it bears the sign of man's complete helplessness, as he can do nothing to subsist alone and by himself in the desert, and thus he discovers his weakness and the necessity of seeking help and strength in God.[5]

We cannot speak of the desert as just a geographical reality for some people. It is, for all of us, a sign of the 'way of the heart'. We all need to create a *poustinia* in the heart – a desert place of silence and prayer.[6] It is a place to which we must withdraw as Jesus did, to be renewed in the midst of a busy world.

Nonetheless, however much this is something we long for, desire itself is not enough. We need a point of entry into the clutter and insecurity of our lives so that they can be simplified for prayer and God.

One way to nurture simplicity is through the discipline of silence. Society is dominated by the inane notion that action is the only reality. Please, for God's sake and your own, don't just do something, stand there! Come in and enjoy his presence.[7]

Sometimes the simplest solutions are the hardest. Henri Nouwen was seeking just this when he went to spend seven months in a monastery. His journal of that time was published as *The Genesee Diary*. In the introduction he discusses what led him to 'stop'.

I realized that I was caught in a web of strange paradoxes. While complaining about too many demands, I felt uneasy when none were made. While speaking about the burden of letter writing, an empty mailbox made me sad. While fretting about tiring lecture tours, I felt disappointed when there were no invitations. While speaking nostalgically about an empty desk, I feared the day in which that would come true. In short, while desiring to be alone I was frightened of being left alone. The more I became aware of these paradoxes, the more I started to see how much I had indeed fallen in love with my own compulsions and illusions, and how much I needed to step back and wonder – is there a quiet stream underneath the fluctuating affirmations and rejections of my little world? Is there a still point where my life is anchored from which I can reach out with hope and courage and confidence?[8]

It is a testimony that also reminds us that, more than we care to admit, the secret lies in rediscovering our freedom to choose – and to say 'no'.

Struggle

For this simplifying to happen, the desert becomes a place of testing – and therefore of struggle. To enter the security of God's love we must first let go of our own securities.

> Much religious life is geared to safety, not to sanctity, for sanctity involves danger, involves launching out into the deep, facing the wilderness, the dark night and the perils of Babylon.[9]

Desert faith is therefore faith 'on the move'. It is nomadic. Abraham is its father (see Hebrews 1:1, 8-10), but Jesus himself completes our understanding. As John writes, 'The Word became flesh and made his dwelling [or pitched his tent] among us' (John 1:14). The word normally translated 'dwelling' is *skenoo*, related to the word *skene*, which means 'tent'. Of his life on earth Jesus once said, 'The Son of Man has nowhere to lay his head' (Luke 9:58).[10] The struggle is not to settle down, giving up the journey too soon, accepting lesser securities and so making idols of them. 'We must take the feeling of being at home into exile. We must be rooted in the absence of a place.'[11] The struggle is experienced in different ways.

We know that as Abraham responded to the call to move out into the strange land, 'a thick and dreadful darkness came over him' (Genesis 15:12). We are not told what it cost Moses, the prince of Pharaoh's court, to live in exile, tending sheep in the wilderness for 40 years, but whatever his struggles were, they changed his life. It was a servant of the Lord who returned to Egypt. Then there is Jacob's struggle at Jabbok and the mystery of a God who comes in the silence and darkness of the night, wrestling a man into his new name and identity (see Genesis 32:22-32). There are many others through the Scriptures whose lives were formed and transformed by their struggles with faith in the wilderness. It was a testing that even the Son of God was not spared.

The wilderness has different moods. There are times when it bursts with promise, an absurd hope of fruitfulness and new life. There are times when its fearful voids speak of a terrifying absence and God-forsaken emptiness. The feature of wilderness faith, however, is its willingness to accept the absence of God without protest. Consider the fury of Habakkuk: 'Why are you silent while the wicked swallow up those more righteous than themselves?' (Habakkuk 1:13). There is a boldness to faith (and doubt) which makes our Western spiritual tradition seem very passive by comparison. Yet the boldness to question and search will lead us directly into the vulnerability and night of desert faith. We will know the darkness of our own fears and the perils of our weaknesses, but that very struggle makes possible a new exposure to God himself. And so it is that out of Habakkuk's wrestling a new strength and vision is born, for God has spoken: 'The LORD is in his holy temple; let all the earth be silent before him' (Habakkuk 2:20).

When we speak of silence in this context, we recognize that it is something much more than those times of stillness in our church worship. The idea of silence in public worship has found much more place in recent years, but it needs to be carefully and imaginatively introduced. Just to suggest 'a time of silence' will leave many people feeling confused as to how to use it. It will feel stressful – rather like being told to hold your breath for a time!

It is a fact that, for many, the experience of entering into silence is one of frightening alienation and inner turmoil. Far from the enticing vision of being 'alone with the Alone', it feels like a dubious invitation to be submerged in personal chaos and darkness. The important thing to note is that in such an event it is not a failure of the person or the silence.

Christian prayer is more often marked by struggle than peace. The presence of blissful feelings when I am silent does not mean that I am actually in God's presence. If we are to encourage each other in the desert of silence, we need to be growing in the maturity of our love and care for one another in the dryness or the night of faith. Someone once said that 'prayer and love are really learned in the hour when prayer becomes impossible'. Struggle is the fruit of faithfulness in the desert – not the failure of it.

We might well find that, once we consent to seeking silence, it has a way of turning the tables and searching us. It is the work of the Holy Spirit to search all things (see 1 Corinthians 2:10). There is a chapel in a monastery to which I used to go for retreats where I knew that, if I went to pray, I would have to submit to the disturbing sensation of being spiritually 'undressed'. That is the only way I can describe it. The Quakers speak of a 'sifting silence', and I imagine that is what they mean.

Waiting

Some years ago I travelled across the Nubian Desert in Northern Sudan and down the Nile to Cairo. It was a journey packed with vivid impressions, but I remember it clearly for the amount of waiting that was involved. Whatever level of life or organization was involved, nothing hurried in the desert – and that seemed right. Waiting was not an interruption to progress; it was an essential part of the journey itself.

In our Western culture we have no positive use for waiting. Much technology and expense goes into reducing the waiting in our lives. It is an intrusion, a frustration, whether it be at the bus stop or by the letterbox. It interrupts our timetables and delays our lives.[12] Yet our God is the God of the desert. He is the 'three-mile-an-hour God'. He walks with his people.

Perhaps Elijah best expresses the dangers in our lifestyle. He too lost the 'stature of waiting'. He learns the hard way that there is nothing to sustain him between the noisy mountain tops of his ministry and the bitter deserts of his own exhaustion. He has to make a journey – from the mountain of his own activities, through the desert of his own emptiness, to Horeb, the mountain of God (see 1 Kings 18 and 19). There he waits in a cave as all the whirlwind, fire and vigour of his ministry passes before him and God is not in it. But there, behind it all, barely discernible, there comes 'a sound of sheer silence' (1 Kings 19:12, NRSV).[13] It is the silence of God. Elijah has returned to the roots of his faith.

There is a frustration that surfaces among Christians when 'silence' is mentioned once too often. Surely God is not silent? He has revealed himself and spoken. We have something to share and proclaim. John the Baptist's father Zechariah must have felt this frustration acutely. He illustrates well the apparent contradiction of Christian silence. Here is an old man who knows the pain and frustration of waiting – all his life he had longed and prayed for a child. Now, in old age, an angel appears and gives him an astonishing message of prophecy – and immediately strikes him dumb for his hesitation in receiving it! The word of the Lord is locked up within him in silence. He is completely alone with the message all the world has been waiting to hear.

We do not know what those months meant to him, but, like Elizabeth and Mary, he was confined with the Word of Life. When signs are made to him to resolve the controversy over the name of his son, however, his response (in the Greek) is emphatic: 'His name is John' (Luke 1:63). There is fire in those bones! When his tongue is loosened, he utters the song that Christian worship has been using ever since. Out of silence has emerged a prophet.

This capacity for taking in what God is saying or doing and 'waiting upon it' is vital. It is a quality that Luke found in Mary (see Luke 2:18-19). We are also familiar with it in the rhythm of withdrawal and activity by which Jesus lived and which he impressed upon his disciples (see Luke 5:16). Even after spectacular miracles of healing, Jesus is found urging people to silence about what has happened (see Luke 8:27-30, 54-56; 9:35-36). Theologians usually step in with an explanation at this point, but the intention may be quite practical:

> Where there was a danger of all deeper impressions being scattered and lost through the garrulous repetition of the outward circumstances of the healing, there silence was enjoined, that so there might be an inward brooding over the gracious and wondrous dealings of the Lord.[14]

There is a time to speak and a time to be silent. We have to learn to resist the pressure to live on the surface of an experience or encounter. We must still ourselves and take it in. This is the fullest understanding of what it means to listen. Thus the desert of silence becomes a place of loving, attentive vigilance to the will of God and of reverent longing for his word:

> I lift up my eyes to you,
>   to you whose throne is in heaven.
> As the eyes of slaves look to the hand of their master,
>   as the eyes of a maid look to the hand of her
>   mistress,
> so our eyes look to the LORD our God.
>
> PSALM 123:1-2

Adoration

Lest it be thought that faith in the desert must be one of grim struggle and endurance, we finally recognize it as a place of worship and hope. For the promise of God's coming salvation is given, not to the cities and the rich places of human achievement, but to the wilderness and waste places. It is the desert that waits in hope for the salvation of our God:

> The desert and the parched land will be glad;
> the wilderness will rejoice and blossom.
> Like a crocus it will burst into bloom;
> it will rejoice greatly and shout for joy.
> The glory of Lebanon will be given to it,
> the splendour of Carmel and Sharon;
> they will see the glory of the LORD,
> the splendour of our God.   ISAIAH 35:1-2

Yet the desert calls us to something fuller and richer still. It calls us to a vision of God – to adoration. Adoration begins when we are captivated by the living God, not for what he does or promises, but just for who he is.

When we contemplate the solitary hours that Jesus spent in prayer in the hills –

> Where Jesus knelt to share with thee
> the silence of eternity
> interpreted by love . . .

or read in Revelation 4:8 of the awesome outpouring of praise in the heavens –

> Holy, holy, holy
> is the Lord God Almighty,
> who was, and is, and is to come . . .

are we not drawing near to this kind of adoration?

There is much worship that stops short of adoration. In doing so it remains on the level of appreciation or another way of offering thanks to God. Adoration, however, is not appreciation but abandonment – abandonment before the wonder and beauty of God in all his glory.

I once spent three months working on a kibbutz in the Negev Desert in Israel. I used to spend all my spare time wandering the sun-baked hills and arid plains around the settlement, but it was the experience of walking at night that I remember most. There would be no one else for miles – the simplicity and solitude were spellbinding. There were moments of deep intensity as I seemed to feel the ancient strength of the wilderness rising to meet the sparkling infinity of the silent heavens. I would be completely lost in it. Although I could not understand what moved me, I knew that I deeply belonged in the mystery of it all. Time and again under those stars, I stood breathless as the night, my whole being alive with wonder and awe.

Adoration of God must be something like that. It means being completely captivated by Love. It means knowing ourselves drawn into the eternal life and love of the Trinity – 'that they may be in us', in the words of Jesus' prayer to the Father (John 17:21).

SILENCE AND THE 'LEAPING WORD'[15]

> Many people ask me to speak; no one asks me for silence.
>
> HENRI NOUWEN

We can now begin to explore what an understanding and experience of silence might contribute to our own living and praying. The possibilities are very diverse, but we will try to consider a variety of them.

Silence as a way of life

A dietician once described fasting as 'the punctuation marks in my relationship with food'. That may be a helpful way of expressing the relationship of silence to lifestyle. There must be punctuation in the script of our lives, giving it its flow, its pauses, its varieties of expression. It brings a subtlety and depth to it all.

At the beginning of this chapter I spoke of the 'spontaneous' moments when we encounter silence. They are, perhaps, the exclamation marks, but life needs the discipline of regular punctuation – moments to pause, to catch breath, to reflect, or just to lie fallow for a time. These will be the times when we get back in touch with our deeper selves, times when we can, with loving suspicion, review the demands and priorities we have laid upon our lives. Finding a personal rule of life (see Chapter 4) can help to provide for more disciplined punctuation of our lifestyle.

It is the 'full stops' that are the most difficult, perhaps – the points at which we decide to halt completely, to sit still and be silent. It may be for an hour, a day, or a longer time away somewhere, but it is not surprising to find that one of our first reactions on entering silence is that we get angry. There may be no apparent reason for it. It is part of the struggle to 'let go'. We are stepping out of all that gives us a sense of worth and security. Silence is an unknown and unfamiliar territory. We are not in control any more. 'The eternal silence of the infinite spaces terrifies me,' said Pascal. Silence itself is an encounter with infinity. That is why we feel so powerless, so empty and unable to do anything. It is very threatening. At such times we must stay in the struggle and allow the Holy Spirit, in the silence, to ease our grip on the controls and yield them afresh to God.

The silence also assaults our notion of usefulness. What is the point of silence? What is the use of it? None at all on the face of it – but our assumptions about worth and usefulness need challenging. Our culture still measures worth by activity and achievement. It is an approach to society that profoundly devalues the most vulnerable in our midst, not least the unemployed and the elderly. Silence must profoundly disturb us in these false estimates of ourselves. It calls us to confess them, to die to them, and so to enter new life in Christ.

Solitude and community

Dietrich Bonhoeffer always taught that the ability to live in community requires the freedom to be alone. Unless we have that freedom, then we will always be using our life together to hide from what we cannot face in ourselves. It is in solitude that we seek our place in community, and it is in community that we find strength for our solitude.[16]

It is sad that our culture, and often our churches, make us feel that spending time alone is selfish. We feel guilty for wanting to 'go off on our own'. Our commitment to each other is measured by our active involvement together. This is quite false. As one writer expresses it:

> We do not go into the desert to escape people but to learn how to find them; we do not leave them in order to have nothing to do with them, but to find out the way to do them the most good. But this is only a secondary end. The end that includes all the others is the love of God.[17]

Without these roots in solitude and silence, our life together will all too easily be sustained by an incessant whirl of activity. Our activity will be all that we have to affirm us. The simple truth is that Christian fellowship sustained in such a way may be exciting for a time, but it cannot truly liberate and give life. It can only enslave us. We will get stuck and exhausted. Alan Ecclestone suggests that we need 'a solvent' for 'those devices and rigid forms which are imposed upon life'. He goes on:

> Silence is such a solvent. There is a kind of silence in which the hard thick shell which normally covers and protects us, the thick shell of fiction and prejudice and ready-made phrases which separate man from man, begins to crack and open. The silence that liberates is among the great needs of our time.[18]

Silence and words

Silence is not an abandoning of words. Silence expresses our reverence for words and reminds us to respect their truth and power. After some weeks of sharing the silent life of a Cistercian monastery, Henri Nouwen was aware of a growing sense of responsibility for the words he used. After one conversation he experienced remorse.

> I felt as if I had touched something that should not be touched, as if I had distorted something simply by talking about it, as if I had tried to grasp a dew drop.[19]

We have a responsibility for the words we use. They are not to be wasted or misused. Nouwen's experience of silence led him to repent of his careless wordiness. Not only does Jesus make clear that we will not be any more heard for piling up words to God (see Matthew 6:7), but James sternly warns us:

> The tongue is a small part ... but it makes great boasts...
> The tongue also is a fire ... It corrupts the whole person ...
> Out of the same mouth come praise and cursing ... this
> should not be. JAMES 3:5, 6, 10

Yet that is the way it is. He is not exaggerating. The same tongue we use to pray and to worship God is compulsively at work at other times to manipulate, to self-justify, to flatter for influence – a ceaseless torrent of communication devoted to the maintenance and control of our own little worlds. 'Silence is one of the deepest disciplines of the Spirit simply because it puts a stopper on all that!'[20]

St Ignatius taught that our silence can point people to God more than our words. He therefore expects this quality most of all in church leaders:

> A bishop should be particularly revered when he is silent.
> The silence of a bishop bears witness to the reality of God,
> both in the mystery of his divine silence and in the silence
> of his passion. The church is the place where all things
> pass over into reality by being plunged into the hidden
> reality of God, so that the outer and inner become one, the
> word and silence are reunited.[21]

Silence deepens communication. I remember the comment of a person who came to a retreat at the Lee Abbey Community in Devon (where I was chaplain for a time) and was dismayed to discover that half of each day would be spent in silence. At the end of the week, however, she said, 'You know, I think I know all these people better now than if I had spent the week talking to them!' Once we have got over our awkwardness, silence seems to bring a new sensitivity to our relationships. In a quiet way, a new society can emerge out of silence in which the eloquent are humbled and the tongue-tied exalted. Then we may find God speaking through people who have never had the courage to contribute before. We will learn to 'honour those parts which appear weaker' (see 1 Corinthians 12:21-26).

> It is in solitude that I find the gentleness with which I am
> to truly love my brothers. The more solitary I am the more
> affection I have for them. It is pure affection and filled
> with reverence for the solitude of others. Solitude and
> silence teach me to love my brothers for what they are, not
> for what they say.[22]

'The language of the mad'

Christianity is not the only faith to speak of silence. Far from it. It is a quality of attentiveness and expression that other cultures and religions have often understood much better. African culture, for example, understands the power and meaning of 'presence' between people, where Western culture would be uncomfortable without words.

We have also seen silence used as both a protest and a political weapon. Louis Fischer perceptively observes of Mahatma Gandhi:

> Sometimes, if he was too tired or the crowd too noisy, he would sit on the platform in silence until the audience, which often numbered two hundred thousand, became quiet. He then continued to sit in silence, and the men and women sat in silence, and he touched his palms together to bless them, and smiled and departed. This was communication without words, and the mass silence was an exercise in self-control and self-searching, a step therefore towards self-rule.[23]

A Christian understanding of silence will also have this note of protest to it. The silent spirit of the Quaker movement has kept it in the forefront of Christian concern on social and political issues.

We are not just concerned for the words we speak. We have a responsibility for the words by which the world is living – a concern for truth wherever it is expressed. In his novel *Proteus* Morris West writes the following conversation between the Russian ambassador and a personal friend:

> ' — what is the thing you are most afraid of?'
>
> ' — politically or personally?'
>
> ' — both.'
>
> ' — it is a thing which has happened already, whose human consequences are already upon us. We have so debased human language that it is impossible to believe any longer what we hear or read. I tell you "yes", the echo answers "no". We state one position and negotiate another. You talk "food", I hear "bombs". We have created a language of the mad. You show on television bodies broken in a railway accident. The next instant some impossibly beautiful

wench is demonstrating how to make floors shine like glass. The illusion is complete. There are no bodies. There could never be blood on so bright a surface.'[24]

We have created a language of the mad. It was with this kind of discernment that Merton would speak of the priority of prayer as 'the unmasking of illusion'. It is to be the place of truth. There is a striking parallel in the comments of a man from Beirut, about prayer for the Middle East:

> The difficulty [concerning the Middle East] . . . is that words have lost their meaning. For instance, if you mention hope, you might as well be talking about despair for all the effect it has on people. Therefore I would talk mostly of waiting upon God and quietly searching for his presence. Real prayer is offering what you can see and grasping what is happening, however painful and beastly it is, and waiting on God with it, almost as though you have it in your hands.[25]

Silence and suffering

One of the most unforgettable impressions I received from watching film of the Ethiopian famine and refugee camps a number of years ago was the silence of the suffering. Silence is a friend of suffering. With his insight from the Jewish Hasidic tradition, Chaim Potok wrote *The Chosen*. In the story a boy is brought up in silence by his father, a Hasid rabbi. He later begins to speak of the experience to a friend:

> You can listen to silence, Reuven . . . you have to want to listen to it. It has a strange and beautiful texture. It doesn't always talk. Sometimes – sometimes it cries, and you hear the pain of the world in it. It hurts to listen then. But you have to.[26]

The difficulty of praying for 'the world' is that its pains and conflicts feel so vast and complex. We are helpless to put prayer into words and generally feel as if the failure to 'say it right' is a failure in the prayer itself. That is not so.

When we seek to pray into the pain of the world, we are drawing near to the cross. We are seeking to join with the intercession of

Christ. That is what Christian prayer is all about. The striking fact is that the nearer Jesus got to his cross, the less he spoke. There is, as one person put it, 'an enormous and dreadful solitude' around those events. He fulfils Isaiah's vision of the servant who suffers in silence. 'He did not open his mouth' (Isaiah 53:7). It is a participation in suffering that words cannot express. It is a suffering completely beyond words as he willingly descends into that hell of man's sin and estrangement.

A faith centred on the cross will certainly feel tongue-tied with its burden at times. We must learn the prayer of silence. There is no other way. Our Western Christian understanding of prayer and intercession is almost completely verbal. This inhibits us. We need alternative ways of expressing our prayer in a suffering world. One helpful idea has been used at Lee Abbey on occasions. The leader invites the congregation to express intercession by using three simple movements of the hands:

- Hands cupped (as if holding something in them). We are invited to give thanks for all that God has given us over the past week; a silence is kept.
- Hands reaching out (as if to show God a suffering world). We are invited to pray for the world in its suffering and pain – there may be particular needs; a silence is kept.
- Hands reaching up (as if in longing and welcome). We express our hope in God for the world he comes to save; a silence is kept.

The combination of silent prayer and simple movement has led some people to a new involvement in intercessory prayer.

Silent for God

While working in a parish in London I was, for a time, a member of a weekly home group. We met each Wednesday evening after a full working day, to plunge into coffee, fellowship and Bible study. As some began to find this simply adding to the activity of the day rather than providing a refreshment from it, we agreed to begin our evenings together with 10 minutes of silence. One person would read a passage of Scripture and then we were still. During the weeks we followed this pattern, we found that our evenings became focused on God in a new way. It was not dramatic, and some of us felt it more than others, but we had (in Quaker language) 'centred down'. We were capable of a new responsiveness to God and to each other. We also found that God would speak during the silence – a guiding word, a picture, or a verse of Scripture.

God is the goal of our silence. It is God himself we are seeking, and we are silent for him. It is very easy to use prayer to invite God into our presence and activity. In silence we seek to enter God's presence and attend to *his* activity. It is also a temptation to seek silence for itself – for the feelings we might have of love and peace. As soon as we do this, however, we are no longer seeking God. Christian silence is the prayer that seeks the living God out of the heart of this broken world.

> As long as we remain interested in nothing but God, we cannot be distracted. [But] suppose my 'poverty' be a secret hunger for spiritual riches: suppose by pretending to be silent, I am really trying to cajole God into enriching me with some experience – what then? Then everything becomes a distraction. All created things interfere with my quest for some special experience ... if my prayer is centred on myself, if it seeks the enrichment of my own self, it will be my greatest potential distraction. Full of my own curiosity I have eaten the tree of knowledge and torn myself away from God. I am left rich and alone and nothing can assuage my hunger: everything I touch turns to distraction.

Let me seek, then, the gift of silence, and poverty and solitude, where everything I touch is turned into prayer, where the sky is my prayer, the birds are my prayer, the wind in the trees is my prayer, for God is all in all. Amen.[27]

CREATIVE SILENCE

> Sarah: I live in a place you can't enter. It's out of reach.
> James: Out of reach? That sounds romantic.
> Sarah: Deafness isn't the opposite of hearing, as you think. It's a silence full of sound.
> James: It's a silence full of sound?

Sarah: The sound of spring breaking up through the death of winter.[28]

Our churches are very diligent in urging us to pray more. Most of us feel thoroughly guilty that we do not. Yet we have been appallingly unimaginative in teaching *how* to pray more, and so it is with dry duty that we labour at what is intended to be the creative heart of our life and vision. We face the same danger in commending silence.

This section makes practical suggestions for exploring silence in prayer, worship and lifestyle. They are made with the conviction that prayer is the offering of the whole of our being. In the Scriptures it finds an incredible range of expression. It involves the physical body, not just the 'soul'. It involves all the senses – sight, touch, taste, hearing and smell. It involves the whole of life. It was through the whole of life that God spoke. The 'word of the Lord' came in myriad ways. To Jeremiah it came through the blossom on the almond tree (Jeremiah 1:11) and through watching the potter at work (Jeremiah 18). For Ezekiel it was a word to taste and eat (Ezekiel 3:3). For Peter it was in a strange dream (Acts 10:9-25). Not least, however, it was through the offering of the daily routine of life in all its ordinariness to God that the word of life would quietly form itself among his people. What we are seeking, in the 'great and ordinary' ways of God, is the quality of quiet attentiveness in all we do that enables us to receive him as the deepest source of our lives.[29]

As a general rule for all the suggestions that follow, remember the advice of Dom John Chapman: 'Pray as you can and do not try to pray as you can't. Take yourself as you find yourself and start from there.'

Dropping anchor (preparing to pray)

A creative use of silence may be the most effective way of stilling ourselves when life is hectic and time is short. It enables us to come before God in gentleness rather than by a violence of will or embattled by distractions. Choose your posture, comfortable but alert. Consider whether a visual focus would be of help – a candle, a picture, or a cross, for example. A verse or short passage of Scripture is a good anchor with which to start.

Breathing

Begin by deepening your breathing slightly into a relaxed, natural rhythm. This will help you to physically 'wind down', but it also helps your prayer. Let it be so. As you breathe you might silently pray, 'Lord Jesus Christ, have mercy on me' – prayed in and out on the rhythm of your breathing. Or you may like to reflect on 'breath' itself. It is the same word as 'Spirit' in the Bible. God breathed into Adam's nostrils and he became a living being (Genesis 2:7). Or you can just relax and let mind and heart lie fallow in God's presence (see Psalm 131).

An act of acceptance

Quietly reflect on the 'world' you have brought with you to prayer – its mood, its problems, its relationships, joys and sorrows. We normally call these distractions. Do not reject them. Gather them up and ask Christ to keep them while you pray. 'Love your enemies' and bring them with you into God's presence.

If 'dropping anchor' is being done as a group, it helps to have someone steering the time. It may help to agree the length of silence before you start. Come out of silence gently. Do not rush into activity. It will have meant different things to each member of the group and there is a need to be sensitive. Someone may need a chance to offer a thought for prayer or discussion – God may have spoken in some particular way. But equally, do not be tempted to analyse the silence for the sake of it.

Silent punctuation (silence and shared worship)

Liturgy

In recent Anglican liturgies (the *Alternative Service Book* and *Common Worship*) there are regular points where it is suggested that 'silence may be kept'. These generally come at points where something has just been received – after the reading of God's word, after the Eucharistic Prayer and after Communion itself. Where congregations grow into the naturalness of such a rhythm, there can be a beautiful ebb and flow to the worship without the need to have it all announced. In this way even a noisy family service can have a quality of stillness about it. There may be other points at which silence will be appropriate. Jean Vanier, founder of L'Arche, once suggested that all Christian celebration should end in silence, to remember those who cannot celebrate.

There is, however, a traditional tendency to fill all gaps in the worship with music. If 'a time of silence' is what is intended, make sure it is allowed to be just that.

> I sat in the church (I'd gone to break bread)
> the pastor began to assure us
> that we could spend time with our minds fixed on God
> – but somebody thought of a chorus![30]

Christ in quiet

A time of quiet meditation may be a helpful alternative to the more formal sermon or even intercession time when we meet as a church. 'Christ in Quiet' is the name given to a daily part of the Lee Abbey programme in the half hour before supper. It is a mixture of music, readings and silence chosen around a theme and led by a member of the community. Over the years it has been an enormous help to many people and it is consistently among the most popular features of the programme. There is no reason why it could not form part of the worship of any congregation.

Body and senses

Movement and imagination

We have already suggested an example of the use of movement in prayer (see under 'Silence and suffering' above). It can be something explored together or in private prayer. It does not have to be clever, it just needs to be 'you'. There are many times in our lives when we express ourselves more through action than words. Why should prayer and worship be any different? Here are some suggestions for 'action' prayers:

1 *The Lord's Prayer*. In groups of no more than six people express the Lord's Prayer in simple movements. You will need to discuss this, but keep moving!
2 *Entering God's courts*. Imagine yourself entering the presence of God as you would be received in a royal audience.

Express this prayer in movement. (This has often been a breakthrough to discovering what an aid to prayer the imagination can be – it is traditionally an enemy).

3 *In awe, in love, in contrition.* Movement can express our sense of awe and God's majesty (with Revelation 4:9-11), our love and trust in his goodness (with Psalm 131), our penitence and humbling before him (with Ezekiel 1:25ff.).

We might also include at this point the creative actions of writing and drawing. To express your prayer through a poem or drawing can help you explore what the heart of your prayer really is. It disciplines the prayer and gives it content. Once again, this is not a question of being 'good at' something. We are simply learning to pray and worship from our true selves.

The senses

Another occasional ingredient to a Lee Abbey programme has been something called a 'Silent Walk'. A small group of people will walk together on the estate for half an hour, in complete silence. The intention is to listen and to be sensitive to the world around. They then meet and discuss their impressions. There is always an awareness that the discipline of silence shared has brought a new intensity to the world in which they have walked. Colours, smells, textures are all received with a new life and vigour. There is always a sense of dismay at how much 'we have been missing' in the normal bustle and wordiness of it all. We neglect our senses to our cost. In silence we can rediscover them. We need hardly add that such a walk will teach us as much about inner cities as countryside.

The senses can also find expression in church worship. In some traditions there is much colour and sensitivity, of course, but it can also become the province of the 'professionals' at the front. I remember the impact, one Good Friday, of finding nails provided for those sitting in the pews. Meditating, through touch, on the reality of the cross was a helpful focus. I have also known it done with cups of vinegar. It may be possible to use darkness and light more imaginatively in some churches, too.

Some church traditions have no place for the nose to worship God! Laurens van der Post wrote, 'Scientists tell us that the nose is the oldest of the organs of our senses and therefore retains an unrivalled power to evoke what is inexpressible.' It may take getting used to, but the occasional use of incense in church worship can contribute an important dimension to our expression of God's holiness.

Silence in the diary

There must be 'full stops' in our diaries when we withdraw for a time to be silent. We must not feel guilty about doing so – in fact, we will need each other's encouragement to keep it up. It is amazing how easily this commitment drops out of the diary before anything else does! There may be places nearby that could be a resource in this way, whether for a day or part of a day, or for a longer period.

To repeat the words of St John of the Cross given earlier: 'One Word the Father spoke, which Word was his Son, and this Word he ever speaks in eternal silence and in silence it must be heard by the soul.'

FURTHER READING

Silence

Mother Mary Clare, *Silence and Prayer* (Fairacres)
Morton Kelsey, *The Other Side of Silence* (SPCK)
Wendy Robinson, *Exploring Silence* (Fairacres)

Solitude and community

Carlo Carretto, *Letters from the Desert* (Darton, Longman and Todd); *The Desert in the City* (Darton, Longman and Todd)
Richard Foster, *Celebration of Discipline* (Hodder and Stoughton); *Freedom of Simplicity* (Triangle)
Henri Nouwen, *Reaching Out* (Fount); *The Way of the Heart* (Darton, Longman and Todd)
Thomas Merton, *Thoughts in Solitude* (Burns and Oates)
Michael Mitton, *The Wisdom to Listen* (Grove Books)

Notes

1 Kenneth Leech, *True God* (Sheldon, 1985), Chapter 5.
2 Henri Nouwen, *The Way of the Heart – Desert Spirituality and Contemporary Ministry* (Darton, Longman and Todd, 1981), p. 33.
3 *Maximus on Love*, no. 21.
4 Leech, *True God*, Chapter 5.
5 Cited by Leech, ibid., pp. 154-55.
6 Catherine de Hueck Doherty, *Poustinia* (Fount, 1977).
7 Richard Foster, *Freedom of Simplicity* (Triangle, 1981), p. 58.
8 Henri Nouwen, *The Genesee Diary* (Image Books, 1981), p. 14.
9 Leech, *True God*, p. 159.
10 Of course, the incarnation itself was not temporary but eternal – the taking of manhood into God.
11 Simone Weil, *Gravity and Grace* (Routledge and Kegan Paul, n.d.), p. 34.
12 See W. H. Vanstone, *The Stature of Waiting* (Darton, Longman and Todd, 1982).
13 The traditional translation 'still small voice' does not reflect the meaning of the Hebrew.
14 Archbishop Trench, *Notes on the Miracles*, commenting on Mk 5.19.
15 'All things were lying in quiet and silence, and night in her swift course was half spent, when the Almighty Word leapt from thy Royal throne in heaven. . .' (Wisdom of Solomon 18.14). Though belonging to a different context, this is traditionally used as a Christian antiphon.
16 Dietrich Bonhoeffer, *Life Together* (SCM, 1954) pp. 77-78.
17 Thomas Merton, *Thoughts in Solitude* (Burns and Oates, 1958) p. 22.
18 Alan Ecclestone, *A Staircase for Silence* (DLT, 1977) p. 42.
19 Henri Nouwen, *The Genesee Diary*, p. 134.
20 Richard Foster *Freedom of Simplicity*, p. 58.
21 Cited by Simon Tugwell, *Ways of Imperfection* (SCM, 1984) p. 4
22 Thomas Merton, *Sign of Jonas* (Sheldon, 1976) p. 268.
23 Louis Fischer, *The Life of Mahatma Gandhi* (Granada, 1982) p. 311.
24 Morris West, *Proteus* (Collins, 1979) p. 184.
25 Alan Amos interviewed in *Grassroots* magazine (February 1983).
26 Chaim Potok, *The Chosen* (Penguin 1970) p. 259.
27 Thomas Merton, *Thoughts in Solitude* pp. 90-91.

28 Mark Medhoff *Children of a Lesser God* (Amber Lane Press, 1980). A fascinating play revolving around the love of a speech therapist (James) for one of his deaf students (Sarah) which was later made into a film.
29 I acknowledge my debt to those guests at Lee Abbey who had joined in workshops on this subject over the year prior to my writing this. Most of the ideas that follow come out of those times of discussion and experiment.
30 From 'But somebody thought of a chorus' by Gordon Bailey, *Patchwork Quilt* (SOL Publications, 1975).

PART 3

PAST AND PRESENT

LEARNING FROM THE ENGLISH MYSTICS

Alison Fry

You have probably done it too. Something convinced you that you really ought to pray more. Spurred on by new-found enthusiasm, you resolved to get up early and devote to God as much extra time as you could muster, so you set your alarm clock for an unfeasibly early (but very self-sacrificial) hour. By day three all your enthusiasm was in tatters and the sense of failure was complete as you crawled back to bed, promising to do better tomorrow, but of course tomorrow never came.

We think we *should* pray more, we think we *ought* to pray better, but our best efforts seem destined to end in apparent failure. This is nothing new. More than 600 years ago, an Englishman called Richard Rolle wrote, 'You frequently awake early, so why don't you find him [that is, God] you say? Well surely, if you look for him in the right place, you are bound to find him.'

We need some help to search in the right place. Prayer is indeed a duty (see 1 Thessalonians 5:17; Luke 18:1), but it is also a delight and a joy (see Psalm 37:4; Philippians 1:4), and neither duty nor delight can survive without the other. Our enthusiasm to get up early and pray more began with a longing for God and a desire to delight in God. Somehow that got lost in the 'shoulds' and 'oughts' of duty. If we are ever going to fulfil our longing for God, we need to reach a point beyond the 'shoulds' and 'oughts' where we can 'want to want' to pray. We need some guidance to reach it, but fortunately the resources already lie within our grasp.

In Chapter 1 of *The Cloud of Unknowing*, we read:

> Our Lord has, in his great mercy, called you and led you
> to him by the desire of your heart ... And so with his great
> grace he kindled your desire and fastened to it a leash of
> longing, and with this led you into a more special state and
> degree of life, to be a servant ... of his.

Richard Rolle wrote in *The Fire of Love*: 'There is delightful warmth
in the loving heart ... for there you, my God and my comfort, have
set up your temple.' Jesus promised, 'You did not choose me, but
I chose you' (John 15:16). Deep within our being God has built a
temple (see 1 Corinthians 6:19), and from it God calls gently and
urgently. The longing we feel, however fleeting, is our inner voice
answering that call. The starting point to 'want to want' to pray is
God's call, not our faltering response.

There is a God-shaped space in all our lives, but it is not one
into which God can be plugged, like a piece in a jigsaw puzzle. Our
God is too exciting to be pinned down and we grow and change as
we are transformed by God. God is constantly revealing something
new. Our yearning, longing and reaching out for God is renewed
throughout our Christian journey. As we explore this journey, our
own resources are never enough. Sometimes we do not know
which way to turn. Sometimes our longing loses its urgency. Then
we need travelling companions, praying people who will join us for
a part of the road which, although new for us, they know well.

The purpose of this study is to introduce one such group of
companions – the so-called 'medieval English mystics'. They acted
as helpers and guides to faithful people who were sincerely seeking
God in their own day; they can help us still.

WHO WERE THE ENGLISH MYSTICS?

Many people have heard of John of the Cross and Teresa of
Avila, the great continental mystics of the sixteenth century. They
are acknowledged spiritual heavyweights. It has never occurred to
most people, however, that there might be an English equivalent.

Some will have heard of the fourteenth-century Julian of Norwich, but they may have no clear idea of who she was or why
people get so excited about her writings. Few know that, contemporary with Julian, there lived a whole series of eminent English

mystics. Highly regarded as spiritual teachers in their day, their writings went on to be prized for centuries after their deaths.

Let me introduce our travelling companions. Most of them never met each other in their own lifetimes, and all have their own individual approach and style. All are at least 600 years old, so some of their habits, their ways of speaking or their assumptions, may seem a little strange to us, as indeed our behaviour would astound them. Yet they share with us an earnest desire which is timeless – to love and to serve God and to share with others the riches of God's grace and gifts.

Richard Rolle (c.1300-49)

Rolle was probably born at Thornton le Dale near Pickering. He was definitely not a dour Yorkshireman. He was an enthusiast, animated and passionate in the sheer excitement of his love for Jesus. Many would label him eccentric.

Rolle seems always to have been a rebel. He left Oxford University before completing his Master's degree. At the age of 19 he returned to Yorkshire but ran away from his parents to adopt the life of a hermit. This was perhaps his protest against a conventional church life, which did not seem to meet his very vivid experience of God. In his writings he was scathing about clerics whom he felt knew nothing of the love of God.

Hermits were quite commonplace in medieval England. They were sometimes members of a religious community, but often they were individuals who lived in solitude in order to be more able to pray. Normally they were licensed by the diocesan bishop and supported themselves by performing a local service (often maintaining a stretch of road or a bridge). Rolle, of course, had to be unconventional. He was neither a member of a religious order nor licensed and, as a consequence, he had to borrow two of his sister's dresses to make a makeshift habit of the kind hermits customarily wore. The standard rules of self-denial and asceticism did not appeal to Rolle either. What mattered over and above all orthodoxy and legalities was a fervent devotion to God.

Without a Master's degree, he could not preach, teach or hold any major church or administrative office. Instead he relied on various patrons for support, and seems to have inspired deep affection among his friends and followers, who included both high-ranking figures and unlearned laypeople. His anti-establishment, unconventional stance may explain his substantial popular appeal for a couple of centuries after his death, since such attitudes were gaining ground as the Reformation approached.

His most famous work, *The Fire of Love*, was not addressed to anyone in particular, but we know that Rolle acted as a spiritual guide to individuals (notably an anchoress, Margaret Kirkby, for whom his *Form of Living* was written) and to the Cistercian convent at Hampole near Doncaster, near to where Rolle ended his days.

The Bible was Rolle's primary authority – he peppered his work with scriptural quotations. He could be explosive in his opinions, but was also understanding and encouraging. He had an ability to joke at his own expense and was not insensitive. Rolle was a prolific writer in both Latin and English. Like the other English mystics, the English he wrote was that of his day – 'middle English', the language of Chaucer. This requires some translation to make it accessible today, but modern versions are available of all the major works by the mystics.

Walter Hilton (died c.1396)

Sadly we know very little about Hilton's life. We are not sure when or where he was born. He seems to have taken a degree at Cambridge and may have practised law for a time. His writings show him to have been a highly educated man with the precise, systematic and thoughtful mind of an academic theologian. His work also portrays someone of deep compassion and immense common sense.

Hilton probably became an Augustinian canon and spent his later life at the priory at Thurgarton in Nottinghamshire. The Augustinians had a particular concern to bring God's word to 'the person in the street'. Hilton was no exception. His major work, *The Scale of Perfection* (or *Ladder of Perfection*), was produced for a devout laywoman who had asked for guidance on living a life of contemplative prayer, and the *Mixed Life* was written for a layman seeking to make time for prayer in the midst of his responsibilities as the head of a medieval household. Hilton also made it clear that he expected both works to be read more widely.

Hilton does not come across as a dry academic, scribbling from his ivory tower. He writes with care and pastoral concern for real people with real spiritual needs. His gentle and practical wisdom fits much more closely the role of a wise friend for the spiritual journey than that of an authoritative tutor schooling us in the way we should go.

The Cloud of Unknowing

We know still less about Hilton's contemporary, the author of *The Cloud of Unknowing* (possibly written around 1370). The generally accepted opinion is that the writer was probably a Carthusian monk and almost certainly a priest. Even today, Carthusians are anonymous authors.

A number of works have been attributed to the same pen. These include *The Epistle of Privy Counsel* (or *A Letter of Private Direction*) and *The Epistle on Prayer*. Like Hilton, this person was a scholar whose advice and counsel had been sought by those for whom he wrote. He had the teacher's knack of explaining complex ideas with simplicity, a caustic sense of humour and a touch of poetry.

He writes with the conviction that God cannot be reached by human reason and is to that extent 'unknowable', but he is accessible to love. Rational thought and careful study can only help us know *about* God. We only truly know God when we love God and recognize that we are loved in return. The author of *The Cloud* gives the impression that he is struggling to communicate with inadequate human words and images what he has discovered of God in silence and stillness. His driving certainty is that it is an absolute necessity to have God at the centre of one's life.

Julian of Norwich (c.1342-c.1416)

Julian was an anchoress, one of those who took vows to remain inside a cell for their natural life. They believed that cutting themselves off from the world enabled them to devote their lives to prayer. Many towns employed an anchorite specifically to pray for the town's welfare. On 8-9 May 1373, Julian lay close to death. She was gazing at a crucifix left by the priest who had come to give her the last rites, when she received 16 'shewings' or revelations from God. She recovered, and at some point in the next 30 years Julian wrote two accounts of these showings and her reflections on them. Her *Revelations of Divine Love* is the best-known work of the English mystics and it is still much studied.[1] Adrian Daffern explores her thought at greater length in the next chapter.

Margery Kempe (c.1373-c.1438)

Margery was a medieval housewife from King's Lynn, where her father was one-time mayor and Member of Parliament. Despite the status of her family, Margery, like most laypeople, was illiterate. A scribe wrote for her the autobiographical *Book of Margery Kempe*.

Many scholars have discarded Margery as a genuine English mystic because she does not quite fit the mould. This antipathy is partly the result of profound disappointment. Until 1934 only a few fragments of her work were known, and these revealed her as another Mother Julian. The myth was exploded when a complete manuscript of *The Book of Margery Kempe* was unearthed in a private collection.

Margery was no holy anchoress. She was a wife, mother to 14 children, and an unsuccessful businesswoman and traveller. Her book begins with her own description of a bout of insanity after the birth of her first child. Today we would probably call it severe post-natal depression. Her spiritual life was marked by extreme emotion – incessant public tears, shouting, foretelling other people's damnation. She was tried for heresy twice and insisted on a vow of celibacy from her husband. The full book revealed someone who was 'an insensitive, completely self-absorbed, bombastic and rather quarrelsome personality'.[2]

The revelations of the complete book led many to dismiss Margery as mad. The reputation has stuck, although it is not necessarily true. It was Margery's healing from madness that began her spiritual explorations. She was driven to tears by penitence (for her own sins and those of the world) and by an acute awareness of Christ's passion and suffering – which ought to be something to shout about!

Although her behaviour startles us, it was accepted by the Church authorities in her day. Heresy charges against her were never upheld. The worst accusation she sustained from her contemporaries was that she was putting it on. Margery was a devout and articulate laywoman, with energy and ambition, but she was also illiterate and barred from the religious life by marriage. How else might she have expressed her overwhelming desire to serve God with heart, mind, soul and strength?

Of all the English mystics, Margery remained the one most in touch with everyday life. She tried to live faithfully in the world, not shut away from it. Rather than being a spiritual consultant, she consulted anchorites and anchoresses (including Julian of Norwich), hermits and other prayerful people. It is perhaps the very 'ordinariness' of her life that is appealing.

An uncertain world

The unusual abundance of spiritual writing that this odd, assorted group has left may relate to the world in which they lived. It was a time of great upheaval. The Hundred Years' War (1337-1453) drained the country. The great plague of 1348-49 killed a third of the population. The discontent which exploded in the Peasants' Revolt of 1381, sparked by poll taxes, was also brewing. The seeds of the great changes of the Reformation were in the wind. Parliament was disputing the payment of papal taxes. John Wycliffe and the Lollards were questioning the nature of the Eucharist, the authority of the clergy and the use of Scripture solely in Latin. Executions by burning for religious opinions were common.

The English mystics seem to have responded to the spiritual needs that people were feeling in this uncertain climate. Our world may be very different from theirs, but we too live in a confusing time of loss, conflict, change and spiritual need. The English mystics offer some wisdom which spans the centuries.

A WORD ABOUT MYSTICISM

A reputation, whether good or bad, is very hard to shift, and the word 'mystic' has a reputation. It conjures up in many people's minds a picture of a turban-clad guru. 'Mysticism' has attached to it various esoteric and mysterious practices ranging from horoscopes and fortune-telling to Stonehenge and the druids. Mysticism is often associated with Eastern religions or groups on the fringes of the mainstream. It seems to belong to strange and alien cultures. This is a reputation that is difficult to change, even though we know that it is a caricature.

Yet there is a long history of *Christian* mysticism. It extends from the pages of Scripture into the lives of all who seek to know and serve their Lord. Christian mysticism is not about chanting mantras, but about singing hymns, psalms and spiritual songs. It is not about physical or breathing exercises, but about discipline in prayer. It is not about focusing on a single object until it occupies the whole of one's consciousness, but about being preoccupied with God. It is not about seeking an experience of heightened awareness, but about an exploration of fellowship with Father, Son and Holy Spirit.

For the English mystics the word 'mysticism' would have had none of today's connotations. All the accumulated baggage of the intervening centuries needs to be jettisoned. Only then can we hear what the English mystics actually said about mysticism, instead of what we fear they might have said.

Meeting the hidden Christ

'Mystic' and 'mysticism' are derived from the Greek *mystikos*, a word referring to things which are hidden. For the English mystics, 'mysticism' referred to meeting Christ hidden in the Scriptures and the sacraments but revealed through the work of the Holy Spirit.[3] In any case, they tended to refer to their way of life as 'contemplative' rather than 'mystical'. Christian mysticism might simply be described as the journey towards a place of contemplative prayer.

Perhaps, therefore, we would be more comfortable with the word 'contemplation' instead of 'mysticism', and 'contemplative' instead of 'mystic'. The two words are used interchangeably when speaking of Christian mysticism. Their meaning may be the same, but the reputation of the words is different. With 'contemplation' we are in the realms of peace and tranquillity, of walking with our God beside still waters, in the silence of eternity.

Many of us have been there, albeit briefly. Deep in prayer, we suddenly catch a glimpse of the nearness of God; in the middle of a moving church service, we sense vividly his presence and peace. This is a glimmer of what the English mystics would have called 'contemplation'.

It sounds idyllic, but it is not a place that is easy to find, especially in a frantic, restless, rush-filled world. The experience comes to us out of the blue and we do not know how to find our way there again. There never seems to be enough time to stop and pray when there's work to be done, the children need collecting from school, and the supper is still in the supermarket.

Is 'the contemplative' therefore something to leave to the experts? It is true that those who have, down the ages, been called 'mystics' or 'contemplatives' were regarded as people with a special gift from God. They can seem to be on a higher plane than the rest of us because of a special calling or vocation from God to a contemplative lifestyle. Yet these 'experts' have spent an extraordinary amount of energy trying to help 'ordinary' people follow the same path.

The English mystics wrote books by hand, at a time before the printing press was invented, when paper or parchment was scarce and expensive. They wrote in English when writing spiritual works in the vernacular ran the risk of imprisonment or burning. Their enthusiasm in their efforts to encourage their fellow Christians to journey towards a deeply reflective relationship with God is evident from their work. They believed that at least a degree of contemplative prayer is available to all, and they did not seem to regard themselves as distinguished contemplatives in any way.

WHAT IS CONTEMPLATIVE PRAYER?

In medieval understanding, the contemplative life was distinguished from the active life. In Chapter 1 of his *Mixed Life*, Hilton said there were 'two manner of states ... in Holy Church, by which Christian souls please God and get them the bliss of heaven: the one is bodily and the other is ghostly.'

This does not mean that salvation was sought through works. Hilton writes here of *Christian* souls whom he assumed were already saved. There were, rather, two equally valid paths towards sanctification. The *Ancrene Riwle* (a thirteenth-century handbook for anchorites and anchoresses) puts it less controversially: 'The rules of this pursuit are two. The first is concerned with the right directing of the heart, the second with the right ordering of exterior things.'

The active life

In *The Scale of Perfection*, Hilton described the active life as a path which 'lies in love and charity shown outwardly in good bodily works, in the fulfilment of God's commandments and of the seven works of mercy – bodily and spiritual – towards one's fellow Christians'. The seven bodily works of mercy were to feed the hungry, give drink to the thirsty, clothe the naked, visit the prisoner, shelter the stranger, visit the sick and bury the dead (see Matthew 25:31ff.). The spiritual mercies were to correct the sinner, teach the ignorant, counsel the doubtful, comfort the sorrowful, bear wrongs patiently, forgive all injuries and pray for the living and departed – all of which have scriptural precedent. The active life also included activities such as holding vigils and fasting. Thus it involved ordering one's outward, bodily affairs in accordance with God's word, and might easily be summarized as 'loving your neighbour'.

The contemplative life

The contemplative life, by contrast, concerned the ordering of one's inner, or spiritual, affairs. The ultimate gift of the contemplative life was the state of mystical union with God. This could only truly be obtained on the other side of the grave, but it could be approached in this life. The author of *The Cloud of Unknowing* explains in the first chapter:

> My spiritual friend in God, you are to understand that according to our rather crude reckoning, there are four degrees and forms of the Christian life ... Three of these can be begun and ended in this life, and one may begin the fourth by grace here below, which is to last without end in the happiness of heaven.

Hilton also helps us to get our modern minds around this concept. In Book 1 of *The Scale of Perfection* he explains that the contemplative life has several parts which approximate to the 'degrees' mentioned by the author of *The Cloud*. 'The first lies in the knowledge of God and the things of the spirit acquired by reason, by the teaching of man and by the study of holy Scripture.' Some have a particular calling to be scholars devoted to 'long study and labour in holy Scripture', but it is in measure open to all Christian people, 'to good and bad alike'. Hilton knows that knowledge without love is worthless (see 1 Corinthians 13:2), so, 'The second part of contemplation lies principally in affection.' This is the will to give oneself to serve God, or simply devotion:

> Sometimes a man or woman meditating on God feels a fervour of love and spiritual sweetness in the remembrance of his passion, or any of his works in his humanity; or he feels great trust in the goodness and mercy of God for the forgiveness of sins, and for his gifts of grace ... He cannot explain what it is, but he feels it plainly ... making him feel that he does not care what then becomes of him provided the will of God is fulfilled.

Devotion is open to all Christian people in the 'active life', in a 'lower degree', as Hilton terms it. A 'higher degree', he says, 'can be had and held only by people who are in great quietness of body and soul'. By this he appears to mean that, although all may find it, it can only be 'held' (or sustained) by those who have chosen to devote themselves to the contemplative life – such as those in religious orders, anchorites and hermits. Practice makes perfect, it seems.

The third and final part of contemplation, Hilton says,

> which is as perfect as can be here, lies both in cognition and in affection; that is to say, in the knowing and perfect loving of God. That is when a person's soul is first cleansed from all sins and reformed to the image of Jesus by completeness of virtues, and afterward he is visited and taken up from all earthly and fleshly affections, from vain thoughts and imaginations of all bodily things, and is as if forcibly ravished out of the bodily sense; and then is illumined by the grace of the Holy Spirit to see intellectually the Truth, which is God, and also spiritual things, with a soft, sweet burning love for him.

This perfect knowing and loving of God is again available to all, whether in an active or contemplative life, but only by God's special gift and grace. The mystics could teach contemplation, but only God could give the 'mystical' experience of union with himself. This is vital to the Christian understanding of mysticism.

Both Hilton and the author of *The Cloud* issue spiritual health warnings. No one is to seek after such experiences. They specifically dismiss any seeking after physical sensations, in which they seem to be having a dig at the excesses of their predecessor, Richard Rolle. In the prologue to *The Fire of Love* Rolle describes the fire of his love for God as warming his heart:

It was real warmth too, not imaginary, and it felt as if it were actually on fire. I was astonished at the way the heat surged up and how this new and unexpected sensation brought great and unexpected comfort.

He appears to think that physical sensations demonstrate the highest devotion, commenting in Chapter 2, 'It would be surprising if anyone without such experience should claim the name of contemplative.'

God will speak to our individual and unique personalities, but we should be wary of seeking any particular physical or spiritual sensation. It is God we are seeking, not an experience.

The mixed life

Since the English mystics aimed to help their readers towards the contemplative path, it can appear that they thought this path was a more important, higher and better way. We seem to have gone to the opposite extreme. It is active life that counts, not just in our world but in our churches too. If I announced to my congregation that I was called to a contemplative life while remaining in my post, I suspect they would feel that they were being short-changed and that I was malingering. After all, there is the Sunday school to oversee, the visiting to be done, the services to prepare – all kinds of activity.

Jesus at Bethany told Martha, 'Mary has chosen the good portion' (Luke 10:42, my paraphrase). This need not be translated as 'better portion' as some would have it; the implication is that Jesus wants his followers to have the opportunity to set aside their busyness and sit and listen to him.

In reality the active and contemplative paths cannot be entirely separated. The English mystics recognized this. Just as the contemplative life required the ordering of one's outward and active life, so the contemplative life could also be brought into the active life. Hilton had a specific pastoral concern for one layperson with many responsibilities, who was not free to devote his entire life to contemplation, but who nonetheless, as Hilton expresses it in Chapter 2 of *Mixed Life*,

yearnest greatly to serve our Lord by ghostly occupation
all wholly, without letting or troubling of worldly business,

that thou mightest come by grace to more knowing and ghostly [spiritual] feeling of God and of ghostly things.

Hilton was certain that the active life was as much a path to God as the contemplative life. Loving God was not the prerogative of the professional contemplative. The journey to self-understanding and awareness of the gift of salvation in Christ and the journey to active love for one's neighbour were both central to all Christian devotion.

People whose lives are professionally devoted to God – the vicar, the nun, the missionary – can seem to be capable of a deeper faith or greater heights of prayer than other Christians. We still need to recognize that such 'professional' Christians are merely called to express their devotion in a *particular* way, not in a *higher* or *better* way that is inaccessible to others. This misconception does not escape the caustic humour of the author of the *Epistle of Privy Counsel*, who writes in Chapter 1:

> Through their blindness and sophistication people have no more insight and understanding of these simple exercises [contemplative prayer] than the child at his ABC has of the knowledge of the greatest scholar in the university ... Yet in truth it is this simple exercise that can unite the soul of the most uncouth man alive to God in love and humility and perfect charity.

Contemplative prayer is there for absolutely anyone.

More importantly, Hilton recognized that a desire for the contemplative life was in the gift of God. God sometimes gave it to those who were not 'professional' contemplatives, but who had worldly responsibilities. In these circumstances it was not necessary to rush to the nearest monastery or hermitage. When we feel drawn to spend time in quiet, contemplative prayer in the midst of our busy lives, we are to live what Hilton calls the 'mixed life'. In Chapter 5 of *Mixed Life* he describes this as:

> sometimes to use the works of mercy in active life, in help and sustenance of themselves, and of their subjects, and of others also; and sometimes for to leave all manner of outward business, and give themselves unto prayers and meditations, reading of Holy Writ, and to other ghostly occupations.

If we were to forsake our worldly business, we would fail in our responsibility to love our neighbour. Equally, to forsake contemplation would be to deny a God-given gift.

The mixed life may seem to be the perfect example of an English compromise, but there is good biblical precedent for spending some time in one practice and some in another (see Ecclesiastes 3:1-9). More than one mystic suggests becoming like both Martha *and* Mary. And of course Jesus himself chose, in his earthly life, to devote some time to prayer and solitude (see, for example, Mark 1:35) and some time in active work.

Most Christians today have a limited amount of time to devote to prayer and meditation on Scripture. Most of us are not ordained or members of religious orders (and so in a sense paid to pray). Neither, however, are we uninterested in prayer and contemplation. We need to find the right balance between our outer, active life and our inner, contemplative life. This search is what fired the English mystics.

'GO THEN ALONE...'

The English mystics have gained that title because of their writing on contemplative prayer and their own evident experience of God's grace and blessing received through it. This was not their only consideration, however. Much of what we can learn from them concerns the basic discipline of prayer. None of the English mystics considers contemplative prayer in isolation. It is, for them, only a part of a whole pattern of prayer.

The first problem is to carve out a time and place. No prayer, whether intercessory or contemplative, individual or corporate, can happen without making space for it, and the English mystics knew that only in solitude is it possible to devote all your energies to contemplative prayer. In Chapter 11 of *Mixed Life* Hilton urges his readers to 'go then alone to thy prayers and to thy meditations'. In Book 1 of *The Scale of Perfection* he writes, 'Whoever has this gift of God fervently needs to escape for the time from the presence and company of everyone, and to be alone, lest he should be hindered.' In Chapter 13 of *The Fire of Love*, Richard Rolle says:

Their sole desire is for the joys which are eternal and so they make time for devotion and contemplation, never wavering in their wholehearted effort to love Christ. Many of their number, although they live physically among people, are mentally remote from them.

Finding a place of solitude for prayer has biblical roots. Jesus took time alone to pray before many of his most important choices (see, for example, Matthew 4:1ff.; 14:13, 23; 26:36ff.; Luke 6:12). He taught his followers to withdraw from the busyness of life and pray alone (see Matthew 6:6; Mark 6:31). If God is moving us to spend time with him, we must not let ourselves be drawn away by distractions. When a friend asks us to join them for an evening, we try to keep our promise even if a better offer comes along, and God's invitation is at least as important. Times of solitude and silence guard our relationship with God.

We need a place where we shall be undisturbed, but the time need not be long – 10 minutes on the walk to work, in the traffic queue, or during a coffee break. There are many pauses that go unnoticed during our busy days that we could claim as time for God. Several of the mystics recommend taking time either first thing in the morning, or closing the day with a review of its activities. Generations of Christians have found this helpful. The important thing is to make sure that the space is feasible and sustainable. It is pointless to set unattainable targets. My piano teacher used to insist that five minutes' practice daily was better than half an hour once a week. I suspect that the same is true for 'practising the presence of God', although it is also appropriate to find longer times now and again, perhaps on a holiday or a retreat.

Avoiding the distractions of the world is only half the benefit of solitude. In a curious way, avoiding temptations brings us face to face with our own shortcomings. Once we have set aside the preoccupations that fill our lives, we are left alone to confront God and have God confront us. Solitude forces us to face our own state before God, and so allows God to deal with us.

Solitude may seem a very uncomfortable prospect. This is partly because it is so unfamiliar and we are all a little bit afraid of the unknown. We have driven out almost all space for solitude and silence in our busy, noisy world. At home the television or the radio is turned on, shops and workplaces are filled with 'muzak', the headphones of a Walkman are carefully positioned to shut out silence.

Solitude also appears uncomfortable because we are afraid of loneliness and isolation, of being alone. That, however, is not at all the same thing as solitude. In Chapter 13 of *The Fire of Love* Rolle writes, 'They [i.e. those who denigrate the solitary life] define "alone" not as being "without God", but understand it to mean "without company". A man is alone indeed if God is not with him.'

If we never face our inmost being or God, we will never allow ourselves to be truly as we are, however 'foul and wretched' we may be (as the *Epistle of Privy Counsel* puts it); nor can we allow God to be as God is. We are then less than the human beings we were created to be. We are not in union with our Creator. We are still running away from the guilt of the garden of Eden. Part of the goal of contemplative prayer is to be open and honest within the security of our relationship with Christ. The *Epistle of Privy Counsel* suggests that solitude is a place to

> take good, gracious God just as he is, and without further ado lay him on your sick self just as you are, for all the world as if he were a poultice! Or to put it in other words, lift up your sick self just as you are, and through your longing strive to touch good, gracious God just as he is. Touching him is eternal health, which is the point of the story of the woman in the Gospel who said ... 'If I touch but the hem of his garment I shall be whole.'

Once we have found this peace, silence and solitude can be carried into the noisiest of circumstances. Hilton hints at this in Chapter 10 of *Mixed Life*, urging his reader that if he is interrupted by the call of his family or work, he is to 'leave off lightly thy devotion, whether it be in prayer or in meditation, and go do thy debt and thy service to thine even-Christians [fellow Christians] as readily as if our Lord himself bade thee do so.'

Solitude will not rob us of precious time which we could spend doing all sorts of useful activities. Rather, peace and stillness will fill our lives – and may draw others towards our God who grants us such serenity, as Margery Kempe describes in Book 1 of her autobiography: 'Many ... wanted to hear her converse, for her conversation was so much to do with the love of God that those who heard it were often moved to weep very sadly.'

It is worth noting that the mystics would have assumed and expected that everyone to whom they wrote was part of a congregation (whether inside or outside the cloister). Time spent in contemplative solitude was not a superior substitute for corporate prayer or service to one's neighbour or community. It was rather something that was a natural response to, and that had its roots in, the worshipping life of the Church. Solitude might mean severing the ties we have with some of the trappings of the world, but for the English mystics it never meant isolating ourselves from our brothers and sisters in Christ. Contemplation could not happen apart from the 'body of Christ'.

'...UNTO PRAYERS AND MEDITATIONS'

One reason for our reluctance to seek solitude and silence may be that we are not sure what to do with it once we have got it. We are uncertain how to go about silent or contemplative prayer.

It is easy to equate prayer with intercession. Even biblical translators can fall into this trap. Hebrews 7:25 is usually translated 'since he always lives *to make intercession* for them'. The same word is also found in Acts 25:24, Romans 8:27, 34 and Romans 11:2. Although it can have the sense of 'petition' or 'plead with', it primarily means 'to fall in with', 'to meet with in order to converse', 'to turn to'. These are phrases which encompass a relationship between two persons involving listening and responding to one another. Prayer is therefore first and foremost our 'meeting in order to converse with' God, and only secondarily is prayer what we ask for, or intercession. The English mystics can help us to reclaim this biblical aspect of prayer, for contemplative prayer is a 'falling in with God', finding ourselves caught up in what he is about rather than what we thought we had come to say. The mystics guide us through practices which are familiar to us – the building blocks of confession, recited prayer and extempore intercession – towards the less familiar contemplative 'being' before God.

Confession

Confession was fundamental to all prayer for the English mystics. Turning to face God inevitably makes us aware of our shortcomings. Chapter 35 of *The Cloud of Unknowing* says:

> God's word, whether written or spoken, is like a mirror
> ... It follows, then, that when a person sees in the bodily

or spiritual mirror, or knows by the information he gets from someone else, just where the dirty mark is on his bodily or spiritual face, he goes to the well to wash it off – and not before. Now if this mark is a particular sin, the well is holy Church and the water confession, with all its elements. And if the mark is simply the blind root with the impulse to sin, then the well is the merciful God, and the water is prayer, with all its elements.

Confession was assumed to include a formal confession before a priest, because this was the practice of the day and of the religious communities to which several of the mystics belonged. Nonetheless, Hilton explicitly states that confession can be a private act of contrition before God (in Chapter 17 of *Mixed Life*), Margery Kempe describes such private confession (in Chapter 5 of *The Book of Margery Kempe*), and Richard Rolle provides an example (in Chapter 16 of *The Fire of Love*), and is soon soaring heavenwards:

> When a man, devout and poor, worries over his sin, he can pray (if he so desires) like this: Jesus Christ, my Lord and God, take pity on me; please consider my body's grievous yoke, which depresses my soul so quickly. My flesh is faltering under the burdens of life, and in consequence my spiritual strength is flagging too. For all that the world ever gave me I have spent, and now nothing remains but for you to lead my soul to that other world where my most precious treasure, where my real and lasting wealth abides ... For truly my treasure is you, yourself.

The first degree of prayer

The 'first degree of prayer' was what followed confession for Hilton, who writes in Book 1 of *The Scale of Perfection*: 'You are to understand that there are three kinds of prayer. The first is spoken prayer.'

He took it for granted that the vocal, daily, recited, formal prayers of the Church were a part of his reader's life. Admittedly, most of the mystics were themselves members of religious orders where set prayers were an obligation. *The Ancrene Riwle* devotes so much space to this that it is difficult to see how the anchoresses had time to eat, never mind make lace – one of their edifying pastimes! We cannot match such diligence, but Hilton suggests in Chapter 29 of *Mixed Life* that it is possible to focus on saying 'thy *Pater Noster*, or thine *Ave*, or else thy *Matins*, or else for to read upon thy Psalter. For that is evermore a secure standard that will not fail: Whoso may cleave thereto, he shall not err.' Such prayers were 'the first degree' because they were the foundation for all other forms of prayer. The mystics believed that formal, spoken prayers were the best forms of prayer for a person beginning a spiritual life, acting as 'a firm staff to support him'.

We have to start somewhere. Prayers gleaned from Scripture, or honed by centuries of faithful people at worship, give us a language with which to begin. We learn to speak, read and write initially by imitation. Only later do we find our own words. The same is true of learning to pray and of exploring new ways of praying. We borrow other people's prayers to equip us with the tools that then enable us to discover our own voice in prayer.

Furthermore, someone else's written prayers can often express things we cannot ourselves find the words for. In Book 1 of *The Scale of Perfection* Hilton explains that such prayers guard against the danger that

> in the quiet of their meditation they imagine and think of spiritual things according to their own wit ... Therefore through their indiscretion they often overstrain their wits and break the powers of their body, and so fall into fantasies and singular inventions, or into manifest errors ... If they only knew how little they feel in comparison with what God gives ... they would be ashamed.

The habit of formal, spoken prayers can also be a lifeline at times when prayer is hard, or when we do not want to pray. Richard Rolle writes in Chapter 10 of *The Fire of Love*:

> Should your prized facility of prayer or meditation desert you and you cannot raise your mind to joyful and holy contemplation or sing as you once did, you are not on that account to give up your reading or praying or whatever other useful thing you do, be it outward or inward, lest you degenerate into sloth.

The English mystics also help us to reclaim our memory here. We tend to read our formal prayers out of books and to assume that most other people can too. The mystics lived in an era before the printing press was invented. There were few books and fewer people able to read them. They therefore assumed that set prayers would be recited from memory. Searching within oneself for the words must have made the prayers more vital than chanting them out of a book.

In spite of increased literacy, the majority in our society belongs to what has been dubbed the 'non-book culture'. A minority buys books and reads them. Our churches have a responsibility to teach people a few memorable prayers that can be learned by heart and carried anywhere (such as the Lord's Prayer). If we do not do this, the whole language of prayer from which could spring the individual's own prayer and spiritual life will literally be a closed book. We will risk depriving people of all spiritual resources.[4]

The second degree of prayer

The 'second degree of prayer' went a step further. Formal, spoken prayers need not be boring. Set prayers allow us to search the heights and depths of written prayers, whether scriptural, liturgical, or other people's wisdom. They are a fuel which sustains our fire of devotion, as Hilton notes in Chapter 32 of *The Scale of Perfection*: 'Nourish the fire of love in [your] heart with holy psalms, pure thoughts, fervent desires, so that it never goes out.' They are a springboard to 'the second degree of prayer'. For Hilton this 'is spoken, but without any particular set words, and this is when a man or a woman feels the grace of devotion by the gift of God, and in his devotion speaks to him as if he were bodily in his presence.'

Christians today often value such extempore prayer as a 'first degree'. There is nothing wrong in that. The empty recitation of meaningless words is frowned upon in the Scriptures (see Matthew 6:5-8). Whether in our own words or someone else's, what is vital is our attitude when we pray. Rolle wrote in Chapter 7 of his *Form of Living*:

> Don't be concerned about how much you are reciting, but rather how well, so that the love of your heart may always be directed upward, and your thought on what you are saying, as far as you are able.

Extempore prayer is triggered and enriched by formal, written or remembered prayer.

The third degree of prayer

The 'third degree of prayer' is wordless adoration. Richard Rolle writes in Chapter 15 of *The Fire of Love*:

> I was sitting in that same chapel, and repeating as best I could the night-psalms before I went to supper ... In my prayer I was reaching out to heaven with heartfelt longing when I became aware, in a way I cannot explain, of a symphony of song, and in myself I sensed a corresponding harmony at once wholly delectable and heavenly, which persisted in my mind.

It is difficult for us with our twenty-first-century, activist lifestyles to see the point of this kind of silent adoration. Surely reciting the Lord's Prayer or the psalms and adding our own intercessions or words of praise is enough? Should we not be out there, active, doing something? Yet across the centuries the *Epistle of Privy Counsel* tells us:

> Your wayward curiosity can find nothing solid to hold on to in a happening of this sort, and so it grumbles and tells you to stop doing it and do something 'useful' in the curious way people understand it – for it seems to these that what you are doing is not at all important: they do not know the first thing about it!

The author of *The Cloud of Unknowing* writes:

> And though all your bodily faculties can find there nothing to feed on because they think that what you are doing is nothing, carry on, then, with that nothing, as long as you are doing it for God's love. Do not leave off, but press on earnestly in that nothing with an alert desire in your will to have God ... Prayer in itself is nothing but a devout reaching out directly to God, in order to attain the good and to do away with evil.

We are summoned to love God with mind and heart, strength and soul. Sometimes this will take the form of Bible study, sometimes

singing his praises, sometimes loving our neighbour, but sometimes love goes beyond words. The English mystics often use the
image of the Christian soul united to her bridegroom, Christ. Just
as in a human relationship words are not always the best way to
express our love, so it is with this 'marriage' for which we were
created. Margery Kempe found that all the wise words in Rolle
and Hilton did not express her experience of God. The living God
exceeds description, and our relationship with him will not always
need words.

Wordless adoration is perhaps the closest we come to 'praying
continually' (see 1 Thessalonians 5:17; Hebrews 13:15). Obviously
it is not possible to focus our thoughts on God every waking
second. We read in Chapter 41 of *The Cloud of Unknowing*:

> I do not say that you should persevere in it [i.e. contem-
> plation] with the same vigour; for that is not possible.
> Sometimes sickness or other disorders of body or soul,
> and many other necessities of nature, will greatly hinder
> you ... But I do say that you should always be either
> doing it or preparing for it; that is to say either actually or
> in intention.

The mystics understood 'pray continually' to mean that through
regular and deliberate contemplative devotion we would develop a
habit of desiring God. Contemplative prayer enables us to adopt
an attitude that is pointing continually in God's direction.

'THE READING OF HOLY WRIT'

Contemplative prayer is not divorced from our whole pattern
of prayer. Neither is it the emptying of one's mind. The English
mystics do not expect our contemplation to start with a blank sheet.
Reading and studying Scripture is part of the pattern of prayer.

Cyprian, the third-century Bishop of Carthage, wrote, 'In
prayer you speak to God, in reading God speaks to you.' Such scriptural conversation was the source of the continual awareness of God
for which the mystics aimed. Something carefully read and prayed
will pop up throughout the day. The author of *The Cloud* wrote:

> There are certain preparatory exercises which should
> occupy the attention of the contemplative apprentice: the

lesson, the meditation and the petition. They may be called, for better understanding, reading, reflecting and praying.

This will be familiar to some as the 'Lectio Divina',[5] that is, reading, meditation and prayer, leading towards contemplation. It is no ordinary reading. First the subject matter is prescribed – the Scriptures, and possibly other devotional works – then the manner of reading. It is to be slow and attentive, not searching for information from the passage but listening for God's voice speaking from it.

Such meditation is more than merely reflecting quietly and prayerfully on the passage. It may include reading several times, allowing words and phrases to speak to us. It may mean imaginatively entering a biblical scene (Margery Kempe frequently reports her somewhat fanciful imaginings). Or a verse or phrase is consciously repeated, carried about throughout the day. Prayer (petition, thanksgiving, praise) grows from such reflections as a response to what we have 'heard' in the text.

Faced with the whole Bible, it can be difficult to decide where to begin. In *Mixed Life* Hilton suggested a series of subjects for meditation – the passion of Jesus, or his life on earth and his humanity. The lives of saints, especially the saints of the Scriptures (i.e. Peter, Paul and various Marys), could also be an inspiration. They were to aid contemplation only in so far as they help to focus on the divinity of Christ, and thence direct our thoughts to God.

We might equally choose a passage from our daily Bible reading notes, or something in our mind from a Sunday sermon. God will already be at work in our choice, as Hilton notes in Book 2 of *The Scale of Perfection*:

> The spiritual presence of Jesus opens the understanding of his lover who burns in desire for him, and by the ministry of angels brings to his mind the words and the insights of holy Scripture, unsought and unconsidered, one after another, and readily expounds them, however hard or secret they may be.

These 'preparatory exercises' do not automatically lead to contemplation in the technical sense. They are our human activities directed towards God. True contemplation is only in God's gift. It can never be attained by sheer effort, or by obedience to patterns and techniques, or by silence, reading and meditation. In Chapter 27 of *Mixed Life* Hilton writes, 'By God's grace you will transform a duty into a delight.'

Each of us is a unique individual, and our Creator will deal with us each in our own way. Prayer is not to be a straitjacket, as Hilton says earlier in *Mixed Life*:

> Not that thou shalt use the same form always that I say, but that thou should have thereby … some warning and wissing [i.e. instruction, direction] for to rule thee in thy occupation … Which are best for thee can I not say.

The mystics' instructions are to form a framework from which the individual can explore his or her own relationship with God.

MYSTICISM REVISITED

We have discovered the English mystics to be deeply committed Christian people. They received God's grace and gifts and attempted to share these with their neighbour. They still show, through their writings, the desire for their fellow Christians to join them on their contemplative journey. Their insight can be as fresh and vital today as it was over 600 years ago.

The English mystics have taught us that prayer is not primarily intercession. It is meeting with God on our journey through and towards his kingdom, and learning to align ourselves in prayer with God's wants and wishes for his world. Archbishop Michael Ramsey, who was much influenced by the English mystics, wrote that contemplative prayer 'was not only a quest for the inner peace of God but an exposure to the love of God with intercessory outreach'.[6]

The mystics have shown us that contemplative prayer does not divorce the Christian from the world, and it is not performed in a vacuum. Contemplation has a place *only* within a context of prayer, Bible study and love of God and our neighbour. It is a context which we cannot achieve in total seclusion. Times of solitude and silence are but a part of our wider involvement in the worshipping community, the Church.

Some are called to devote themselves to contemplative prayer and join appropriate religious communities. Most of us are called to pray as we can, not as we cannot – to direct our lives towards

God in contemplation as far as we are able. There will be times of difficulty and darkness as we seek to probe the mystery that is God, but the person of Jesus Christ is our focus and the glorious dawn of his resurrected presence is our encouragement in our endeavours.

The mystical experience

Contemplation may grow into a vivid experience of God's nearness, an intense awareness of God and our relationship with him. It is a God-given insight which, if anything, is what might be termed the 'mystical experience'. Michael Ramsey, however, warns:

> The effect of the experience . . . is not to cause a person to long to have the experience again but to serve God and to do his will. Those who have had mystic experience will not want to tell everyone about it; they will have a longing to serve God in daily life, for his *will* is our peace.[7]

Hilton also warned his reader in *Mixed Life* not to attempt to grasp the moment of meditative union so much that other duties suffered. Nor are we to be kept from sleep, food or other duty by our meditation – prayer is not to become an excuse for inaction. We are not to seek after the experience or to be discouraged if it does not come. The *Epistle of Privy Counsel* advises:

> Though God does sometimes withdraw this sense of sweetness, these enthusiastic feelings and these burning desires, he never on that account withdraws his grace from his chosen.

The fact that we pray is sufficient witness to our wanting to pray. The final words should belong to the English mystics:

> Lord, you say that no man shall come to you without you, nor shall any man be drawn to you unless you draw him. And therefore, Lord, if there be any man who is not drawn, I pray you draw him to you. You have drawn me, Lord, and I never deserved to be drawn, but according to your great mercy you have drawn me.
>
> THE BOOK OF MARGERY KEMPE, BOOK 2, CHAPTER 10

When you are about to pray, make your intention and your will at the beginning as complete and as pure toward God as you can, briefly in your mind, and then begin and do as you can. And however badly you are hindered in your first resolve, do not be too fearful or angry with yourself, or impatient against God for not giving you that savour and spiritual sweetness with devotion which (as it seems to you) he gives to other creatures. Instead, see by it your own weakness and bear it easily, holding your prayer in your own sight (simple as it is) with humbleness of heart, also trusting confidently in the mercy of our Lord that he will make it good – more than you know or feel; and if you do so, all shall be well.

SCALE OF PERFECTION, BOOK 1, CHAPTER 33

Do not hang back then, but labour in it until you experience the desire. For when you first begin to undertake it, all that you find is a darkness, a sort of cloud of unknowing; you cannot tell what it is, except that you experience in your will a simple reaching out to God.

THE CLOUD OF UNKNOWING, CHAPTER 3

So I can declare that contemplation is a wonderful enjoying of the love of God, and this joy is [a way of] worshipping God which cannot be described. And that amazing worship happens within the soul, and because of the overflowing joy and sweetness, it rises up to the mouth, so that the heart and voice combine in unison, and the body and soul rejoice in the living God.

A FORM OF LIVING, CHAPTER 12

FURTHER READING

R. Allen (ed.), *The English Writings* (SPCK)

Anon., ed. M. B. Salu, *The Ancrene Riwle* (Exeter)

Anon., ed. J. Walsh, *The Cloud of Unknowing* (Paulist Press)

S. Bhattacharji, *God is an Earthquake: The Spirituality of Margery Kempe* (Darton, Longman and Todd)

T. Hall, *Too Deep for Words* (Paulist Press)

Walter Hilton, eds. J. P. H. Clark and R. Dorwood, *The Scale of Perfection* (Paulist Press)

D. Jones (ed.), *The Minor Works of Walter Hilton* (Burns, Oates and Washbourne)

Margery Kempe, ed. B. A. Windeatt, *The Book of Margery Kempe* (Penguin)

D. Knowles, *The English Mystical Tradition* (Burns and Oates)

Julian of Norwich, ed. Clifton Wolters, *Revelations of Divine Love* (Penguin)

T. Park, *The English Mystics: An Anthology* (SPCK)

G. Pigott, *Prayers to Remember* (Grove Books)

Michael Ramsey, *Canterbury Pilgrim* (SPCK); *Be Still and Know* (Fount)

J. Robertson, *Praying with the English Mystics* (Triangle)

Richard Rolle, ed. Clifton Wolters, *The Fire of Love* (Penguin)

Clifton Wolters (ed.), *The Cloud of the Unknowing and Other Works* (Penguin)

Notes

1 See the following chapter, for example, Adrian Daffern, *The Cross and Julian of Norwich* (Grove Spirituality Series 46, 1993), and references in T. Park, *The English Mystics: An Anthology* (SPCK, 1998).

2 S. Bhattacharji, *God is an Earthquake* (Darton, Longman and Todd, 1997), p. xviii.

3 Park, *The English Mystics*, p. 6.

4 See G. Pigott, *Prayers to Remember* (Grove Spirituality Series 52, 1995).

5 For a fuller treatment, see T. Hall, *Too Deep for Words* (Paulist Press, 1991), pp. 36ff.

6 Michael Ramsey, *Be Still and Know* (Fount, 1982), p. 13.

7 Michael Ramsey, *Canterbury Pilgrim* (SPCK, 1974), pp. 59-60.

THE CROSS AND
JULIAN OF NORWICH

Adrian Daffern

Julian of Norwich has been described as the most popular of the English mystics, and it is not hard to see why. Julian's interpretation of her experiences into simple, everyday language while using such vivid and striking images has won her a wide and appreciative following. Many Christians have warmed to her portrayal of a God who shows characteristics of both Mother and Father, a God who is deeply in love with his creation, a God of hope who reassures his people that 'all shall be well, and all shall be well, and all manner of thing shall be well'. These truths about God that Julian illuminates through her infectious and moving writings have an obvious appeal. They reflect a God of love, a God who seeks to save, not to judge, his people.

Yet Julian is more than an attractive spiritual writer. She is an important theologian, and her theology is rooted in her reflections on the visions which she received in the late spring of 1373. These visions, mostly of the passion of Christ, are striking in many ways, not least because they were received as a result of Julian's earnest prayer that God might grant her three gifts: first, to have a greater understanding of the passion of Christ; second, to suffer to the point of dying while still a young woman; third, to receive three wounds from God.

It was while she suffered *in extremis* that a priest held a crucifix before her eyes and recommended that she gaze upon it as she lived her last few moments. It was as she did this that she began to receive her 'shewings'. She reflected on these over many years before producing the longer version of her account of these visions, which not only gives a lucid description of what she saw and heard, but is full of theological insight that is refreshingly free from technical language and speaks simply and clearly of the love of God shown supremely in the death of Christ on the cross.

THE LESSON OF LOVE

Julian is a model for us to look to in our Christian lives today. Very few of us will be able to follow her vocation exactly and lead the solitary life as part of our discipleship, but an increasing number of people continue to benefit from silence and meditation as part of their life of prayer. In an increasingly noisy and demanding world, Julian's profound and approachable writing provides an oasis of peace and prayerfulness, and leads us to be still. In silence, we are able simply to rest in God's presence for a while, as Julian did, and know his acceptance, not condemnation; his love, not his anger.

Julian presents us with a challenge, too – a challenge to remain faithful to Christ despite the evil and malice which we find in the world. It is through suffering that Julian experiences a God of vulnerable love, and we are invited to do the same, not unquestioningly or without integrity, but faithfully. In our faithfulness to God, and in our compassion for our neighbours, we are led to prayer and to lives of love in action.

JULIAN IN CONTEXT

Julian was living at a time when mystical thought and writing was flourishing in Northern Europe. In England, this writing stemmed largely from experience of the solitary life. Alongside Julian, there are three distinctive contributors to the particular spirituality of this period.

The first of these is Richard Rolle, a Yorkshireman who died in 1349. His most famous work, *The Fire of Love*, was translated from Latin into English in the fifteenth century. Rolle was extremely popular in England right up to the Reformation. The second is the anonymous author of *The Cloud of Unknowing*. This is a work of far greater sophistication than Rolle's output, and its author shares many similarities with Julian, such as the belief that the highest forms of mystical experience are available to ordinary people as a gift from God. The third is Walter Hilton, about whom little is known, although his *Scale of Perfection* shows him to be a man of considerable education. These three are explored in greater depth in Chapter 9.

While there are considerable similarities between Julian and other English mystical writers of the period, Julian remains distinctive, not least because of her vigour, down-to-earth imagery and turn of phrase. This is particularly true in her understanding of the passion of Christ, which is central to her writings and her understanding of God and God's dealings with his creation. In this chapter we will examine Julian's understanding of the cross and the place it holds in her spirituality and theological thought. To do this, it is necessary to learn something of Julian, her background and life as a 'recluse atte Norwyche', the social and ecclesiastical context of her day and, of course, the nature of the visions which she received.

JULIAN'S LIFE

We know very little of Julian's life; indeed, we do not even know her name (the name Julian is taken from the dedication of the church to which her anchorhold was attached). Apart from the information which we can glean from her own writings, there is a reference to her in a book by Margery Kempe,[1] and some mention of her as a beneficiary of some wills of the period.[2] We know that she was probably born in late 1342 or early 1343, and that at some stage she took the decision to become an anchoress.

An anchoress (or an anchorite, if male) was someone who led a life of prayer and sacrifice completely shut off from the world (the word comes from the Greek *anchoreo*, 'I withdraw'). Such recluses lived in an anchorhold which was usually attached to a church, where their everyday needs were met by one or more domestic servants. The anchorhold was probably not the small, uncomfortable cell often conceived by popular imagination, and could well have been several small rooms with some land attached. The life led by the anchoress was one of rigorous and disciplined daily prayer, following a similar pattern to that of a monastery or convent with seven or more offices a day. When an anchoress took possession of the anchorhold there was a complicated ceremony, involving the celebration of the mass coupled with many rites that were similar or identical to those of the burial services of the church. This was because the anchoress, from the moment of her entry into the anchorhold, was 'dead to the world'. The anchorhold would be sealed up at the outside, just as Christ was sealed in his tomb. There could be no release from the anchorhold until death, on pain of excommunication. We can only guess at the extent of the psychological impact of such a ceremony on the anchoress.[3]

The solitary life

From our twenty-first-century perspective, the solitary life seems rather harsh, even impossible, although in the Middle Ages it was very popular, being deeply rooted in the eremitical traditions of the Desert Fathers of the fourth century. Most large towns could boast a 'solitary', and many rules and regulations for the solitary life were produced. Indeed, many of the great spiritual writings of the time were written either by or for hermits and anchorites. One of the most famous of these rules was the *Ancrene Riwle*, which was written anonymously sometime in the thirteenth century. It stands out from some of the earlier rules for anchorites because it concentrates on the inner life of prayer rather than on the external affairs of solitary life, such as arrangements about food and clothing. The *Ancrene Riwle* gives us some indication of what the daily pattern of solitary life was like, including extremely detailed instructions on daily prayer.

Nonetheless, the life of the anchoress was not one of total isolation from the world around her. She would hear gossip and news from her domestic servants (although many of the rules advised that such talk should not be allowed to interfere with the daily life of prayer). More importantly, the anchoress would have a 'window onto the world' to which people would come seeking advice and spiritual counsel. Many anchoresses built up formidable reputations for their counselling skills – but this was not their chief concern. The anchoress was called to do the following:

Embrace the whole world with the arms of your love and in that act at once consider and congratulate the good, contemplate and mourn over the wicked. In that act look upon the afflicted and the oppressed and feel compassion for them ... In your love take them all to your heart, weep over them, offer your prayers for them.[4]

The anchoress was called to enter deep into the heart of God, and only as one who was close to the heart of God could the anchoress exercise a compassionate and pastoral counselling ministry. People would come to the anchoress for counsel precisely because they knew that they were talking to someone who had the ability to communicate the peace and presence of God.

It is not surprising that the anchoress should be such a popular consultant when the affairs of Church and State outside the anchorhold were in such turmoil. Julian's own bishop, Henry Despenser, was feared for his aggression and autocratic style; in the aftermath of riots in Norwich at the time of the Peasants' Revolt, the bishop had many tortured and executed. This was at a time when the population of England was feeling vulnerable and insecure. The events of 1369 had been preceded by the calamitous plague known as the Black Death, which began in the south of England in 1348, spread quickly, and reduced the population of the country by dramatic proportions. Julian had much time to contemplate the repercussions of such catastrophic events and, while there is no explicit mention of them in her writings, it would be foolish to imagine that her spirituality and theology were not affected by them.[5]

We can say very little further about the life of Julian for certain, although many people have different ideas about her life before she became an anchoress. The date of her death is unknown; some place it as late as 1429, when Julian would have been 87 years old. We can be sure, however, that Julian ended her days within the anchorhold at Norwich.

JULIAN'S VISIONS

Julian of Norwich received her 'shewings' as she lay ill, apparently at the point of death, on 8 May 1373. Nearly all the visions which she received were concerned with the passion of Christ, and all were received while she gazed at her crucifix. With startling reality, she saw the full horror of the effects of the crucifixion of Jesus. In Chapter 4 of *Revelations of Divine Love* she writes:

> And at once I saw the red blood trickling down from under the garland, hot, fresh, and plentiful, just as it did at the time of his passion when the crown of thorns was pressed on to the blessed head of God and Man, who suffered for me. And I had a strong, deep, conviction that it was he himself and none other that showed me this vision.

It was this vision that began the series of 16 'shewings' that were to be revealed to Julian. They followed one another, the final vision appearing the following night when her feeling of illness returned. It is impossible to do justice to the visions by summarizing them, for to do that would inevitably mean losing the freshness and intensity of Julian's own account. Nonetheless, it is worth briefly outlining what they were.

The shewings

The first two visions are of Christ's passion, the crowning with thorns and the discolouring of his face. The third vision is of the Godhead concentrated in a single point, before moving on to two more visions of the passion, the flogging of Christ's body and the victory over Satan brought about by the crucifixion of Jesus. The sixth vision is one of God's servants being rewarded in heaven, while the seventh is of the 'recurring experience of delight and depression' that is constantly experienced in the spiritual life. The eighth vision is a graphic illustration of the suffering and death of Jesus. The ninth vision follows on from this, and recounts the 'pleasure that the Blessed Trinity has in the grievous passion of Christ'. The tenth vision is of the heart of Christ riven in two, with its simple message of 'see how I have loved you'. The eleventh is a vision of Mary, and the twelfth is a vision of Christ's glory, with Christ proclaiming, 'It is I; I whom you long for, I whom you delight in.' The thirteenth is a vision of the value of God's creation and speaks much of Julian's understanding of the place of sin and suffering. The fourteenth vision concerns prayer, especially the place of Jesus as the foundation of Christian prayer. The fifteenth vision speaks of the pain we feel in this life because of our absence from the full and glorious presence of God, but looks to heaven where we shall know that presence to the full. The final vision, the sixteenth, acts as a conclusion, referring back to Julian's earlier visions, and looking forward to the glory of the Triune God and the victory over 'the Fiend' that we have because of God's love.

Bodily sight and spiritual sight

There are many interesting features concerning the visions which Julian received. One of these is the way Julian herself makes distinctions between the 'sight' with which she saw specific aspects of certain visions. For example, in the eleventh revelation Jesus asks Julian if she wishes to see his mother. Julian replies that she would indeed like to see Mary, and then she tells us, in Chapter 25 of *Revelations of Divine Love*, 'I thought I was going to see her in person. But I did not see her in this way. Jesus in that word, gave me a spiritual sight of her.'

Julian evidently kept a clear distinction between the visions that she actually saw with her 'bodily sight' and the things that she saw in her imagination. Indeed, at the end of her description of the first revelation in Chapter 9, she claims that she received the vision in three different ways, 'in actual vision, in imaginative understanding, and in spiritual sight'. This is important to us because it reinforces the power and reality of the visions which she claims to have seen in 'bodily sight'.

Others have written on the nature of Julian's sickness and the nature of the visions which she received, and we need not go into that here.[6] In preparing to examine Julian's perception of the cross of Christ and its place in her spirituality, however, we need to be assured that Julian herself was convinced that the visions which she received were most certainly from God, and not the distorted imaginings of a sick woman. Indeed, Julian had difficulty in coming to terms with the supernatural nature of the revelations which had been given to her. When visited by a priest after she had made some recovery from her illness, she commented that she had 'raved that day', although she later came to repent of those doubts. There can be no doubt that Julian, after many years of reflection and, significantly, no further revelations (at least, no further revelations that we are aware of), was convinced that her 'shewings' were God-given. Furthermore, Julian sees that revelations are worth nothing in themselves except that they speak of God's love, and it is this love of God shown in the life of the Church that is her main concern. She is emphatic that her revelations are to be shared and understood by all her fellow Christians, and that they do not make her out to be more important or special than she is. She writes in Chapter 9:

> The fact that I have had this revelation does not mean that I am good. I am good only in so far as I love God the better: if you love God more than I do then you are by that much better than I ... When I look at myself in particular I am obviously of no account, but by and large I am hopeful, for I am united in love with all my fellow Christians.

Such a statement gives authenticity to Julian's writings and the teaching that she gives in them. Julian's motivation for sharing the experience of her visions is wholly selfless; her sole concern is that her fellow Christians might have a greater understanding of the nature of the love of God. It is surely significant that Julian can identify so readily with her fellow Christians from a position of solitary living. We might imagine an anchoress becoming quite preoccupied with her own spiritual journey and spiritual needs. Not so with Julian: her solitary lifestyle merely intensifies her desire to ally herself with all Christian people and to place her own experiences of God alongside theirs.

Holy Church

The holiness which shines through Julian's writing stands in stark contrast to the brutality of the church in Norwich at that time. She does not, however, seek to be at odds with the Church; on the contrary, she sets herself firmly within it – the phrase 'as Holy Church teaches' recurs throughout her writings. Grace Jantzen comments:

> The church is the Body of Christ in whom we are grounded: to do violence to the church would in Julian's thinking be to do violence to ourselves ... Julian's account of the church, therefore, is integral to her total theological understanding: it is not token loyalty to avoid a heresy hunt.[7]

The absence of any kind of 'tokenism' in Julian's writings is a further strand in the rich tapestry of Julian's nature that we see evolve. She is extraordinarily humble, and stands in great contrast to some of her mystical contemporaries who regarded themselves as particularly special in God's eyes because of the understanding of him that they had received. Yet what is truly special about Julian is her burning desire for others to deepen their faith in the reality of God, a reality which Julian strives to communicate throughout her writing.

Julian's visions of the passion of Christ are stunning in their realism, and it is hardly surprising that it is the supreme sacrifice of Christ on the cross that should dominate her spirituality and permeate everything she has to say about the nature of the love of God. There are many striking themes in Julian's understanding of the passion, and it is by a thematic approach that we shall move on to look at the place of the cross in Julian's spirituality and the inevitable effect that it has on her theology.

JULIAN'S UNDERSTANDING OF THE CROSS

The first thing we need to consider is that the visions of the cross she received came as an answer to her own prayer, repeated in Chapter 2 of *Revelations of Divine Love*:

> ... to be actually there with Mary Magdalene and the others who loved him, and with my own eyes to see and know more of the physical suffering of our Saviour ... I would be one of them and suffer with him.

Even before she had received any visions, she had a great desire to suffer with those who stood at the foot of the cross, and even to share in the sufferings of Jesus himself. Julian understood that the cross was the ultimate revelation of the love of God, as did many other Christian thinkers and mystics of her time, but what is different about Julian is the way that she approaches the cross.

> The *Revelations* are not, like every other devotional piece of the time, a description of the Crucified written to invoke pity and repentance; they are not in the tradition of the Stabat Mater; they are serious theology of the love that is God.[8]

It is therefore impossible (and it would be wrong to attempt) to divorce Julian's spiritual understanding and her theological understanding, for the two are wholly integrated in a single systematic approach. As we progress we shall see that, when Julian gives us an account of her spiritual understanding of the cross, such as its being a revelation of the humility of God, she is also making a theological statement.

The humility of God

Christians have always been struck by the vulnerability and suffering of the cross, particularly as it was the result of hatred engendered because of the ministry of Jesus. Julian has a true understanding of the cross as a means of revelation of God's essential nature – a nature of sacrificial love and identification of the Creator with that which he has created. In Chapter 7 she writes:

> Surely there can be no greater joy – at least as I see it – than that he, the most supreme, mighty, noble, and worthy of all, should also be the most lowly, humble, friendly and considerate.

This might seem to be such an obvious feature of Christian belief that it is hardly worth mentioning, but it is the humility of God, shown through the death of Jesus on the cross, that is central to Julian's theological scheme. Julian believes that it is the fact that the death of Jesus was such an expensive price to be paid that makes the gift of God's love worth receiving. She argues that if the love of God was, as it were, handed to us on a plate, it would be devalued and not truly representative of its full worth. God had given her an analogy to make clear what this revelation meant, as she explains in Chapter 7:

> The poor man will think something like this, 'What greater honour or pleasure could my noble Lord confer on me than to show a simple man like me such marvellous friendliness? Indeed, it gives much more pleasure than would the greatest gifts if they were bestowed condescendingly.'

Here Julian is making a profound theological statement concerning the dealings between God and man. God is wholly and inexorably committed to his creation because of his nature, which is love – but this is not to say that God exercises an absolute control over our everyday dealings. Julian is clear that it is God's will that all people should come to know him, but this can only be so when people respond through faith to the love which God has shown them. As Julian herself puts it in Chapter 7:

> The revelation shows that it all depends on faith, no more and no less; for as we can see from our Lord's teaching on the same matter, it is faith that counts at the last.

Julian's argument is that the humility of God shown by the suffering and death of Jesus on the cross enables the believer to make the leap of faith, just as the spectacle of the cross brought the centurion to faith. If it were not for the humility of God, we would never have known the revelation of Jesus as God-made-man. Julian refers to this aspect of God's nature as 'unpretentious and considerate', and she is not on her own in this understanding of the nature of God. The author of *The Cloud of Unknowing*, while differing essentially from Julian in respect of the theology of God's revelation of himself to the world, sees 'perfect' humility as caused by God, and because of this he sees the essential nature of God as being this 'perfect' humility. It is, he believes, attainable by those who come to a true knowledge of God, which he perceives to be found by coming to a true knowledge of oneself:

> Two things cause humility. One is the degradation, wretchedness, and weakness of man to which by sin he has fallen: he ought to be aware of this, partially at any rate, all the time he lives, however holy he may be. The other is the superabundant love and worth of God in himself.[9]

Elizabeth Ruth Obbard suggests that Julian regards the primary expression of humility as being found in the figure of Mary, Jesus' mother.[10] While Mary is important to Julian, it is actually the suffering and death of Jesus that is the primary expression of humility, and it is because of that 'divine' humility that we are able to receive the love of God.

Matter for lasting joy

The realization that the humility of God leads to joy and to rejoicing in our salvation is another vital aspect of Julian's understanding of the cross. We have already read that Julian differs from devotional writers of her day in her approach to the cross. This is largely due to the fact that Julian sees the passion of Christ as cause for rejoicing, not because of Jesus' suffering and death but because of what that suffering and death has brought about, which is the end of death and atonement for humankind with God. More than that, of course, the cross reveals the love of God in all its glory, and that is cause for great rejoicing. The ability to find joy in God stems from Julian's understanding of the love of God that the cross reveals. Just as Christians are called to enter into the knowledge of the love of God, so they are called to enter into the joy that such a knowledge inevitably brings. She writes in Chapter 53:

> The result is that we now have both matter for mourning –
> for sin is the cause of Christ's sufferings – and matter for
> lasting joy – for his unending love made him suffer.

It is important to establish here that the actuality of the suffering and death of Jesus is something that causes Julian great pain, and because of the extraordinarily vivid nature of her visions she participates in that pain to a very great and real extent. When we talk of the joy that stems from the passion of Christ, it is specifically about the joy that we should feel because of the love of God shown to us in the death of Jesus on the cross.

There is, however, something more significant even than this. Just as we can love God because he has loved us, so we can delight in God because he has delighted in us. Grace Jantzen puts it like this:

> God invites our rejoicing; he wants us to be happy, not
> just in the sense of putting a good face on carefully hidden pain, but in the far deeper sense of letting him resolve
> the pain, so that our joy is deep and real.[11]

Here Jantzen is uniting the joy which we feel in God with the desire of God for us to be healed. The ultimate place of healing is the cross, where the divisions which kept humankind and God at a distance were broken down for ever. It is in this knowledge that Julian can write such a joyful book, even though it centres so greatly on the passion of Christ. Julian does not seek to avoid the question of the reality of sin and suffering; on the contrary, she has a very clear and developed approach to the problem. But she has an equally realistic approach to the fact that it is because of the death of Jesus that joy may be found in God and in our relationship with him. Julian understands the salvation won for us by Jesus' suffering and death as a present reality involving human wholeness and healing, not just as a means of entering into eternal life. The salvation offered to the Church in Christ is a means for present joy, and it is this present joy which is so characteristic of Julian's writings.

> To know Christ, therefore, is to know joy ... Julian sees great significance in human joy; as a reflection of our relationship to the Trinity we are meant to be full of joy and to know God in his love, though, in fact, we can never appreciate the full extent of God's love for us.[12]

Julian's understanding of Christian joy is closely tied to her understanding of the Trinity, and it is to this we now turn.

The joy of the blessed Trinity

In approaching the trinitarian basis of the faith, Christians tend to divide the creating, redeeming and animating actions of God between the three Persons of the Trinity. This is nowhere better expressed than in the Creed (introduced in the Anglican *Alternative Service Book* and included in *Common Worship*), where we affirm our faith in 'God the Father who made the world, God the Son who redeemed mankind, and God the Holy Spirit who gives life to the people of God'. Nonetheless, while it is unlikely that any Christian is going to disagree with it, this statement of faith, as it stands, does not tell the whole story. For it is not just God the Son who suffers on the cross, but the whole Godhead; not just God the Father who creates, but the whole Godhead. Western Christians, on the whole, have considerable difficulties in coming to terms with the theological subtleties of trinitarian belief, and they can hardly be blamed for that. It is interesting to note that Julian had no such difficulties, and that it is the cross which is a focal point for her trinitarian faith. So it is that in the very first of her revelations of the passion of Christ, described in Chapter 4 of *Revelations*, she is able to say:

For the Trinity is God, and God the Trinity; the Trinity is our Maker and keeper, our eternal lover, joy and bliss – all through our Lord Jesus Christ. This was shown me in this first revelation, and, indeed, in them all; for where Jesus is spoken of, the blessed Trinity is always to be understood as I see it.

Julian's theology is Christocentric. In Christ, Julian sees the 'considerate' nature of God uniquely expressed, the miraculous union of 'God-and-humanity', the humility of God shown through the compassion of Jesus. Julian firmly believes that we see in Jesus the totality of God Incarnate, a truly Johannine understanding of the Christ in whom dwells the fullness of God. Julian believes that Jesus is the way to the Father, the truth about God, God himself. As such, Jesus does not just point the way to God, but reveals in himself everything that God is; and this being the case, Jesus does not merely point to God the Holy Trinity, but actually reveals and embodies God the Holy Trinity. In Chapter 58 she writes:

God the blessed Trinity is everlasting Being. Just as he is eternal, without beginning, so has his purpose been eternal, namely to make mankind. This fine nature was prepared in the first instance for his own Son, the Second Person. And when so he willed, with the concurrence of each Person of the Trinity, he made all of us at one and the same time.

From this we can see that the suffering and death of Jesus on the cross is not simply an act of God the Son in his suffering for us, or even an act of God the Father in allowing his only Son to be sacrificed for the sins of the world. The passion of Christ is an essentially trinitarian event, an expression of the total love of God. As Julian explains in Chapter 57:

For Christ means the Holy Trinity in whom our higher part is rooted and grounded; and he, the Second Person thereof, has taken our lower part, which had already been prepared for him ... For love he made mankind, and out of the same love he willed to become man.

There is nothing unorthodox in this; classic patristic theology speaks of *perichoresis*, a technical term which refers to the dynamism that exists within the Godhead. The Early Fathers were acutely aware that the nature of God is community, and that the saving acts of God were not to be perceived as actions of one or other Person of the Trinity, but of the entire Godhead acting in unity. Julian sees this very clearly; just as it is the Trinity which is bound up in the death of Jesus, so it is the Trinity that rejoices over the salvation brought about by the passion of Christ, and as such it is both the source and focus of our joy. She explains further in Chapter 23:

> As far as we can manage it, our delight in our salvation should be like Christ's. The whole Trinity was involved in the passion of Christ, giving us an abundance of virtue and grace by him, though only the Maiden's Son suffered. And because of this the whole Trinity rejoices eternally.

Thus it is clear how Julian's spirituality of the cross of Christ is inextricably interwoven with her theology of the Trinity.

'Love was his meaning'

Integral to Julian's theology and spirituality of the cross are the themes of love and compassion. We have already seen how Julian sees the love of God the Holy Trinity shown through the suffering and death of Christ, but we have not yet explored how she perceives the nature of that love.

When Julian talks of love, suffering is never far away; she understands the psychology of human emotion in the realms of joy and pain. What is important about Julian's spirituality is that she has an underlying optimism in her approach to God. Like the psalmist, she can readily believe that 'even the darkness is not dark to you; the night is as bright as the day, for darkness is as light to you' (Psalm 139:11-12 NRSV). Julian's optimism is not simplistic, but a true Christian hope grounded in an experience of God through faith. In Julian's understanding, the Christian should desire to be close to God, as God desires to be close to his creation. The whole point of the incarnation, as Julian perceives it, is that God should share in both the joy and the pain which are integral to human experience. The love of God, shown in the suffering and death of Jesus, is mediated to us because it is in our suffering and death that God, through Jesus, is participating. Julian writes in Chapter 18:

Here too I saw a close affinity between Christ and ourselves – at least, so I thought – for when he suffered, we suffered. All creatures capable of suffering pain suffered with him.

Just as God participates in our own sufferings, so the Christian is called to participate in God's sufferings, and this means coming to a relationship with the crucified Christ. It is by entering into the reality of the suffering of our Lord that we shall learn about his love, because it is in his suffering that the very nature of his love is to be found. This love is not the result of his suffering, but the cause of it. There is a beautiful passage in Chapter 22 of *Revelations* where Julian describes the extent of God's suffering love:

> If he [Christ] were to say that for love of me he would make a new heaven and a new earth, this would be a comparatively simple matter; something he could do everyday if he wanted, with no great effort. But for love of me to be willing to die times without number – beyond human capacity to compute – is, to my mind, the greatest gesture our Lord God could make to the soul of man.

Julian believes that this is the love for which Christians should strive. Indeed, she believes that it is only in striving for and gaining this love that the Christian is truly able to participate in God. Thus for Julian, the event of the passion of Christ speaks of the mutuality of the relationship between God and creation. As Christ suffers for us on the cross, so we are called to share in his suffering – but the difference in this relationship of mutual suffering is that it is God's will that he should suffer for us, and Julian sees this as cause for great rejoicing. She writes in Chapter 21:

> He suffers because it is his will and goodness to raise us even higher in bliss. In exchange for the little that we have to suffer here, we shall have the supreme unending knowledge of God which we should never have without it. The sharper our suffering with him on the cross, the greater our glory with him in his kingdom.

Julian accepts the inevitability of suffering in a relationship of love. She seems to say that it is only when we truly suffer with Christ – that is, when we are prepared to love to the extent that he loved – that we can have a true knowledge of the love of God. This is how Julian perceives the mystery of the passion of Christ. It was necessary for Christ to suffer because that was the only way his love would allow him to go, but the cross, while being the utmost expression of God's love for his people, was also necessary for us to be released from the bondage of sin and death. The rejoicing of the Holy Trinity in the cross of Christ is because of what that cross has meant for our salvation. When Julian recounts in Chapter 23 how God rejoices over the redemption of mankind, she tells us that 'he rejoices that by his passion he has bought us out of the eternal pain of hell'.

Julian understands that the cross is the pattern of Christian love – it shows us the depth of God's love and the measure of the love that we are called to show to the world. It also speaks of an enormous truth – that true love has no end. There can be no parameters, no starting or finishing posts, simply love. This is hard for the Christian to understand, and even harder to put into practice in the everyday Christian life. Julian knows this only too well, and tries to point out that we need to take the example of Christ and apply it to ourselves. The cross of Christ is the benchmark by which we need to measure all that we do and say in his name.

Realism and optimism

Julian is always a realist. Whether she is talking about prayer or sin, suffering or love, she speaks from the depth of human experience. Yet her realism does not defeat her optimism, and she is convinced that every Christian has the potential to live and love as Christ did. This hope is built on faith and, for Julian, is constantly fuelled by the vision of the cross of Christ which has been given to her. It is in this cross that we must put all our trust if we are to live our faith with any sincerity or value. The cross of Christ must be our centre, because it is there that we will find his love. Thus she writes in Chapter 40:

> For Christ himself is the foundation of all the laws by which Christians live, and he taught us to prefer good to evil. He himself exemplifies this love, and practices what he preaches. His will is that we should be entirely like him in our continuing love for ourselves and our fellow Christians.

Christ at the centre, Christ revealing the totality of God in the Holy Trinity, Christ revealing the true nature of the love of God – this is the consistent pattern at the heart of Julian's view of the relationship between God and humanity. Paul Molinari suggests that it demonstrates a progressive union of God and humanity throughout the *Revelations*. God has shown us all that we need to embark on a true relationship with him; our task is now to play our part by doing our utmost to become one with God.

> God is seen [by Julian] as the principal agent, the inspirer, the first to act (he is 'the Ground'). But man has to play his part by following the movement begun in him by God. That is to say, man has to unite his will to the will of God, so as to be 'fastened' to him and in perfect accord 'with him in all things'.[13]

Molinari is right when he speaks about this uniting of wills, but for Julian the truth of the matter is rather deeper than a clinical exercise. Julian's spirituality is full of emotion, and this is hardly surprising as it is a spirituality which has the suffering and death of Jesus as its core. So when we speak of uniting the will of humanity to the will of God, we have to know that Julian would see this in terms of a mutual relationship in suffering love. This is first because of the love that God has shown to us through the passion of Christ for our salvation, and second because of the suffering that is ours because of our humanity, a suffering which is redeemed as, in Christ, it becomes an integral part of what it means to truly love in Christian terms. At this point we may well be laying ourselves open to accusations of unrealism and attempting to cope with suffering by somehow making its centre external to ourselves. To that there are two responses.

First, Julian is too much of a realist. She is quite clear that there is much that she does not understand and much that no one will ever be able to understand. Yet at the heart of her spirituality lies a real event, a dramatic event, an event which speaks the truth about God. Basing her whole understanding on that event, she finds not an answer to suffering, but a clue as to what lies at its heart. The compassion of God for humankind enables him to enter into human experience, and thus we are given something of a revelation – that it is in loving that we will necessarily suffer, but that it is in suffering that we will inevitably find glory.

The pain which we bear, Julian says, is directly related to the reward, because it is through the pain that we develop the 'wounds' of contrition, compassion, and the longing for God without which we could never be receptive to the delights of his love.[14]

Second, Julian is too much of an optimist, in that she has an unshakable trust in God. Where there are holes in her understanding she has to accept them, setting them against the vision of God's love which she has received. It is because she is able to trust in the love of God that she faces the questions of human suffering and human loving so frankly and concisely, as she explains in Chapter 31:

> Thus our good Lord answered all the questions and doubts that I could produce. Most reassuringly he added, 'I may make everything all right; I am able to; I intend to, and I shall. You will see for yourself that every sort of thing will be all right.'

Julian's optimism is grounded in the cross. She portrays a God who has committed himself in a selfless way to the needs of his creation. For this she can be grateful, and because of this she can be free to love God in return. Thus it is in the cross of Christ that Julian finds the reality of the mutual relationship of suffering love that must exist between God and humankind if there is to be true theology, true spirituality and living faith.

JULIAN TODAY

When examining the place of the cross in the spirituality of Julian of Norwich, in many respects one is faced with an endless task because the cross is the centrepiece of what Julian has to say. If she speaks of any aspect of the Christian faith, whether it be prayer, suffering, salvation or whatever, the answer that Julian gives is this: 'There were times when I wanted to look away from the cross, but I dared not. For I knew that while I gazed on the cross I was safe and sound.' As Gordon Mursell has so succinctly put it, 'The passion of Christ is literally the crux of Julian's theology.'[15]

The cross at the centre

We have seen that the cross is for Julian the great symbol of the humility of God, a primary focus for meditation on the extent of the love of God that should drive him to experience humanity as one of us. We have seen the joy that is revealed through the cross because of the salvation that it has brought about and the depth of the love of God that it shows to us. We have seen how the cross is central to Julian's understanding of the Trinity, and how she has been able to incorporate complex theological systems into a workable and honest spirituality. We have seen how the cross is a model for us as a pattern for Christian love, standing before us not as a warning as to the consequences of our actions, but rather as a sign that we are conforming to God's will for his people and as a reassurance that, in so far as we share in Jesus' sufferings, so we shall also share in his resurrection. Finally, we have seen how the cross stands as the ultimate symbol of the love and compassion of God, and how we need to conform to his will and identify with his love.

Many might wonder if such an exercise is worthwhile. After all, Julian received her visions and wrote her *Revelations* in the fourteenth century – how can such spiritual writings, however sincere and forward-looking, speak to us today? Are our own reflections on the sufferings and death of Jesus not more relevant to our own needs?

The relevance of Julian

The answer to these questions are to be found in the writings of Julian herself. There are many reasons why Julian and her writings are as relevant today as they were 600 years ago.

First, they proclaim an eternal truth – that in the suffering and death of Jesus we can see the love of God in a unique and wonderful way, and that it is when we seek to understand that suffering and death and to enter into that love that we shall be able to embark on the relationship with God that he would wish us to have.

> Julian helps man to look at himself with the eyes of God, and thus to experience the ultimate joy of a creature: his consciousness of being the object of his Creator's love.[16]

This is done within a loving relationship, a relationship which has love at its centre and, because this love is a gift from God, it is a relationship which also has the cross at its centre. If Julian has done anything at all, she has helped us to realize the full horror of the act of the crucifixion, the full extent of the pain that Jesus suffered, and the full measure of the love that is at the centre of the whole mystery. In a world which has sentimentalized love to a dreamy romanticism, and in a Church which has often failed to reassert the truth of God's love and put it into practice, Julian's voice speaks with a clarity and a freshness which cannot go unnoticed.

Second, Julian has a wide vision. If our world can be accused of sentimentalizing love, it can also be accused of emphasizing the self, in that personal achievement and success lie at the heart of everything. Julian's position is far removed from this. Although her visions were intensely personal, she sees them only in the context of the Christian family, of which she has a deep awareness – her 'even-Christians' for whom she has so much concern. Those who seek to follow Christ today are gently reminded by Julian that selflessness is at the heart of the gospel. Julian's message also applies to the wider world, for it is a God of universal love to whom she bears witness.

Third, Julian is accessible because of her humanity. Her imagery is drawn from the world around her, a world which was, in many ways, in as much turmoil as ours is today. Through her experience of that world, and through her suffering, she depicts a God who loves endlessly. We are able to identify with Julian because she writes, in one sense, for us. We are her 'even-Christians' today, and we are able to benefit from the compassion which she feels and sees as a true expression of the suffering love of God.

So we end, as we began, at the cross. The cross lay at the centre of Julian's experience of God, as it lies at the centre of all Christian experience. Julian encourages us to look at the cross, not in a vacuum but in the context of the world around us, to see the suffering of Jesus as a sign of hope, a sign of God's commitment to a world which has the potential to be beautiful. Our task is now to discover afresh for ourselves the love which is the meaning of that cross. If, with Julian, we fix our eyes on the suffering love of God, we may find our heaven, as she surely found hers.

> Ever since, this has been a great comfort to me that by his grace I chose Jesus for my heaven, and him in all his passion and grief. It taught me to choose only Jesus for my heaven, come what may. CHAPTER 19

FURTHER READING

Aelred of Rievaulx, 'A Rule for the Life of a Recluse', in *Treatises and the Pastoral Prayer* (Continuum)

Marion Glasscoe (ed.), *Julian of Norwich, A Revelation of Love* (Exeter)

Grace Jantzen, *Julian of Norwich* (SPCK)

Cheslyn Jones, Geoffrey Wainwright and Edward Yarnold (eds), *The Study of Spirituality* (SPCK)

David Knowles, *The English Mystical Tradition* (Burns and Oates)

Kenneth Leech and Sister Benedicta Ward SLG, *Julian Reconsidered* (Fairacres)

Robert Llewelyn (ed.), *Julian: Woman of our Day* (Twenty Third)

Paul Molinari, *Julian of Norwich* (Longmans, Green)

Gordon Mursell, *English Spirituality: From Earliest Times to 1700* (SPCK)

Julian of Norwich, ed. Grace Warrack, *Revelations of Divine Love* (Methuen)

Julian of Norwich, trans. and ed. Clifton Wolters, *Revelations of Divine Love* (Penguin)

Jill Raitt (ed.), *Christian Spirituality* (Routledge)

Richard Rolle, trans. and ed. Clifton Wolters, *The Fire of Love* (Penguin)

Martin Thornton, *English Spirituality* (Cowley)

Gordon Wakefield (ed.), *A Dictionary of Christian Spirituality* (SCM)

James Walsh (ed.), *Pre-Reformation English Spirituality* (Burns and Oates)

Clifton Wolters (ed.), *The Cloud of Unknowing* (Penguin)

Notes

1 Grace Jantzen, *Julian of Norwich* (London, 1987), p. 13.

2 Sister Benedicta SLG, 'Julian the Solitary', in *Julian Reconsidered* (Fairacres Publication 106, 1988), p. 18.

3 Jantzen, *Julian of Norwich*, p. 33.

4 Aelred of Rievaulx, 'A Rule for the Life of a Recluse', in *Treatises and the Pastoral Prayer* (Michigan, 1971), pp. 77-78, quoted in Jantzen, *Julian of Norwich*, p. 46.

5 Kenneth Leech, 'Contemplative and Radical: Julian meets John Ball', in Robert Llewellyn (ed.), *Julian: Woman of our Day* (London, 1985), pp. 91-92.

6 For more detail on the nature of Julian's sickness, see Paul Molinari, *Julian of Norwich* (London, 1958), p. 21ff.

7 Jantzen, *Julian of Norwich*, p. 101.

8 Sister Benedicta SLG, 'Julian the Solitary', p. 29.

9 Clifton Wolters (trans.), *The Cloud of Unknowing* (London, 1961), p. 78.

10 Elizabeth Ruth Obbard ODC, 'God Alone Suffices', in *Julian: Woman of our Day*, p. 116.

11 Jantzen, *Julian of Norwich*, p. 216.

12 Anna Maria Reynolds CP, 'Woman of Hope', in *Julian: Woman of our Day*, p. 22.

13 Molinari, *Julian of Norwich*, p. 140.

14 Jantzen, *Julian of Norwich*, p. 187.

15 Mursell, Gordon, *English Spirituality: From Earliest Times to 1700* (London: SPCK, 2001).

16 Jones, Wainwright and Yarnold (eds), *The Study of Spirituality* (London, 1986), p. 336.

PART 4

FORGIVENESS AND FREEDOM

How Forgiveness
Works

Jonathan Baker

Forgiveness is still an everyday word, and roams at large outside the ghetto of theological jargon. It is a dangerous word, at
once familiar and mysterious, comforting and subversive. We talk
about it lightly, we say 'sorry' to each other every day, we think we
know what it means, until suddenly we are confronted with a profound need either to ask for forgiveness or to offer it to another –
and then it becomes elusive and disturbing. 'Nothing is less obvious
than forgiveness,' is the verdict of one authority.[1] Yet at the same
time it can take us right to the heart of the Christian faith and of
human experience.

When we see people forgiving each other, overcoming deep
injury and outrage in order to do so, it can be striking and memorable. Who could fail to be moved by the words of Gordon
Wilson, in the aftermath of the bombing of the Remembrance Day
parade at Enniskillen in 1987, publicly tendering forgiveness to
those who killed his daughter? By contrast, who could fail to be
troubled by the dilemma of the Jewish nation after the Holocaust,
expressed on the fiftieth anniversary of the liberation of Auschwitz
by the president of Israel, as he said, 'We do not hate, but neither
do we forgive'?

Such statements underline the fact that forgiveness is, by its very
nature, controversial. This has always been so. Bede records an early
example from the mid-seventh century of the devout King Sigbert
of the East Saxons, 'who was murdered by his own kinsmen ... who,

on being asked their motive, had no answer to make except that they hated the king because he was too lenient towards his enemies and too readily forgave injuries when offenders asked pardon'.[2]

Precisely because forgiveness is such an important and controversial word, it is perhaps presumptuous to try and consider it usefully in a study of this size. I have tried to give a simple outline of how forgiveness works, focusing especially on the way human expressions of forgiveness need to reflect the divine pattern as it is revealed to us in Christ. In the nature of the case, forgiveness cannot tidily be restricted to our relationship with God, but keeps on spilling over into our relationships with others. It is on this area of overlap that I have tried to concentrate my attention.

THE PROBLEM OF FORGIVENESS

Not everyone sees forgiveness as necessary or even desirable. Some have suggested that forgiveness is at best irrelevant to the quest for human wholeness, and at worst an immoral refusal to take evil actions seriously. As we try to identify the real quality of Christian forgiveness, it may be helpful to clarify some of the negative or inadequate ways in which the word is commonly used.

For many people, forgiveness can only be offered when the grievance has not been deeply felt. It applies in situations where we can say, 'I do not feel angry and resentful towards you, even though you have done me harm'. At a subjective, emotional level the offence has simply not made an impact and has left no scars. It is assumed that forgiving must involve forgetting.

This explains why people can talk about the possibility of forgiveness on an everyday basis, and expect to experience it, while at the same time finding its prospect scandalous and upsetting in more serious situations. When I step on your toe, you say, 'It's all right, I forgive you.' What you really mean is, 'It's all right, I wasn't hurt.' The offence was trivial, and forgiveness in this context is simply an expression of good manners. Yet if we suggest that forgiveness is an appropriate response to serious and malicious hurt, many will find this outrageous, not least because it seems to imply that the offence was unimportant and did not really matter.

Many Christians are crippled by guilt because they share this inadequate understanding of forgiveness. They believe that they should be willing to forgive others, and that God's ability to forgive them is bound up with that willingness to forgive others. Yet they cannot bring themselves to forgive, because to do so would imply that the injury somehow did not matter. The hurt they have suffered is compounded by a sense of guilt and inadequacy, because they feel they cannot be real Christians. Often those who say, 'I could never forgive him for what he did,' are simply stating that they cannot imagine their strong feelings of hurt or bitterness ever subsiding.

Forgiveness and denial

For some, forgiveness is a dangerous concept precisely because it suggests to them a reluctance to acknowledge the extent to which someone has been hurt. It implies a repression of those feelings of anger, pain and resentment which need to come to the surface if there is to be any genuine healing. So when you deliberately and malevolently stamp on my toe, and I say, 'It's all right, I forgive you,' I am failing to acknowledge that our relationship has gone seriously wrong and I am denying the existence of problems which need to be dealt with. Far from being a means of establishing acceptance, wholeness and reconciliation, such forgiveness avoids having to face up to the offender honestly. It involves ducking the seriousness of the situation, perhaps because it is too painful to come to terms with, and forgiveness becomes a dishonest shield behind which the victim can retreat.

It would appear that much modern psychology takes this view of forgiveness as denial. The late Bishop Stephen Neill used to say that whenever he came across a book on psychology he would always turn to the index to see if there was an entry under 'forgiveness'. It was invariably absent, a fact which he found most disturbing. Part of the reason for this absence is that modern consciences tend to be untroubled by sin and guilt. We worry about our low self-esteem, our inadequacies and insecurities, our feelings of alienation, but it never occurs to us that such feelings might be more than mere illusion, that we might actually be morally responsible for our own disorientation. If the connection between sin and self-esteem were recognized, forgiveness would be much more fashionable, not least because it offers healing for our relationships and thus for our self-image, which depends so much on our ability to trust and to bond.

The right to forgive

The charge of unreality can be made at a moral level as well as a psychological one. In the first place, forgiveness is said to be a moral impossibility because the past cannot be changed. What's done is done and cannot be undone, and whatever actions and events we may lament and regret, they are locked away in the past, beyond our reach and inaccessible. So when I stamp on your toe, the pain is real and unrelieved, and my guilt is fixed and irremovable, whatever form your reaction might take. Forgiveness is therefore pointless, and changes nothing. As I hope we shall see, however, Christian forgiveness is in fact a creative process which not only breaks us free from the destructive grip of the past, but creatively uses the rubble of past failure as the foundation for a wholly new set of opportunities.

In the second place, there is the objection that an individual wishing to offer forgiveness may not have any right to do so, because often there is more than one person affected. It is repeatedly said, for example, that the survivors of the Holocaust are not in a position to forgive their tormentors, because they have no right to forgive on behalf of those who died. The dilemma has been expressed by Simon Wiesenthal, the hunter of Nazi war criminals. In 1942 he was summoned to the deathbed of an SS officer who wanted to receive the forgiveness of a Jew before he died. Even though he believed the man was genuinely sorry, Wiesenthal refused, on the grounds that he was simply not in a position to do what was asked of him: 'What would have given me the right,' he asks, 'to forgive on behalf of those whom I had watched die?'[3]

The problem was explored by Dostoevsky in *The Brothers Karamazov*, where Ivan Karamazov argues that a mother who witnesses the horrifying murder of her child may be able to forgive the suffering caused to herself, but she cannot forgive on behalf of the child, and to that extent the crime must remain unabsolved. The response of Ivan's brother Aloysha, however, is a genuinely Christian answer:

> You said just now, is there a being in the whole world who could or had the right to forgive? But there is such a being, and he can forgive everything, everyone and everything, and for everything, because he gave his innocent blood for all and for everything.[4]

The death and resurrection of Christ is not just a moment in history, of limited importance; it is of universal significance, and it has the capacity not only to bring about forgiveness for and between people, but also to make good the inadequacies and limitations of human forgiveness.

Perhaps the most serious objection to the whole notion of forgiveness is not that it is a moral impossibility, but that it is actually immoral, because it appears to disregard ethical norms. If any act, however brutal and selfish, can be redeemed by forgiveness, then the distinction between right and wrong is threatened and justice itself is subverted. We have turned full circle and are back at our original objection – that forgiveness in the end does not take wrongdoing seriously enough. An emphasis on forgiveness can appear to make wrongdoing acceptable or even desirable, if its consequences can be avoided and all made well again. This is the view implicit in the cynical remark attributed to the philosopher Heinrich Heine on his deathbed: 'God will forgive me – that is his business.'

It is a charge that is as old as the gospel itself, and was made against St Paul: 'What shall we say, then? Shall we go on sinning, so that grace may increase?' (Romans 6:1). The apostle thinks not, and as we turn to consider the way forgiveness actually works, we shall begin to see why.

THE FOUNDATION OF FORGIVENESS

Bishop Lesslie Newbigin tells the story of how, as a young missionary in India, he went to classes with a teacher of the theistic form of Hinduism (sometimes called India's theology of grace). On one occasion the teacher asked Newbigin what he meant by salvation; Newbigin gave his answer in terms of sin and forgiveness, upon which the Hindu remarked that 'apart from the personal name of Jesus, what you have said is exactly what I would have said'. 'If that is so,' Newbigin asked, 'what is the basis for your confidence that your sins are forgiven?' 'If God would not forgive my sins,' came the reply, 'I would go to a god who would.'[5]

The story is shocking to Christian ears, not just because of the idea that there might be more than one God, but because of the way forgiveness is made into a quality detachable from God's character. In the Old Testament it is clear that forgiveness is deeply rooted in the character of God; it is not negotiable. Forgiveness is repeatedly linked to the very name of Yahweh. 'For the sake of your name, O LORD [Yahweh],' cries the psalmist, 'forgive my iniquity, though it is great' (Psalm 25:11). Forgiveness as a central quality of God's very being is embedded in the creeds of Israel. 'You are a forgiving God, gracious and compassionate, slow to anger and abounding in love' (Nehemiah 9:17).

Here we find the reason why divine and human forgiveness are so closely related. If humankind is made in the image of God, then the ability to forgive is essential for a full and rounded human life, because it reflects the attitude of God himself. By contrast, unforgiveness can lead to an impaired life, because it implies estrangement from God.

A further point illustrated by Lesslie Newbigin's story is that Christian forgiveness is not a response to the need of sinners to feel good about themselves. The Hindu's point is that a god should be selected on the basis of his ability to meet our need as sinners, for which purpose forgiveness is a useful quality for a god to have. In Christian understanding, however, the problem is how to repair broken relationships with this particular God and with particular people. The key words in Christianity are relational words: faith, love, forgiveness. The process of forgiveness is not for the benefit of the sinner alone, but always aims at restoring fellowship.

Yet the question remains: on what basis does God forgive? 'Does something *happen* for forgiveness? Or is it just a word?' asks one of Iris Murdoch's characters in her novel *Bruno's Dream*. The question implies that some sort of event is necessary, and Christians naturally see such an event in the death and resurrection of Christ. Nevertheless, this has been challenged.

> How miserably all those finely constructed theories of sacrifice and vicarious atonement crumble to pieces before this faith in the love of God our Father, who so gladly pardons! The one parable of the Prodigal Son [Luke 15] wipes them all off the slate.[6]

The father of the prodigal simply forgives, out of his own generosity of heart; the parable contains no plausible reference to anything equivalent to the cross (despite the suggestion that in a Middle Eastern culture the father's loss of dignity in running to meet his son is suggestive of the cross).[7]

Such a view comes perilously close to the superficial understandings of forgiveness examined in the previous section. The parable of the prodigal illustrates the compassion of God, but does not explore the basis of forgiveness. Something decisive and objective must underlie our concept of forgiveness if it is to have any real transforming power. 'Can't you forgive me?' implores the adulterous central character in Tom Wolfe's novel *Bonfire of the Vanities*. 'I suppose I could,' replies his wife. 'But what would that change?'[8] Forgiveness is not some abstract pardon; it is the process by which a broken relationship is creatively restored and once again made healthy and life-giving for both sides. Such a transformation does not take place simply by uttering the magic words, 'I forgive you.' Something more than that is needed.

Forgiveness in the Old Testament

The Old Testament itself finds the notion of forgiveness problematic, not because it might be too easy and superficial, but because it seems impossible. From earliest times the Hebrews believed sin to have irreversible consequences, both for the individual sinner and for the community of which he or she was a part.[9] Sin was not seen as an action distinct from its consequences; it was the beginning of a chain of events which would inexorably lead to disaster for the sinner and his people, even 'to the third and fourth generations'. The sin and its penalty could be spoken of as if they were the same thing, as in Numbers 32:23, 'You may be sure that your sin will find you out.' Furthermore, guilt was real; sin was an objective barrier placing the sinner outside the fellowship of God.

The possibility of forgiveness was therefore limited, at least until the exile. There were particular difficulties with crimes covered by the Decalogue, such as idolatry (see Joshua 24:19) and murder (see 2 Kings 24:3ff.). More alarmingly, King Saul could not be forgiven for his disobedience in failing to annihilate the Amalekite livestock, even though he begged Samuel to absolve him (see 1 Samuel 15:24-26).

Yet God is the God of his people and will remain faithful to his covenant promises, which means that the possibility of forgiveness must be present. Even so, forgiveness seems to be quite compatible with the continuation of judgement. At any single moment God may be experienced both as the One who forgives and as the One who avenges wrongdoing, as expressed in Psalm 99:8, 'You were to Israel a forgiving God, though you punished their misdeeds.'

The combination of forgiveness and judgement is enshrined in some of Israel's earliest credal statements. For example, 'The LORD is slow to anger, abounding in love and forgiving sin and rebellion. Yet [and here comes the catch] he does not leave the guilty unpunished; he punishes the children for the sin of the fathers to the third and fourth generation' (Numbers 14:18-23, echoing Exodus 34:6ff.).

It is as if the Old Testament writers are acutely aware of two apparently irreconcilable truths: first, that sin is utterly destructive and must be treated by God with absolute seriousness; and second, that God is forgiving and will not ultimately allow sin to frustrate his covenant promises. In such circumstances it is far from clear what forgiveness actually means. What can it mean for God to forgive if judgement continues?

Against this background, two developments help to resolve the paradox. The first of these is the growth of the sacrificial system, which was intended to provide a way to remove sin and restore fellowship with God.[10] The offering of animal sacrifices to atone for sin dramatically conveyed the reality that the sinner need not inevitably be destroyed by his or her sin. Instead, the destructive consequences of sin were symbolically redirected onto the sacrifice when the worshipper laid hands on it before killing it. In this way sin could be put to death without destroying the sinner. It made forgiveness possible without winking at sin. Sacrifice dealt with sin vicariously, but not painlessly.

Alongside the development of the sacrificial system there was also a growing emphasis on spiritual sacrifice, which identified the sacrifice even more closely with the sinner. 'The sacrifices of God are a broken spirit; a broken and contrite heart, O God, you will not despise' (Psalm 51:17). In their different ways, both understandings of sacrifice stress the seriousness of sin and the costliness of eradicating it.

The second Old Testament development which helps to resolve the paradox is Israel's experience of exile and her theological response to it. Israel's prophets, historians and priests all interpreted the destruction of Jerusalem in 587 BC and the exile which followed as Yahweh's judgement on his people for the accumulated sins of several centuries. It is as if the destruction of the nation was the only way by which the effects of sin could be exhausted and disarmed and the people brought to repentance.[11] Once Israel had been humiliated and rendered powerless, her armies defeated, her cities in ruins, her national institutions destroyed and her ruling class carried off into captivity, the stage was set for forgiveness to be considered. Thus it is that the prophets who speak most clearly of unconditional forgiveness and the grace of God are Jeremiah, Ezekiel and Isaiah (see Chapter 40 onwards), all of whom speak from the midst of the ravages of exile. Only from the depths of judgement can the word of forgiveness be spoken, because only in a situation of alienation and exile can sin be put away and repentance be deep and lasting.

Forgiveness from the cross

In the New Testament, Christ's death is the perfect sacrifice. John the Baptist cries, 'Look, the Lamb of God, who takes away the sin of the world!' (John 1:29). The letter to the Hebrews identifies the blood of Christ as the supreme sin-offering, far surpassing the blood of goats and bulls shed on the Day of Atonement (Hebrews 9:12-14). At the Last Supper Jesus himself interprets his coming death as a sacrifice creating a new relationship with God: 'This is my blood of the covenant, which is poured out for many for the forgiveness of sins' (Matthew 26:28).

Such language makes a clear link between sacrifice, the death of Christ, the forgiveness of sins and reconciliation with God. Christ dies 'for us', bearing our sins and taking them down into death. He goes as our representative where we cannot go, in order that our sin and guilt may be destroyed in death. In his death he removes the barrier disrupting our fellowship with God, and in his resurrection he opens up the way of forgiveness.

If we then identify ourselves with Christ by repentance and faith, like the Israelite worshippers of old, we find in his death an effective sacrifice. The entail of sin has been broken, because its destructive inheritance has been vested not on the sinner but on Christ. By means of such a sacrifice, God is able to offer forgiveness without sparing the sin. As George MacDonald put it, 'What is usually called "forgiving the sin" means "forgiving the sinner and *destroying* the sin".'[12] Such forgiveness is infinitely costly to God, but completely free for the sinner.

Indeed, all the New Testament evidence underlines the cost of offering forgiveness as well as the fact that it is free to those who receive it. The parables that use the imagery of debt make this especially clear. The king who cancels his servant's huge debt in Matthew 18 does so at enormous cost to himself. Forgiveness in this story may be free for the servant, but it is certainly not free for the king.

Human love instinctively follows the same pattern. For example, the loving parents whose child rejects them do not retaliate in kind. They might feel entitled to cut off all contact and cast the child off, but instead they absorb the child's anger and ingratitude, not throwing it back but taking it upon themselves, where it can cause pain to no one else. Such action is sacrificial; the parents take on their own shoulders the cause of the estrangement, so that there is no longer any barrier to the relationship. Their attitude is certainly costly, but it allows them to hold out to the child the possibility of forgiveness and reconciliation.

Such forgiveness involves the surrender of that to which we are morally entitled. It involves resisting the impulse to pay back our assailants with interest. It involves breaking the cycle (or is it more often a spiral?) of tit-for-tat by accepting the injury done and determining that it shall go no further. In this respect it mirrors the forgiveness offered at Calvary.

Forgiveness and forsakenness

The New Testament also picks up the theme of exile. Christ is crucified as King of the Jews, and so on the cross he enters the ultimate state of exile on behalf of God's people. Just as the Israelites were unable to receive forgiveness before they had come under judgement and learned repentance in the midst of destruction and exile, so God's final word of forgiveness is not possible apart from the destruction of sin in Christ's body as the representative of his people, setting them free to repent.

It is no accident that the word of forgiveness must be spoken from the cross, which is the place of exile, nor that 'Father, forgive them' (Luke 23:34) is spoken alongside 'My God, why have you forsaken me?' (Mark 15:34), since forgiveness is only possible where there is forsakenness. Sin is sent away into exile on the cross, while the exiles are set free to return to God.

Crucified between criminals, Jesus was indeed 'numbered with the transgressors' and died the death of a runaway slave or a violent terrorist. Yet by identifying with exiles in his death, one of them is moved to faith, and Jesus is able to promise him, 'Today you will be with me in paradise' (Luke 23:43). By entering exile with his people, the Messiah is able to bring that exile to an end.

The story of Zacchaeus in Luke 19 illustrates this well. Zacchaeus is a 'sinner'; not only is his trade likely to involve dishonesty and extortion, but as a tax collector he is effectively working for the enemies of God's people. He is apparently quite beyond the pale of God's favour. By going to Zacchaeus's house and sharing a meal with him, Jesus should have become tainted with Zacchaeus's sin. In fact, the opposite happens and instead of Jesus becoming an outcast, Zacchaeus is declared to be a true Israelite, no longer a sinner and no longer exiled. This is the meaning of Jesus' declaration, 'Today salvation has come to this house, because this man, too, is a son of Abraham' (Luke 19:9). Jesus has entered Zacchaeus's exile in order to identify with him in his sin and move him to repentance.

The New Testament, of course, interprets the cross of Christ in other ways besides those of sacrifice and exile. St Paul in particular speaks little of forgiveness as such, but his treatment of justification and righteousness amounts to the same thing, namely the reconciling of sinners to God.[13] In all these different approaches to forgiveness, three things are clear and consistent. First, forgiveness is offered to us freely and unconditionally; it is God's gift and can only be received as such. Second, forgiveness is a gift which is immeasurably costly for God to provide. Finally, it is a gift which prompts a response. To this we shall shortly turn.

The pattern of forgiveness

We have focused on the biblical material because it is here that we see what authentic forgiveness consists of, in contrast to the counterfeits considered earlier. The cross of Christ is constitutive not just of our experience of God's forgiveness, but also of our understanding of what forgiveness actually is. By pondering God's forgiveness we begin to understand what the word means, and there we find a pattern which human forgiveness must follow. As Mackintosh puts it:

> Let the man be found who has undergone the shattering
> experience of pardoning, nobly and tenderly, some awful
> wrong to himself, still more to one beloved by him, and he
> will understand the meaning of Calvary better than all the
> theologians in the world.[14]

The cross also shows that forgiveness is more than an attitude in
the mind of God; it demonstrates that genuine forgiveness involves
action. The journey into exile is a journey with a purpose – not
merely to offer forgiveness, but to establish it. The risen Christ
returns from exile not alone, but leading the exiles home. Hence
God's purpose is to offer forgiveness creatively, so that the offender
is enabled to respond with repentance and faith. Forgiveness is
therefore not a one-off event, but involves a process, a journey –
what Mackintosh calls 'voyages of anguish'.[15]

From this we begin to get a picture of forgiveness as something
that flows outwards from the heart of God. It is a missionary
impulse, and is expressed both concretely and cosmically at Calvary; it gives shape and direction to the mission of the Church; it
refuses to accept that the future must inevitably be determined by
failures and omissions made in the past; and it refuses to stop with
the recipient, but insists on breaking the grip of unforgiveness in
the hearts of the forgiven. The experience of divine forgiveness
leads not only to fellowship with God in Christ, but to a willingness to forgive others, not just in principle but in action.

Of course, this does not always happen. E. M. Forster
describes how forgiveness can break down when the recipient
refuses to forgive another:

> 'Not any more of this!' she cried. 'You shall see the con-
> nection if it kills you, Henry! You have had a mistress – I
> forgave you. My sister has a lover – you drive her from
> the house. Do you see the connection? Stupid, hypocriti-
> cal, cruel – oh, contemptible! ... Men like you use repen-
> tance as a blind, so do not repent. Only say to yourself:
> 'What Helen has done, I have done.'[16]

Henry's wilful inability to 'see the connection' drives his wife to the
point where she announces, 'I am unable to forgive you and am
leaving you,' and so the relationship breaks down totally.[17]

Here, perhaps, is one of the profoundest problems with forgiveness. Many people are unwilling to receive it, not simply because that would involve the humiliation of acknowledging that they have done wrong in the first place, but also because it would imply having to forgive in return – for in human relationships forgiveness is rarely one-sided, but often needs to be mutual. Might it be that we often refuse to accept forgiveness, not because we are convinced that we are in the right, but because we cannot bear to pay the price of responding to forgiveness with forgiveness?

'Forgive us our sins as we forgive those who sin against us,' we pray. Yet the Lord's Prayer makes a connection that is radical in its implications. It makes God's willingness to forgive us conditional on our willingness to forgive others. The two stand or fall together. We cannot find the strength to forgive others unless we have experienced being forgiven for ourselves; neither can we expect to receive forgiveness if we are unwilling to offer it. Such teaching surely makes sense only within the context of the Church, where the support of word, sacrament and the fellowship of the forgiven gives it concrete expression.

THE ACCEPTANCE OF FORGIVENESS

We have considered the quality of forgiveness so that we can tell the genuine article apart from its many counterfeits, and we have looked at the foundation God has laid to make forgiveness possible. Yet the knowledge both that we can recognize forgiveness and that God has made it possible is still not enough to bring it about. Forgiveness must necessarily involve two parties, and it makes no difference to what extraordinary lengths God may have gone in order to hold out the hand of forgiveness, if in the end his creatures refuse it.

In human relationships the problem is common enough: what can be done when forgiveness is refused? When this happens it may feel like a personal failure for the one wishing to forgive, and may even lead to a sense of guilt because the relationship cannot be repaired single-handedly. The limited ability of one party to establish forgiveness and reconciliation was poignantly brought home by a survivor of the massacres in Rwanda in 1994, who, speaking to a television news reporter, asked, 'How can we forgive when no one will admit they have done wrong?' The attitude of those being offered forgiveness is every bit as important as that of those making the offer. Willingness to forgive must be matched by a willingness to be forgiven. What is involved when this happens? How is forgiveness received? And what happens when it is refused?

The forgiving gift

If we look to God in order to gain insight into how forgiveness works, we find that there is a trinitarian quality about it. If the Father is the one with whom we must ultimately be reconciled, and if the Son is the one through whom this is made possible by his death and resurrection, then the Spirit is the one who works to bring about a response in the life of the sinner. It is as if God is present on both sides of the Creator-creature relationship. The Holy Spirit is able to go round the back, as it were, in order that love may respond to Love and the estranged children may be drawn back to their heavenly Father. This means that the balance between God and his creatures is not an equal one; the right of veto enjoyed by human beings in the face of their Creator, although real enough, is circumscribed by the Holy Spirit. When God offers forgiveness it is not left passively on the table, as if God then walks away, saying, 'Take it or leave it.' The involvement of the Holy Spirit in the work of forgiveness makes it a much more powerful and creative process than we sometimes imagine.

The key New Testament passage which explores the relationship between forgiveness and the Holy Spirit is John 20:21ff.

> Again Jesus said, 'Peace be with you! As the Father has sent me, I am sending you.' And with that he breathed on them and said, 'Receive the Holy Spirit. If you forgive anyone his sins, they are forgiven; if you do not forgive them, they are not forgiven.'

The extraordinary implication of this passage is that the trinitarian life of God can be described simply in terms of forgiveness. The Father sends the Son, the Son sends the Spirit, the Spirit empowers the Church, and the result is forgiveness. This means that we can relate forgiveness to the rich activity of God at every level.

In particular, the activity of God in forgiving is continuous with his activity in creating the world in the beginning, and in calling Israel into being as God's new humanity, his creative response to the fall. The Spirit, or breath, of God broods over the waters of chaos in Genesis 1:1 and responds to the word of God in creation. Ezekiel, the prophet in exile, has a powerful vision of the Spirit of God breathing new life into the dead bones of God's people, a vision preceded by promises both of forgiveness and of the gift of God's Spirit. Following this Old Testament image of creation and resurrection, it should come as no surprise to see the risen Christ similarly breathing out God's Spirit in order to recreate the people of God.

The implication is clear. The gift of the Spirit of forgiveness, coming as it does in the context of Christ's resurrection and echoing the imagery of Genesis 1 and Ezekiel 37, is an act of new creation, an act of cosmic power and significance. Forgiveness in this context is no mere retrospective pardoning of sins. It fulfils God's creative purpose. It is an eschatological event, offering us a glimpse of the new heaven and the new earth, like the resurrection itself.

When we forgive each other, we are participating in the resurrection life of Christ. The Church as the special creation of the Holy Spirit is charged not only with the task of proclaiming forgiveness, but is especially to embody forgiveness. The Church of Christ is to be known as the community of forgiveness within which the end-time promises of reconciliation, healing and peace can become present realities. Those who are forgiven are in turn empowered by the Spirit to forgive others. Hence Peter in his Pentecost sermon is able to say, 'Repent and be baptized, every one of you, in the name of Jesus Christ for the forgiveness of your sins. And you will receive the gift of the Holy Spirit' (Acts 2:38). The involvement of the Spirit ensures that forgiveness is not a one-off gift, but is a continuing process and a repeated opportunity. In all the emphasis in recent decades on the work of the Holy Spirit, it is remarkable how little has been said about forgiveness as a gift of the Spirit. As the charismatic movement develops, more will need to be said about the link between fresh experiences of the Spirit's power and forgiveness.

The community of forgiveness

The Church as the community of forgiveness makes both the experience and the need for forgiveness more visible. It should embody an ethos of forgiveness, an expectation that forgiveness is both necessary and possible, which can encourage both the offer and the acceptance of forgiveness. In this way we can speak meaningfully of the Holy Spirit being active on both sides of a human reconciliation, as well as when we receive forgiveness from God. Even if there is only one mutual friend between two people who have quarrelled, that may be enough to create the expectation that forgiveness and reconciliation must come about. When forgiveness is given a setting in a community, it is not simply an issue between two individuals. It is something which affects the whole community, and towards which the community can work.

The visible bones of the Church are meant to express its true nature. So, for example, the gospel it preaches is 'the knowledge of salvation through the forgiveness of . . . sins' (Luke 1:77), while the sacraments are visible pledges of forgiveness. In the Creed it is no accident that the statement, 'We believe in one holy, catholic and apostolic church,' is immediately followed by, 'We acknowledge one baptism for the forgiveness of sins.' Calvin noted the appropriateness of this, saying, 'Forgiveness of sins, then, is for us the first entry into the church and kingdom of God. Without it, there is for us no covenant or bond with God.' Having received us into the Church,

> [God also] preserves and protects us there. For what would be the point of providing a pardon for us that was destined to be of no use? . . . unless we are sustained by the Lord's constant grace in forgiving our sins, we shall scarcely abide one moment in the church.[18]

Here again we see the need for a strong doctrine of the Holy Spirit if we are to grasp the nature of forgiveness as a continuing reality sustaining our fellowship.

The boundary of the Church is marked by baptism, which is supremely a sign of forgiveness, of spiritual cleansing, and of the new relationship with God and his people that forgiveness entails. Moreover, it is in the waters of baptism that we are united with Christ in his death and resurrection. When Paul answered the accusation that free forgiveness encourages sin, he did so by pointing to baptism (see Romans 6:1ff.). The language of dying and rising with Christ is not meant to be merely figurative, but indicates a real putting to death of sin in the life of the Christian and a real sharing in the resurrection life of Christ. Forgiveness that follows the pattern of baptism (which itself follows the pattern of the cross and resurrection) is not open to the charge of immorality, because it does not allow for 'cheap grace'. The Church's orientation is fixed and sustained not only by baptism, but also by Holy Communion, as the community identifies with Christ in his death and resurrection in the breaking of bread and pouring out of wine, the 'blood of the covenant, which is poured out for many for the forgiveness of sins' (Matthew 26:28).

Celebrating forgiveness

To the extent that the Church is not in practice a community where forgiveness is experienced and expressed, it denies its own nature. At times the Church's role as the guardian of public morality has obscured its true gospel identity; it is not a community of the righteous, but of the forgiven. It was a weak doctrine of the Spirit that led the Church in the second century to teach that there could be no forgiveness for sins committed after baptism, and especially not for adultery, idolatry or murder.[19] In response to the pastoral problems this caused, the sacrament of penance developed, although for many centuries even that was permissible only once in a lifetime after baptism.

Perhaps the problem with the word and sacraments is that they are so multifaceted that their united witness to the centrality of forgiveness can be obscured. We might consider ways in which our worship and corporate life might celebrate the reality of forgiveness more explicitly. In the Anglican Church, it is a weakness of Cranmer's liturgy, for example, that it expresses so little assurance of forgiveness. Even the Gloria at the end of the Holy Communion service is marked more by its pleas for mercy than by its celebration of reconciliation and new life. Similarly, in the new *Common Worship* service, the invitation to receive the bread and wine, the tokens of our forgiveness, is immediately followed by the Prayer of Humble Access, which effectively undercuts any sustained celebration of this forgiveness. Yet the celebration of forgiveness should be a hallmark of the Church's worship and needs always to be borne in mind by those planning services.

Where there have been particular occasions of forgiveness, it may be appropriate to celebrate them in rites designed for that purpose. For example, a rite of penance and forgiveness following a divorce might be held prior to a remarriage, or a rite of penance and restitution following public scandal.[20] One church devised its own moving ceremony for the reconciliation of the sexes as part of a teaching series on sexuality, which enabled members of the congregation to offer each other forgiveness.[21]

The politics of forgiveness

The placing of forgiveness in a community context raises the important question of corporate forgiveness. How can forgiveness work in society? The question is difficult, not least because communities, tribes and nations rarely express penitence, let alone forgiveness. Yet Christ's forgiveness is political. The cry from the cross, 'Father, forgive them' (Luke 23:34), 'releases his followers from any obligation to avenge him'.[22] Christ's example offers a striking model for politicians. Charles I's 13-year-old daughter Elizabeth recorded her father's words to her the day before his execution. 'He told me he had forgiven all his enemies, and hoped God would forgive them also, and commanded us, and all the rest of my brothers and sisters, to forgive them.'[23] When Charles II was restored to the throne 11 years later, his reign was marked more by tolerance than by the settling of old scores.

When the Italian vice-president Vittorio Bachelet was murdered by the Red Brigade, his family expressed their forgiveness at the televised funeral. Years later Bachelet's brother received a letter, signed by 18 imprisoned members of the Red Brigade, saying, 'We want you to come ... We remember very well what your nephew said at his father's funeral ... that ceremony when life triumphed over death and we, too, were overcome.'[24]

Individual leaders may also represent their people in asking for forgiveness. We may think perhaps of Willy Brandt kneeling before the memorial to the Warsaw ghetto, or the Czechoslovakian president Victor Havel who, in his first statement on foreign policy, asked forgiveness of the German Sudeten minority for their expulsion from Czechoslovakia.[25]

Such gestures cannot be backed with significant action, which limits their value. In contrast, there has been much more talk of forgiveness and reconciliation in South Africa since the dismantling of apartheid than there was before. The political removal of unjust structures acted as a sign of repentance, allowing space for forgiveness to be offered. There, too, people are amazed at the absence of a backlash against the former white rulers. But to have offered forgiveness before would have been to condone the sin, and could neither have succeeded nor been tolerated.

The Church as a community clearly has a role in the politics of forgiveness, since by living as a community of reconciliation in a world torn by hatred and division it can act as an effective sign and symbol of another kind of society. Especially potent are communities such as those at Rostrevor and Corrymeela in Northern Ireland, set in the midst of sectarian divisions.

The Church also has a role in prompting repentance.[26] When Christians speak out and are willing even to suffer for the truth, society becomes aware of injustice, and pressure for change can build up. Furthermore, faith and hope in the coming kingdom of God, joyfully expressed in the midst of suffering and oppression, 'exasperates the agents of the system ... it destroys their morale'.[27] Finally, suffering for justice keeps alive the hope of liberation in the reformer's heart, so that the desire for peace and justice becomes ever more urgent, and is held ever more tenaciously.

In such ways the Christian enters the exile of the cross and bears the burden of society's sin in order to exhaust its power and bring it to repentance. South Africa stands as an example of a place where the Church has followed this calling. Yet at the same time it must be remembered that reconciliation is the aim, not victory. When a decisive political advantage is gained, the dynamic of forgiveness requires that it should not be overexploited and turned into an oppressive victory.

Forgiveness can thus express salvation in the broadest sense. Jeremiah makes a connection between forgiveness and social stability, peace and prosperity, and also health and healing (see Jeremiah 33:6-9). The same connection is made explicitly in James 5:16: 'Confess your sins to each other and pray for each other so that you may be healed.' Both forgiveness and healing are aspects of the Spirit's work of reconciling, healing and bringing to completion the creation which God has begun.

The place of penitence

Forgiveness must be received as well as offered if true reconciliation is to take place. When Gordon Wilson memorably forgave those responsible for his daughter's death in the Enniskillen bombing, the offer was never taken up. There was some expression of regret that Mr Wilson's daughter should have been killed, but no regret for the planting of the bomb and certainly no sign of repentance. No discussion of forgiveness can be complete without giving some thought to the place of penitence, for this describes the process by which forgiveness is received and blossoms into restored fellowship.

Faith and penitence are two sides of the same coin. Faith draws one into fellowship with God; penitence is faith overcoming the barrier of sin to restore fellowship. The penitent heart is not one deserving of forgiveness, it is simply the sinful heart which is capable of receiving forgiveness. We can therefore say that faith and penitence are alike in this further respect: they are both received as gifts of grace. There is consequently nothing to be gained by asking whether forgiveness is conditional on repentance, any more than there is by asking if the resurrection of Christ is conditional on faith. Yet without faith the resurrection is meaningless to the individual, and without repentance forgiveness cannot restore a broken relationship.

A brief glance at the Gospels reveals that Christ does not look for repentance before holding out forgiveness. He does not ask the tax collector Matthew to repent before calling him (see Matthew 9:9-13), neither does he tell the sinful woman who anointed his feet to repent (see Luke 7:36-50). On the contrary, he assures her unconditionally that her sins are forgiven. What he does say, most significantly, is that it is her faith that has saved her, which suggests that he is aware of the woman's penitent heart and her capacity to receive forgiveness and be restored to fellowship.

The notion that repentance is a gift of God needs to be understood in the context of what was said earlier about the work of the Holy Spirit and the role of the community in forgiveness. Perhaps this makes more sense if we recognize the connection between awareness of God and awareness of self. Calvin argued that 'without knowledge of God there is no knowledge of self' – and vice versa.[28] Only by measuring ourselves against the perfection of Christ can we gain true self-awareness, and so be moved to repentance.

Such self-knowledge comes to us as a gift. Left to ourselves, we should never be moved to repentance, for 'what man in all the world would not gladly remain as he is ... so long as he does not know himself?'[29] Saving knowledge of God and oneself is the gift of the Holy Spirit as he shines on the dark places of our hearts with the light of Christ. The experience may be described variously (but not exhaustively!) with words like guilt, emptiness, need, alienation, fear and longing. Such knowledge comes most frequently through contact with the lives and witness of Christians in the community of the Church.

Repentance and grace

The Westminster Shorter Catechism asks the question, 'What is repentance?' 'Repentance unto life,' goes the answer, 'is a saving grace, whereby a sinner, out of a true sense of his sin, and apprehension of the mercy of God in Christ, doth with grief and hatred of his sin turn from it unto God, with full purpose of and endeavour after new obedience.' In other words, repentance involves the whole personality with its intellect, emotions and will. The need for all three modes of consciousness to be involved is succinctly summarized by Mackintosh:

> Recognition of sin by itself is not repentance; it may be defiance. Nor is sorrow for sin repentance, if it be alone in the mind; it may be remorse or despair. Abandonment of sin, by itself, may be no more than prudence. The regenerating fact is all three, as a unity, baptized in a sense of God's personal grace to the sinful.[30]

The crucial importance of repentance in forgiveness further answers the charge that forgiveness is immoral. That charge has already been answered by stressing the need for the sinner, by faith, to identify with Christ crucified, so that, in St Paul's terms, 'I have been crucified with Christ and I no longer live, but Christ lives in me' (Galatians 2:20). In practical terms, being 'crucified with Christ' means repentance, the putting to death of sin in one's own life. Such repentance must come by grace, or else forgiveness becomes dependent on our own effort, and is transformed into a work of self-righteousness, whereas the whole point of the gospel is that forgiveness is being offered to sinners and outcasts, with repentance as part of the gift. Grace has power to set the sinner free to repent.

This can also happen in human relationships, where repentance is sometimes drawn forth simply by holding out the hand of forgiveness. Michael Bordeaux tells the story of two prisoners sharing the same cell in the Russian gulag. One was a Baptist Christian, the other an atheist who taunted the Christian and tried to break his faith. On one occasion it seemed that the atheist had nearly succeeded and the Christian was reduced almost to the point of despair and cried out to God for strength. Then,

> Suddenly he looked at me and smiled. I was amazed at his face: there was something joyous about it, pure, as though it had just been washed clean. The weight immediately fell from my soul. I understood that he had forgiven me.[31]

However, those offering forgiveness need not feel responsible if it is not accepted. W. H. Auden, writing about the refusal of Shakespeare's character Antonio to receive forgiveness from Prospero in *The Tempest*, sums up Antonio's position thus:

> Your all is partial, Prospero,
> My will is all my own:
> Your need to love shall never know
> Me: I am I, Antonio,
> By choice myself alone.[32]

Conversely, the offer of forgiveness may be met with a false repentance. Antony Bridge gives an example in his autobiography:

> My father's ... understandable and in some ways rather endearing habit of confessing to my mother that he had yet again succumbed to an adulterous temptation, while begging her to forgive him, did not help the marriage; for when she did indeed forgive him, he was able to go happily to sleep, while she lay awake in misery and heartache.[33]

There we see the full cost of forgiveness being paid, but it does not lead to a reciprocal putting to death of the sin in repentance. What can at least be said is that, despite the pain (or perhaps because of it) the mother is in a better position than if she had withheld forgiveness altogether. That would have been to shut the door on the possibility of healing and to retreat, like Antonio, into lonely resentment, 'By choice myself alone'.

Confession

Confession can play a vital role in the process of repentance and forgiveness, as Psalm 32:5 and James 5:16 suggest. When sin is confessed to God, or to another Christian, or to the offended party, responsibility can be taken for it and the demons of guilt, isolation and self-deception can be brought out into the open and exorcized.[34] It is characteristic of sin that it hates to be made public. It prefers to dwell in the dark corners of the human heart, where it can remain secret and unacknowledged and where its grip is strongest. By failing to confess our sins we fail to be open with God, with ourselves and with our fellow human beings. It impairs our relationships and our self-knowledge.

Confession, on the other hand, involves coming to terms with the past and with our distorted or selective memory. It is in my memory that my own unique experience and story are stored. My identity, my self, is bound up with my memory, as Augustine explored at length in his *Confessions*: 'In the vast hall of my memory ... I meet myself and recall what I am, what I have done, and when and where and how I was affected when I did it.'[35]

Where my memory is of sin and broken fellowship, the result is a personality which is to some extent distorted and impaired, often involving a reluctance to come to terms with the full extent of my sin. Part of the process of forgiveness must therefore have to do with the healing and restoring of memories by bringing them out into the open where they can be acknowledged and owned. As Rowan Williams argues,

> The word of forgiveness is not audible for the one who has not 'turned' to his or her past; and the degree to which an unreal or neutralized memory has come to dominate is the degree to which forgiveness is difficult.[36]

He goes on to point out the impossibility of forgiveness for those whose crimes are so great that the memory has 'neutralized' them.

One such was Adolf Eichmann, who apparently blotted out his crimes from his memory and so was unable to come to terms with them later. Repentance is impossible if we cannot, for whatever reason, acknowledge the sin for which we are responsible.

The mere articulation of memories of sin and failure does not by itself lead to forgiveness. It is the confession of sin to the risen Christ or to the fellow Christian (as a representative of Christ) that brings healing. In John 21 Jesus painfully reminds Peter of his denial of Jesus, not in order to exploit his moral advantage and crush Peter with guilt and despair, but in order to bring his exile to an end, to help him acknowledge the past and take responsibility for it, so that he can be restored to fellowship and have his vocation reaffirmed without any trace of self-deception or unreality.[37] Peter receives his apostolic commission not as a faithful follower of Jesus and a saint, but as a repentant betrayer. As such, his future ministry is built on a firm foundation, because Peter knows from experience that he can never fall beyond the reach of grace, and so he will be less likely to trust to his own limited strength.

Thus confession drags sin out from the dark places of the heart and exposes our withered memories to the restoring light of truth. It allows us to place ourselves in Christ's presence knowing what we are, and being willing for him to nail our sin to his cross. As Bonhoeffer put it:

> The expressed, acknowledged sin has lost all its power. It has been revealed and judged as sin. It can no longer tear the fellowship asunder. Now the fellowship bears the sin of the brother. He is no longer alone with his evil for he has cast off his sin in confession and handed it over to God. It has been taken away from him.[38]

Such confession does not have to involve other human beings, but where the community dimension is ignored there is a risk of superficial repentance, like that of Antony Bridge's father, because it is so easy for us to confess our sins only to ourselves while at the same time imagining that we are confessing to God. According to Bonhoeffer:

> Is not the reason perhaps for our countless relapses and the feebleness of our Christian obedience to be found precisely in the fact that we are living on self-forgiveness and

not a real forgiveness? Self-forgiveness can never lead to a breach with sin; this can be accomplished only by the judging and pardoning Word of God itself.[39]

CONCLUSION

In order to forgive, God enters our state of sin and exile so as to bring us home. The story of the incarnation is the story of forgiveness, as God seeks the response of repentance and faith and finally wins it through the passion and Pentecost. It is a supremely costly journey, and one which involves identifying even to the point of death with those who need to be reconciled. It is a journey in which Love confronts the estranged and Innocence confronts the guilty, not in order to gloat or condemn, but to woo and to welcome.

The response of confession, repentance and faith entails its own perilous voyage. In one sense this, too, is a costly journey, involving painful self-discovery and hard discipline, yet it is a voyage for which the passage has ultimately been paid and a safe anchorage guaranteed. The experience of forgiveness with God is supremely an experience of freedom – freedom from the tramlines of past failure, freedom from fear of the future, freedom from the isolation of pride. Yet forgiveness is not just freedom *from*, it is also freedom *for* – freedom to take risks for God, freedom to offer ourselves for others, freedom to become forgiving. It is at that point, where those who find freedom can unlock dungeons for others, that we see the outworking of forgiveness.

Notes

1 E. Brunner, *The Mediator* (Lutterworth Press, 1934), p. 488.
2 Bede, *A History of the English Church and People* (Penguin, 1955), p. 179.
3 Quoted in M. Hubaut, *Forgiveness* (St Paul's, 1994), p. 13.
4 F. Dostoevsky, *The Brothers Karamazov* (Penguin, 1958), p. 288.
5 Bishop Newbigin told this story during questions following a talk entitled 'Why Christianity and not another philosophy?' at Croydon Parish Church, 21 February 1994.
6 Paul Wernle, quoted in D. M. Baillie, *God was in Christ* (Faber, 1961), p. 172.
7 Kenneth Bailey, *Poet and Peasant and Through Peasant Eyes* (Eerdmans, 1983).

8 T. Wolfe, *Bonfire of the Vanities* (Picador, 1988), p. 485.

9 G. von Rad, *Old Testament Theology, Volume 1* (SCM, 1975), p. 264ff.

10 L. Morris, *The Atonement* (IVP, 1983), Chapter 2.

11 See, for example, Walter Brueggemann, *Hopeful Imagination: Prophetic Voices in Exile* (SCM, 1986).

12 C. S. Lewis (ed.), *George MacDonald: An Anthology* (Bles, 1946), p. 27.

13 H. Vorlander, 'Forgiveness', in C. Brown (ed.), *Dictionary of New Testament Theology, Volume 1* (Paternoster, 1975), p. 702.

14 H. R. Mackintosh, *The Christian Experience of Forgiveness* (Nisbet, 1927), p. 191.

15 Ibid., p. 188.

16 E. M. Forster, *Howards End* (Penguin, 1983), p. 300.

17 Ibid., p. 324.

18 J. Calvin, *Institutes of the Christian Religion, Volume II* (Westminster Press, 1960), p. 1034f.

19 J. N. D. Kelly, *Early Christian Doctrines* (A. C. Black, 5th ed., 1977), p. 198.

20 See the discussion on services of reconciliation of the penitent in Grove Ethics booklet E 89, Oliver O'Donovan and Michael Vasey, *Liturgy and Ethics* (Grove, 1993).

21 This was at Holy Trinity, Coventry, under its then vicar Graham Dow.

22 Una O'Higgins O'Malley, quoted in B. Frost, *Women and Forgiveness* (Fount, 1990), p. 45.

23 M. Mayne, preface to Frost, ibid.

24 Ibid., p. 15.

25 Hubaut, *Forgiveness*, p. 8.

26 The following points follow P. Fiddes, *Past Event and Present Salvation* (Darton, Longman and Todd, 1989), p. 203.

27 L. Boff, quoted in Fiddes, ibid., p. 203.

28 Calvin, *Institutes, Volume I*, pp. 35-38.

29 Ibid.

30 Mackintosh, *The Christian Experience of Forgiveness*, p. 234.

31 M. Bordeaux, *Risen Indeed* (Darton, Longman and Todd, 1983), pp. 89-90.

32 W. H. Auden, 'The Sea and the Mirror', in *Selected Poems* (Faber, 1979), p. 137.

33 A. Bridge, *One Man's Advent* (Fount, 1985), p. 3.

34 On the subject of confession to another, see the following chapter by Mark Morton.

35 St Augustine, *Confessions* (Oxford University Press, 1991), p. 186.

36 R. Williams, *Resurrection* (Darton, Longman and Todd, 1982), p. 21.

37 Ibid., p. 35.

38 D. Bonhoeffer, *Life Together* (SCM, 1954), p. 88.

39 Ibid., p. 91.

Personal Confession Reconsidered
Making Forgiveness Real

Mark Morton

This chapter is about the ministry of reconciliation, the means by which the Church formally mediates the grace of God's forgiveness to those who turn from their sin in penitence and faith. In particular, it is about auricular confession, the confessing of sin to God in the presence of a confessor, usually an ordained minister who then (normally) grants absolution. It is written with the conviction that this ministry has much to offer and should be a part of any church's pastoral provision.

Within the limitations of the space here, it is not possible to deal with the subject in great depth, or even to mention all the issues involved. I offer here a basic introduction; those who require a fuller historical or theological perspective, or who need detailed practical guidance, should consult the list of suggested further reading.

I do not write as an experienced confessor. My experience is largely as a penitent, having first been introduced to Confession while at theological college. Although I had been a Christian for many years, I still felt guilty about things which I had done in the past. Every time I moved into a new area of ministry or sought to grow spiritually, my conscience would trouble me and I would be overwhelmed by feelings of unworthiness and inadequacy. Despite the counsel of friends and ministers, despite hours spent in confessing and reconfessing to God and to others, and despite reasonable attempts to make reparation, the problem would not go away. Finally, I shared my predicament with the spiritual counsellor at college. She suggested what she called 'Sacramental Confession' and recommended I go to see a local, very senior priest, with years of experience of hearing confessions. At first I was sceptical – my evangelical convictions recoiled at the very thought – but I agreed to explore further. Within a few weeks, I met with the priest and explained something of my background and the way I felt. After some initial advice and encouragement, he asked me to go away and to prepare a confession, covering all those areas about which I felt guilty. This I did, and I still remember my anxiety as I knelt beside my confessor and bared my soul. I was determined to be as honest as possible and to act on whatever counsel I received. My only desire was to do the right thing and to know the forgiveness of God.

As I look back, my introduction to Confession was a major turning point in my life. For the first time since becoming a Christian, I was able to look people in the eye and not be overcome by guilt. My initial scepticism, based on prejudice and misunderstanding, gave way to an appreciation of the biblical foundations of Confession and of the role it has played in the lives of Christians from many traditions.

Before proceeding further, I would like to make a point about terminology. For convenience I shall use 'Confession' (with a capital 'C') as shorthand for the whole process of auricular confession and absolution. When I write of 'confession' (with a small 'c'), I refer to confession more generally.

A PRACTICE RECONSIDERED

Many Christians outside the Roman Catholic tradition tend to have a jaundiced view of Confession. Perhaps they have heard anecdotes about drunks, inveterate gamblers, wife-beaters and others of dubious moral propriety who live as they please, go to Confession, attend Mass and then start the cycle all over again. Possibly they recall the sketches of Dave Allen and others, casting the priests who hear Confession in rather less than complimentary light. Tut tut, they think to themselves – how can this charade have anything to do with real Christianity?

At a more fundamental level, it is often remembered how the Reformers struggled to free the Church from medieval superstition and to return it to sound biblical faith and practice. One of their earliest targets was a rotten penitential system which included the sale of indulgences and made regular Confession essential to salvation. This system obscured the gospel and enslaved individual consciences to a frequently wicked and corrupt ecclesiastical hierarchy. Against all this, the Reformation upheld certain essential truths: justification by faith, the priesthood of all believers, and so forth. Therefore, any suggestion that those in the Church of England or any other Protestant Church should contemplate using Confession is regarded as both unnecessary and as a betrayal of the Reformed tradition.

Over recent decades, the use of Confession has also been increasingly out of favour among Roman Catholics. This probably stems from fundamental changes in Western society, combined with disillusionment among Catholics which has led them to feel that Confession is largely irrelevant. When there was a widespread fear of hellfire and an unthinking acceptance of the Church's authority, it was relatively easy for priests to encourage their congregations towards Confession. Now, however, better education, widespread secularization and social mobility have all taken their toll. Few people these days are prepared to accept moral absolutes simply on the basis of dictate, and – to take just one example – the widespread use of contraception by Catholics shows that they are no exception. Moreover, whereas Confession once provided the only opportunity that many people had to 'get things off their chests', its place has now been supplemented by modern psychotherapy and counselling which offer alternative, 'non-judgemental' means of psychological unburdening.

This decline in Confession has also been reflected in the Catholic wing of the Church of England, and for many of the same reasons. There was a time, early in the twentieth century, when queues for the confessional regularly formed outside some of the larger Anglo-Catholic churches. Now it appears to be only a small minority who avail themselves of this practice, and they do so in a less ostentatious way.

Given the historical connections between Confession and the perceived errors of medieval Catholicism, as well as its decline even among practising Catholics, there may seem scant reason for commending it. This, however, is only half the story. First, there has been something of a theological rethink of its place and purpose. Second, with the recent resurgence of interest in spirituality among Christians of all denominations and traditions, opposition to Confession purely on the basis of Church tradition has greatly reduced. Increasing numbers of those who go are from outside the Catholic tradition, including evangelicals. While overall numbers of those attending Confession may be down, therefore, there is evidence that a reappraisal is taking place.

There is now a greater emphasis on Confession as a means of reconciliation and spiritual growth. The confessor is not so much a judge who passes a verdict as one who comes alongside, shares your burden and helps you along the way. In tandem with this changed focus, there have also been changes to the way in which Confession is now made. The box confessional was once common, with confessor and penitent separated by a screen. It was all very formal and confessions were made according to a set pattern. Some confessions are still made like this (there are people who find the formality a help), but confessions are increasingly face-to-face affairs, rather like other pastoral interviews. Where the confessor also acts as the person's spiritual director, Confession may form part of a wider discussion covering a range of personal issues. This variety of practice draws attention to an important point – that Confession is not a fossilized ritual but a discipline to be used naturally and flexibly according to individual circumstances and needs.

The gospel and the confession of sin

The message of the gospel is centred on the cross. It is a message about full and free forgiveness that we do not deserve and which we cannot earn. It is a gift – a token of generous, unconditional love – and it is simply to be accepted through faith. This unmerited generosity on God's part is the basis for Christian assurance. If there was the slightest part for us to play in winning forgiveness, there would always be the possibility that we had not done enough, that we had fallen short and that our contribution had been inadequate. Regardless of our repentance and our faith, room for doubt would still exist and the awful prospect of divine displeasure would hover over us until the day we died.

As it is, the New Testament reveals to us that the Living God is also our loving Father. He did not send his Son to condemn the world but to save it. Jesus Christ came to share our humanity, to live among us and to die for us, not because God was angry but because God is love. He took our sins upon himself and suffered for them in an act of supreme self-sacrifice that stands as totally sufficient for all time. There is no sin, no matter how big or heinous, that is greater than the love of God eternally demonstrated and sealed on the cross of Calvary.

It is essential that any discussion about confession is rooted here, in the gospel itself. Never should it be imagined that confession is a means of earning forgiveness. God's pardon depends not on what we do but on what Christ has already done. This is quite fundamental. Self-examination and confession are nevertheless vital to our wellbeing and to the wellbeing of the Church as a whole. Sins, until they are acknowledged and confessed, distort our lives and prevent us from living authentically before God – as Jonathan Baker explored in Chapter 11. They can create all sorts of inner tensions, they can poison our relationships with others, and they can prevent us from hearing God. The psalmist knew this well:

> While I kept silence, my body wasted away
> > through my groaning all day long.
> For day and night your hand was heavy upon me;
> > my strength was dried up as by the heat of summer.
> Then I acknowledged my sin to you,
> > and I did not hide my iniquity;
> I said, 'I will confess my transgressions to the LORD,'
> > and you forgave the guilt of my sin.
>
> PSALM 32:3-5 NRSV

By acknowledging our sin and confessing it, we are recognizing the problem, affirming our desire for change, and inviting the Holy Spirit to execute that change. The process of confession is therefore a process of healing through which we are reconciled to ourselves, to our neighbours and to the Lord.

Primarily, we confess to God. Whatever we have done or neglected to do, our sin is basically an offence against him. Again, we find the psalmist expressing this very point. Calling on the mercy of God, he declares, 'Against you, you alone, have I sinned, and done

what is evil in your sight' (Psalm 51:4 NRSV). In fact, if its historical heading is authentic, Psalm 51 relates to King David's murder-
ous adultery with Bathsheba (see 2 Samuel 11–12). The king had
very much sinned against others, but he recognized that the primary offence was against the Lord.

When our sin has affected other people, we may need to confess to them as well. Where they have suffered some kind of loss
as a result of our wrongdoing, such confession might include an
offer of reparation or restitution, not as a bribe but as a way of
helping to right the wrong and showing the sincerity of our contrition. Normally, our confession will be made in private to the individual or group concerned, but occasionally a public confession is
appropriate (for example, if we have publicly slandered somebody). The essential thing for the Christian in all this is that his or
her relationships with other people are maintained in as healthy a
condition as possible. It is sheer folly to expect that we can enjoy an
intimate relationship with God while there is enmity or injury
between us and another. So far as it is in our power, we need to
ensure that we live in love and peace with all (see Romans 12:18).

Given the importance of confession to our spiritual lives, it is
wise to examine ourselves regularly and to confess our sins as soon
as is reasonably possible. Many Christians set aside a short period
each day and, perhaps, a longer period each week for this purpose.
They also join in the general confession during public worship and
receive God's promise of forgiveness in the absolution. Auricular
confession is not a substitute for these things, but a complement to
them; it does not remove an individual's responsibility before God,
but enhances it.

Assurance and forgiveness

What distinguishes Confession from ordinary pastoral counselling (during which sins are also frequently confessed) is that the
former concludes with an absolution. In other words, the confessor
not only reassures the penitent and prays for him or her, but actually pronounces the person forgiven. It is this assumption of
authority, rather than Confession as such, to which some Christians object. In 1983 a modern-language Rite of Reconciliation of a
Penitent failed to secure a majority in the House of Laity of the
Church of England General Synod because of evangelical objec-

tions to the words 'I absolve you' in the absolution. (The 1986 *Lent, Holy Week, Easter* includes an agreed form of absolution on page 56 that many find more acceptable.)

Words are important, but they can mean different things to different people. The essential thing is not the precise formula adopted, but the understanding that lies behind it. For example, some churches of the Orthodox tradition use what is known as a deprecative form of absolution, 'May God forgive', but this is regarded as authoritative, not just a pious hope. So far as they are concerned, Christ has given his Church the authority to forgive sins, and when this is exercised it works. This is the bottom line. The whole rationale of the ministry of reconciliation is that in it the Church is acting as God's agent and the mediator of his forgiving grace. It is vital that the penitent comes away from the absolution not just hopeful of forgiveness but assured of it.

New Testament foundations

How does this square with Scripture? It is certainly not possible to find Confession in the New Testament *per se*, but neither is it possible to find episcopacy, infant baptism or any other number of things that large sections of the Church have found useful and proper. The important issue is whether Confession is a valid development from biblical principles, or whether it stands in contradiction to them. In particular, what is the nature of the authority granted by Christ to his Church? Is it only an authority to preach and to teach, or does it go further?

Jesus caused offence by pronouncing the forgiveness of sins, and he was accused of blasphemy. The religious teachers of those days believed that forgiveness should be preached, but they regarded the declaration of absolution as presumptuous. In Matthew 9:6, Jesus' answer is that the Son of Man (a title that emphasizes his humanity) does possess the necessary authority and, to prove it, he commands the paralytic to stand up, take his bed and go home. In Luke 7:50, Jesus appears to ignore objections and simply tells the forgiven woman that her faith has saved her and that she should go in peace. Presumably, the reality of God's grace is to be verified by the subsequent way in which she lives her life. These episodes from the ministry of Jesus can, of course, be explained in terms of his uniqueness. In view of the union of Christ with his Church, however, perhaps they have something to teach us about the granting of forgiveness today.

There is certainly strong biblical support for believing that Jesus' authority to minister absolution has been passed to the Church. In John's Gospel we read:

> Again Jesus said, 'Peace be with you! As the Father has sent me, I am sending you.' And with that he breathed on them and said, 'Receive the Holy Spirit. If you forgive anyone his sins, they are forgiven; if you do not forgive them, they are not forgiven.'   JOHN 20:21-23

In Matthew's Gospel, there are two passages in which Jesus appears to anticipate the Church and to speak of its authority in this area:

> And I tell you that you are Peter, and on this rock I will build my church, and the gates of Hades will not overcome it. I will give you the keys of the kingdom of heaven; whatever you bind on earth will be bound in heaven, and whatever you loose on earth will be loosed in heaven.
> MATTHEW 16:18-19

> If your brother sins against you, go and show him his fault, just between the two of you. If he listens to you, you have won your brother over. But if he will not listen, take one or two others along, so that 'every matter may be established by the testimony of two or three witnesses'. If he refuses to listen to them, tell it to the church; and if he refused to listen even to the church, treat him as you would a pagan or a tax collector. I tell you the truth, whatever you bind on earth will be bound in heaven, and whatever you loose on earth will be loosed in heaven.
> MATTHEW 18:15-18

A plain reading of these texts suggests that Jesus granted to the Church the authority to forgive sin. Of course, this was not a power to be exercised lightly, but only within the context of the Church's overall understanding of the Lord's teaching. What is primarily in view here, at least in Matthew, is the need to preserve good church order through the operation of a disciplinary system.

In the letters of Paul, we read of examples of this at work – the case of the infamous sinner of 1 Corinthians 5; the 'consigning to Satan' of Hymenaeus and Alexander mentioned in 1 Timothy 1; the advice given in 2 Thessalonians 3 and Titus. If the Pauline churches are anything to go by, 'forbidding and allowing' (or 'binding and loosing') was a known and accepted practice, although not necessarily a common one.

From the evidence of Matthew, 'binding and loosing' is not restricted to the temporal realm, but has heavenly implications as well. Jesus makes clear that what has been loosed on earth will be loosed in heaven, and what has been bound on earth will be bound in heaven. It is true that the Greek here is ambiguous – some commentators argue that what is loosed or bound on earth has *already been* loosed or bound in heaven – but the context clearly implies real authority on the part of the Church, an authority with eternal validity. Beyond the examples already given of how this applied in protecting good order, we do not know how the Early Church exercised this authority. Nonetheless, some form of mutual confession is suggested in James 5:13-20, and it appears that the local church elders had a role to play in ministering God's forgiveness through prayer. This evidence is too flimsy to suggest that Confession existed in the modern sense, but the New Testament certainly provides two important foundations for later development – the authority of the Church to minister absolution, and the appropriateness of Christians confessing to one another, at least in certain circumstances.

HISTORICAL DEVELOPMENT

Beyond the New Testament, we know that by the third century there existed a penitential system for dealing with baptized Christians who had fallen into serious sin. Particularly pressing at the time was how to readmit to the Church those who, under the weight of persecution, had fallen away and offered sacrifices to Roman gods. Adultery and murder were also considered 'serious' in this context. Either voluntarily or under threat of excommunication, the sinner would privately confess to the bishop, the senior pastor of the locality, and would be admitted to the order of penitents. Penance would involve exclusion from Communion and a strict regime of spiritual discipline, including prayer, fasting and almsgiving. After a period of time, determined according to the gravity of the sin, the penitent was readmitted to the congregation. This frequently carried a number of conditions – lifelong prohibitions on marriage or military service being common – and it was understood that absolution and reconciliation of this kind could not be repeated.

The severity of this system eventually led to its breakdown. Converts increasingly postponed their baptism until the eve of death, as did baptized Christians their penance. Through the influence of Celtic and Anglo-Saxon monasticism, a new system began to emerge. Although this could also be extremely harsh in practice, it offered a number of advantages over the old system. Most crucially, penance was now normally private and the penitential period tended to be relatively short. Previously, penance could only be undergone once in a lifetime, but now it was regarded as repeatable. Reflecting this development, the authority to minister absolution was no longer the preserve of bishops, but was extended to priests in general. In this they were guided by various manuals that sought to bring a degree of uniformity to the setting of penances. Such were the roots from which modern Confession grew.

It would be a mistake, however, to think that the new system was accepted without a struggle. There was strong opposition from some bishops and it took hundreds of years before practice became reasonably uniform throughout the Western Church. Only in 1215 did it receive full official backing, when the Fourth Lateran Council decreed that all Catholics were to confess to their pastors each year.

The old system, with its emphasis on harsh public penance, had been judicial in its tone and was primarily geared at keeping the Church pure and holy. Having developed during a time of frequent persecution, when apostasy and other serious sins were seen as severe internal threats to the Church's already precarious survival, there was a premium on good order and discipline. Once the Church had gained political acceptance and respectability, however, it was possible for the emphasis to change. The new system was more concerned with spiritual health, and medical metaphors were not uncommon. Sin, for example, was seen as an ulcerating wound that required to be laid bare before the physician (the priest) so that it might be healed.[1]

Medieval theologians were keen to examine the whole process of contrition (the sorrow a person feels for past sin which leads to amendment of life), confession, absolution and penance. At what point was a person forgiven? On what basis was he or she forgiven? Some, like Peter Abelard (1079-1142) and Peter Lombard (c.1100-64), emphasized the importance of inner contrition arising from a love for God. Abelard believed that forgiveness preceded Confession, since it was a penitent's sorrow that mattered most. Lombard, however, emphasized Confession as crucial, since it was the outward sign of the inner sorrow felt by the penitent. An alternative school of thought was championed by Hugh of Saint Victor (d. 1142), who considered absolution as essential. Contrition had a part to play, but only as a means of removing the bond of sin and hardness of heart.

As with so much Catholic theology, it was Thomas Aquinas (c.1227-1274) who had the greatest influence on future generations. His position was something of a synthesis. He recognized the need for contrition and stated that a priest might not absolve a penitent in whom the signs of contrition were not apparent. He also insisted, however, that priestly absolution was essential, because it was the Church that had been given the authority to forgive sins. He also held that the formula *Ego te absolvo* ('I absolve you') was part and parcel of the absolution and could not be substituted by alternative wording.

The legacy of the Reformation

Despite the teaching of its theologians, the penitential system of the medieval Church was often unduly concerned with externals and tended, in practice, towards superstition. It is not surprising, therefore, that there was a critical reaction. As early as the fourteenth century, the doughty John Wycliffe (c.1302-84) held a theology of forgiveness that differed markedly from that of contemporary Catholicism. He believed that compulsory Confession to a priest was without biblical warrant and he rejected the necessity of either Confession or penance. While Confession was commended as useful, it needed to be both voluntary and made to a suitable person. Such ideas were to be taken up over a century later by the great Reformers.

Martin Luther (1483-1546) was angered by the sale of indulgences, which was little more than a fundraising exercise for the

Vatican, and by the way in which penance had become divorced from faith. It had become a 'work', an act required to appease God. Luther believed that only the faith of a contrite heart could receive God's promise of forgiveness and that this should precede absolution. Without faith, absolution was void. Any notion of penance as punishment or as a means of satisfying God was preposterous. While denying that penance was a dominical sacrament (i.e. one commanded by Christ), however, he enthusiastically endorsed the practical benefits of Confession and ministerial absolution:

> Christ placed absolution in the mouth of his Church and has commanded it to release us from our sins. Therefore when a heart feels the burden of its sins and aches for consolation, the Christian finds here a sure refuge when he hears the words of God and learns that God, through the ministry of a man, releases and absolves him from his sins.[2]

There were significant differences between Luther and John Calvin (1509-64). Luther always remained an advocate of a reformed Catholicism, whereas Calvin went further, both in his criticisms of the Church and in his prescriptions for reform. With respect to auricular confession, he described it as 'a pestilential thing and in so many ways pernicious for the Church'.[3] He rejected the sacramental nature of penance because there was a lack of 'matter' (the equivalent of water or bread and wine), and he objected to Confession being obligatory or even normative. Despite his reservations and characteristically strong terminology, however, Calvin appears to have held that pastors are joined with Christ in his high-priestly office and that they stand surety for the promises of Christ.[4] In particular, they possess the authority to loose souls by the good news of the gospel in absolution. This is the confirmation and seal of God's grace and it is rightly and effectively received through faith. There is a place for those with troubled consciences to voluntarily make confession to their pastors and to receive the assurance of God's forgiveness.

Confession and the Church of England

The traditional Anglican position towards Confession has been summed up in the words, 'All may; some should; none must.' This upholds the authority of the Church and the spiritual benefits of Confession on the one hand, while defending the freedom and responsibility of individuals before God on the other. It is a characteristically English solution and one that should work well. Unfortunately, there is a tendency for clergy of different parties to twist the tradition to their own way of thinking. Some Catholic-minded priests have stressed the obligation to confession, whereas most evangelicals have ignored it altogether. It is important to restore the proper balance if the ministry of reconciliation is to be widely accepted and used.

For over 300 years, the 1662 Book of Common Prayer was in regular weekly use in parishes throughout England and, indeed, throughout the world. To this day, it remains an essential resource for understanding Anglicanism. It was the product of over a century of theological and liturgical revision and sought to maintain catholic faith and practice while accepting the main thrust of the Reformation. This can be seen quite clearly in its approach to confession.

Unlike the Prayer Book of 1549, written when the break with Rome first happened, the BCP does not specifically mention 'auricular confession'. Personal self-examination followed by general confession and absolution during public worship was the normal pattern laid down. However, provision was made for those who were unable to quieten their own consciences. In the Exhortation (included in the Communion Service), the minister declared:

> . . . if there be any of you, who . . . cannot quiet his own conscience herein, but requireth further comfort or counsel, let him come to me, or to some other discreet and learned Minister of God's Word, and open his grief; that by the ministry of God's holy Word he may receive the benefit of absolution, together with ghostly counsel and advice, to the quieting of his conscience, and avoiding of all scruple and doubtfulness.

Similarly, the Visitation of the Sick includes a rubric that allows a sick person to make a 'special Confession of his sins, if he feel his conscience troubled with any weighty matter'. Moreover, the form of absolution used in this case is very strong indeed and leaves no doubt about the authority of the minister to forgive sins:

> Our Lord Jesus Christ, who hath left power to his
> Church to absolve all sinners who truly repent and believe
> in him, of his great mercy forgive thee thine offences: And
> by his authority committed to me, I absolve thee from all
> thy sins, In the Name of the Father, and of the Son, and of
> the Holy Ghost. Amen.

These provisions of the BCP were, it is true, highly specific and did
not endorse Confession as a regular practice. They were for use
when the normal pattern had in some way failed and a person was
left troubled before God. Their importance, however, was in
recognizing the authority of the Church to hear confessions and to
grant absolution. The continuation of Confession was also recognized by a proviso to Canon 113 of 1603, requiring a minister not
to disclose any crimes or offences confessed to him except in certain
specified circumstances. This proviso was never repealed and
remains part of canon law to this day. Such were the foundations
on which later Anglican thinking was to be built, especially in the
nineteenth century.

The Oxford Movement

The leaders of the Oxford Movement, like the evangelicals,
wanted to see a revival of spirituality and holiness within the
Church. Edward Pusey and others argued that the practice of Confession had a vital part to play in this, encouraging contrition and
strengthening the inner life. Such teaching bore much fruit and in
1866 Pusey was able to write, 'The use of confession among us all,
priests and people, is very large. It pervades every rank, from the
peer to the artisan or the peasant.'[5] Inherent in these developments
was the perception that Confession had something to offer every
Christian, not just the sick or the guilty, and that it was an important element in spiritual growth.

For most of the twentieth century, Confession in the Church
of England remained a predominantly Anglo-Catholic practice. As
noted earlier, however, the days are now long since gone when
people could be found queuing outside the larger Anglo-Catholic
churches for Confession, and over recent decades the practice in
the Church of England has been in decline. Nonetheless, in opposition to this trend, the last 20 years have seen a growing interest in

Catholic spirituality among Anglicans in general. Inevitably, Confession has come to be practised and appreciated by those for whom, 30 or 40 years ago, it would have been out of the question. While the numbers of Anglicans going to Confession remains relatively small, those who are going are much more varied in their Church tradition than was once the case.

One difficulty that arises from the current situation is that Anglicans who want to make their Confession often find it difficult to find clergy willing to hear it. It is to be hoped, therefore, that ministers will not shy away from this area, but will recognize the value it has and the spiritual benefits it offers their congregations.

Confession as sacrament

Restricting the term 'sacrament' to the two rites instituted by Christ is understandable from a historical perspective. In theological terms, however, it is somewhat arbitrary. The word 'sacrament', let alone a definition of it, does not occur in Scripture and the Church has struggled with different definitions at different times. Common to these has been the idea of an outward action signifying an inner reality. On a broader use of the term 'sacrament', it could be argued that Confession or reconciliation can be seen as sacramental. The confessor, acting on authority granted by the Lord Jesus, hears a confession and gives the absolution specifically and individually. The outward action is the uttering of the words of assurance; in some contexts these may also be accompanied, following ancient precedent, by the laying on of hands. No one else is in the room; the words cannot refer to anybody else and there can be no mistake about the person to whom they are directed. That this can be the source of immense comfort and joy is beyond dispute.

It is sometimes argued that such human assurance is not necessary. After all, the Christian who repents and confesses can simply stand on the promises of Scripture without the intervention of a third party. This, of course, ignores the essential role that sacramental actions play in our Christian faith. They are outward signs of what God has done for us and of the new life that he gives us. When received in faith, they are effective reminders of divine grace. Sacramental Confession is essentially no different.

Protestant theology has been slow to recognize this. The definitions of 'sacrament' proposed by Calvin and others were restrictive, drafted in reaction to the specific events of their times rather than as guidelines for all time. There appears to be no good reason why, as Calvin asserted, a sacrament should have to be characterized by 'matter'. Why should a sacrament not be equally a sacrament if it consists of an action of some kind such as the laying on of hands or of a form of words such as the giving of absolution?

Confession and baptism

Perhaps one way forward is to regard Sacramental Reconciliation or Confession as a return to baptism – as both the Early Church and Luther did. At baptism, the drama of our redemption is sacramentally portrayed in a dramatic way as the apostle Paul reminded the Christians at Rome:

> Don't you know that all of us who were baptized into Christ Jesus were baptized into his death? We were therefore buried with him through baptism into death in order that, just as Christ was raised from the dead through the glory of the Father, we too may live a new life. (Romans 6:3-4)

To be baptized is to identify with Christ, both in his death and in his resurrection. It is an outward sign of what God has already accomplished, a tangible and (if we are true to the New Testament) an efficacious reminder of redemptive grace. The person who has been baptized can look back, as Luther was inclined to do at times of doubt, and draw comfort from the objectivity of what has taken place.

What we need when we sin is not to be rebaptized, but to be reminded of the baptism that we have already undergone. We need to be reminded of God's love for us and of the forgiveness that he grants to us. This is where the ministry of reconciliation comes into play; it is a sacramental reminder of our baptism, a means by which we ask our Father's forgiveness and receive his blessing. As our baptism was conducted on Christ's behalf by a minister of his Church, so in Confession we receive Christ's absolution in the same way.

WHY AURICULAR CONFESSION?

If Confession possesses sacramental value, it is reasonable to ask how this translates in practical terms. I suggest the following:

- It emphasizes the community aspect of church life and reminds the sinner that all sin, no matter how private, has social consequences. The confessor acts as a representative of the whole body and hears the confession and pronounces absolution on the body's behalf.

- It guards against self-deception, something all of us find only too easy. We can convince ourselves that a sin is not a sin or, even if it is, that we have good grounds for committing it. A confessor is able to offer an impartial judgement and to bring the light of God's word to bear. On the other hand, we may imagine we have sinned when we have not and the confessor can help dispel our false sense of guilt.

- It can help a penitent to identify the root causes of his or her sin. Sometimes a confessor is able to discern that individual sins are merely symptoms of a bigger underlying problem. Only when this is accepted and turned over to God is there free access to healing and growth. It may be, for example, that there is a problem of pride or greed or, alternatively, there may be deeper spiritual, emotional or psychological difficulties that require professional help. Either way, left to our own devices, we can more easily remain blind to the reality of the situation.

- It helps us to concentrate more carefully on self-examination and the process of confession itself. If we are honest, confessing to God (who knows about our sin before we tell him) can seem rather pointless and dull. From my experience, this is especially true when we are tired or busy. There is a tendency to cut corners in our self-examination and to make do with a rather generalized, ill-defined admission of guilt. Once again, the effect is to leave sins hidden and unconfessed and therefore (effectively) outside the transforming power of God's Spirit. Having to prepare a confession to present to a confessor is an excellent incentive to do the job properly.

- It provides immediate access, at the point of confession, to counsel about what to do next. Penitents may be uncertain whether they need to say sorry to somebody or to make reparation. Such decisions often require great wisdom and sensitivity, and the penitent, who is emotionally entangled, may feel pulled in different directions. The confessor, from a standpoint of detachment, is in a position to offer advice.

- It can greatly assist new Christians to come to terms with their past lives and truly to repent. The practice of the Early Church, whereby converts spent long periods in prayer, fasting and self-examination, was clearly excessive, but the underlying principle was sound. There is much to be said for new Christians, under the guidance of their minister or some other mature Christian, spending time looking back over their lives to identify their sin before laying it bare in Confession. As they do so, they will be able to receive immediate counsel and the reassurance of an absolution. This will require a high level of personal commitment, but it will help the convert better to break with the past and live the new life in Christ.

- Confession has an invaluable place in the comfort of the terminally ill and dying. As life draws to a close, the mind can be full of past regrets and sorrows and there can be a powerful desire to make amends. Very often this is not possible, but the confessor is able to hear what the person has to say and is able to give assurance of God's forgiveness.

- All these practical advantages of Confession can be summed up as 'burden sharing'. There is a positive value to being listened to, to confessing our worst and yet still to experience the love and acceptance of God through another human being. This strikes very close to the incarnational heart of Christianity – that God became flesh in Jesus Christ and continues today to minister healing and forgiveness through the Church. It is one thing to pray to an unseen God; it is quite another to experience the love of God through the smile and touch of another person. Those who have experienced it will know that it is a healing encounter.

To whom should Confession be made?

In line with the teaching of James 5:16, some Christian groups have practised mutual confession. This was true, for example, of the early Methodists and, more recently, it was a prominent aspect of the East African revival. It is also a feature among some charismatics. Certainly, openness and honesty is a vital part of Christian fellowship and the prayer, support and encouragement of our brothers and sisters in Christ is of immense value as we make our journey of faith. Mutual confession is especially valuable where, for instance, members of a particular group have argued among themselves and where a restoration of relationships needs to take place. Mutual confession is not so helpful where deep confidences are involved or where careful, patient listening and counselling are required. In such cases, an individual confessor is called for.

Both Leslie Weatherhead and Paul Tournier have argued that the role of confessor can be taken on by any reasonably mature Christian.[6] Tournier points out, quite correctly, that the authority to minister absolution was given to the whole Church and not just to the clergy. Personally, I have no quibble with this and I am sure that there are many laypeople who could hear confessions and absolve just as well as, if not better than, many clergy. Even so, it is well to remember that those who have been ordained have a specific pastoral responsibility which includes (in the case of both Anglican and Catholic priests) the authority to absolve.

If we look at the New Testament, elders or overseers were appointed over each congregation (as, for example, in Acts 14:23) and Christians were encouraged to heed their authority (see Hebrews 13:17). In particular, James 5:14-15 implies that elders had a specific role to play in praying for the sick and possibly, given the context, in hearing confessions. They were probably not the only Christians so engaged, but they seem to have been prominent. Indeed, if Confession is to be linked to the receiving of counsel and is to include the ministering of absolution, it is not surprising that those charged with the teaching of God's word should be the ones most closely involved. As we have already seen, this is the position of the Book of Common Prayer which states that confession should be made to a 'discreet and learned Minister of God's Word'. It could be argued with some justification that this should include experienced deacons and even lay readers, but the Church of England has limited the hearing of formal confessions to priests.

The question sometimes arises as to whether we should confess to our local pastor or to another. There must be room for flexibility here, for at least two reasons. First, some clergy simply decline to have anything to do with Confession. Second, it can be helpful to make our Confession anonymously or to a minister who is outside the immediate local situation. Many cathedrals, retreat houses and religious communities now provide Confession and it should not prove too difficult to find a confessor within easy reach of where we live. The advantage with this is that the minister concerned will be familiar with Confession and will normally possess the qualities which distinguish a good confessor from a poor one. Even so, in most circumstances, it is good to approach our own local minister first, even if only to discuss the options. This is common courtesy and recognizes the pastoral responsibility that the minister has for the congregation to which we belong.

How regular should Confession be?

There can be no hard-and-fast rules. The Roman Catholic teaching that Confession is obligatory and should be habitual is without biblical warrant and has never been accepted by the Church of England or by any other mainstream Protestant Church. It is there within the Church's treasure chest for those who wish to use it, when they wish to use it. Many Christians get by without ever doing so and they should be under no pressure to change. Their relationship is with God through Christ, and it would be wrong to imply an absolute need for a human go-between to act as confessor, spiritual director, intercessor or anything else. This is quite fundamental and we should guard against pushing a good idea too far.

Among those Christians who do use Confession, a variety of patterns exist. Some make their Confession regularly, once a month, once a quarter, or just prior to the major festivals. Others go to Confession at major points of life – baptism, confirmation, marriage, ordination and so forth – or while on annual retreat. For some, the making of a Confession will be a one-off event to deal with some specific sin, or else it will be an occasional event whenever the conscience is troubled. We are all individuals and our individual needs will vary. If we are uncertain what to do, the confessor will gladly offer advice.

The important thing is that the process of self-examination and confession in some form is built into our spiritual discipline. It is only by recognizing our sin, owning it and repenting of it that we avail ourselves of God's forgiving and transforming grace. The extent to which Confession contributes to this process will vary from person to person.

Before moving on, it is well to mention the danger of making Confession an obsession. The young Luther did this and spent hours in the confessional, dredging up all manner of perceived sin and exhausting his confessor in the process. It was only after he came to understand that salvation is by grace through faith that his fear of dying with some sin unconfessed began to subside. He was then content to rest on the love and mercy of God. This is a lesson for all of us. Confession is a means to spiritual growth; if it becomes a legalistic obligation or the source of obsessional fear and anxiety, it is counter-productive and harmful. Should this happen, it is important to discuss the problem with the confessor and to take advice.

WHAT DOES GOING TO CONFESSION INVOLVE?

Those who have not made their Confession before probably find the whole idea rather daunting. Indeed, some of those who *have* made their Confession before may still find it so! It takes courage to bare your soul to somebody else, and if the exercise did not cause some apprehension, it might be asked how seriously it was being taken. The actual method of making Confession, however, has changed dramatically in recent times, with a new emphasis on informality. Confessions frequently resemble other pastoral interviews, with penitent and confessor sitting next to each other. Sometimes the penitent is asked to kneel beside the confessor as a mark of contrition and humility, but the old box confessional is largely a thing of the past, except for those who seek the anonymity it provides. Because practice does vary from church to church (and even from Confession to Confession), it is sensible, before making one's first Confession, to visit the confessor a week or two beforehand. This not only provides an opportunity for you to ask questions about method, but it also enables the confessor, where appropriate, to get to know a little of your background and context.

Where a Confession is made informally, the penitent may use his or her own words without any recourse to a written formula of any kind. There should always be the flexibility for this to happen, but, if it does, there is a danger that the encounter will become little more than a chat and its sacramental value will be undermined. It is always helpful, therefore, for the penitent to be provided with an Order of Confession; this makes it clear when the Confession begins and when it ends, and the pattern is generally conducive to the Confession being given in a systematic and understandable matter. A simple Order of Confession is given at the end of this chapter for illustration purposes, although most confessors will have their own version.

There is a significant overlap between Confession and what has come to be known as 'spiritual direction'. The precise nature of this overlap is an issue of some controversy among confessors and directors. There are those who believe that the two disciplines should be kept completely separate; others are prepared to act as confessor and director to the same person, but they set aside separate times for the exercise of each role; and some directors may minister absolution even where it has not been specifically sought, if it is felt that Confession has been made. In all of this, it needs to be recognized that the confessional has a specific spiritual and legal status that should not be violated. Matters disclosed under the seal of the confessional should not be passed on to a third party under any circumstances. This is right enough, since the confession is made to God with the confessor acting as God's agent. If there is any doubt whether an interview is covered by the seal of the confessional, the matter should be clarified immediately. An experienced director should realize this and act accordingly, but the penitent should always feel free to seek whatever clarification he or she considers necessary.

Preparing for Confession

Your confessor will offer guidance about the best way to prepare. As a general rule, however, it is wise to set aside a generous period of time for prayerful reflection; so far as possible, this should be free of distractions and interruptions. Different people will approach this in different ways. In the past, it was common to use manuals written for the purpose of jogging the memory. These contained long lists of sins and searching questions designed to unsettle even the cleanest of consciences! The problem with these was that they encouraged the view that every remembered sin must be brought to the confessional if it was to be forgiven, and they did not highlight those specific areas where spiritual growth was being held back.

It is important not to get so bogged down in detail that the broader picture is lost. While it is right, as part of our private prayer and Bible study, frequently to recall and confess the wrong things we have thought, said or done, the most important thing at Confession is to bring our sin as it impinges on our spiritual growth. In other words, we should concentrate on those sins which are especially serious in their nature or especially persistent in their recurrence. We need to identify what is holding us back in our walk with God. Very often this will be quite obvious, because our conscience will be troubled.

Where a Confession covers a period of a month or two, half an hour may be sufficient for preparation, but the preparation of a life confession could take half a day or even longer. Sometimes it is useful to spread the preparation out over several sessions, since this can aid the process of reflection and recollection. Of course, it may be that there is one specific sin that is weighing heavily on our conscience and which is driving us to Confession. Even so, it is still good to examine ourselves and to see how this sin is related to other aspects of our life.

While Confession should be specific and honest, it is not necessary to give intricate details. Neither should we blame or implicate others (it is our confession, not theirs). A confessor will normally ask for clarification where this is necessary and will be happy to discuss whether a particular act is or is not a sin. Therefore, when preparing our confession, it is a good idea to place a question mark against anything that we are not sure about.

One final point: once Confession has been made and absolution granted, any written list of sins that has been prepared should be destroyed. Its contents are no longer of concern to anybody, including the penitent.

Penance

Those who are unfamiliar with Confession and have heard about 'penance' sometimes confuse it with punishment or with an attempt to earn forgiveness. Whatever the historical reasons for this, penance is not to be seen in this way. It is intended to reinforce the healing process and often consists of a prayer or a Bible reading or some other devotional act. It may consist of performing some act of kindness, and the confessor will attempt to make the penance fit the sin.

In exceptional circumstances, a confessor may make absolution conditional on some duty being performed. This might, for example, be the case where some serious crime needs to be confessed to the police. The reason is not to restrict the grace of God, but to emphasize the relational obligations we have to our fellow human beings. Repentance is not just a matter of feeling sorry, but a change of direction. It will be demonstrated by its fruit and the confessor will want to be certain that there has been true repentance before granting absolution. The confessor will make the position quite clear and the penitent will be encouraged to put things right quickly so that absolution can be granted.

CONCLUSION

Confession has a chequered history. Abuses of the confessional have sometimes been serious and the Reformers were certainly right to repudiate the penitential practices of their day. It is important, however, to recognize the contribution that Confession can make to the spiritual life of the Church and to the spiritual growth and development of those within it.

We live in times when, for example, Roman Catholics are increasingly aware of the need for personal conversion and evangelicals are increasingly aware of the body of Christ. As they both share with each other, in the light of Scripture and their respective traditions, it is to be hoped that much common ground will be discovered and built on. Both desire holiness and maturity in the Christian life, and they have a shared interest in whatever contributes to these things.

It is so easy for Christians, approaching a subject from different angles, to disagree on forms of words and details of practice. While in no way wishing to devalue the importance of clarity and precision, I do hope that the value of Confession will not be obscured in that way. In the final analysis, the contribution it has to make to the life of the Church stems from the personal and direct way in which absolution is addressed to the penitent. This allows for a wide variety of styles and liturgical patterns and I urge those Christians who cannot, in good conscience, accept the existing forms of Confession to use a little imagination and to develop their own.

From my own experience, and from the experience of others with whom I have spoken, Confession has much to offer. My prayer is that it will find its place in the regular parochial life of the Church of England and of other denominations where, until now, it has not been common practice.

A SIMPLE ORDER OF CONFESSION

This example is taken from page 56 of *Lent, Holy Week, Easter*, published by the Central Board of Finance of the Church of England, 1986.

Penitent: Please give me your blessing, for I have sinned.

Minister: The Lord be in your heart and on your lips, that you may truly and humbly confess your sins, in the name of the Father, and of the Son, and of the Holy Spirit. Amen.

Penitent: I confess to Almighty God, the Father, the Son and the Holy Spirit that I have sinned in thought, word and deed, through negligence, through weakness, through my own deliberate fault.

My last confession was...

Since then, I have... (the sins are listed simply and clearly).

For these and all my other sins which I cannot now remember, I am truly sorry. I intend to amend my life, and I humbly seek God's pardon. From you, I ask for penance, counsel and absolution.

Minister: (Questions may be asked at this point and counsel may be given. Where appropriate, the priest may suggest a penance.)

God, the Father of all mercies, through his Son Jesus Christ forgives all who truly repent and believe in him. By the ministry of reconciliation which Christ has committed to his Church, and in the power of the Spirit, I declare that you are absolved from your sins, in the name of the Father, and of the Son, and of the Holy Spirit.

(The absolution may be accompanied by the laying on of hands.)

And the blessing of God Almighty, the Father, the Son and the Holy Spirit, be upon you and remain with you always. Amen.

The absolution used was specifically written for use with individuals. There is no reason why, if preferred, the absolution from Holy Communion in the *Alternative Service Book* should not be used. The most important thing is that the absolution should be addressed specifically to the penitent.

After the confession is over, the absolved penitent is recommended to spend some time in personal prayer and thanksgiving. This may take any form, although the canticles from the Book of Common Prayer or the *Alternative Service Book* are especially appropriate. Where a penance has been suggested, this should also be performed as soon as is reasonably possible.

SUGGESTED FURTHER READING

Dudley and Rowell (eds), *Confession and Absolution* (Liturgical Press, 1990) – an excellent introduction to the subject, setting confession in its biblical and historical contexts.

Hollings and Konstant, *Go in Peace* (McCrimmons, 1990) – a survey, by two Roman Catholic authors, of the theology and practice of Confession today. It is a good basic read and contains much useful devotional material linked to Confession.

Max Thurian, *Confession* (Mowbray, revised edition, 1985) – approaches the subject from a Reformed perspective and seeks to reconcile auricular confession with Protestant theology.

Ian Petit, *Your Sins Are Forgiven* (Darton, Longman and Todd, 1993) – for those who are especially interested in modern Roman Catholic practice; well written and a quick and easy read.

Catechism of the Catholic Church (Geoffrey Chapman, 1994) – somewhat heavier than the titles given above, but there is a good section on the sacrament of penance and reconciliation.

All the above books are in support of auricular confession. For an alternative point of view, the finest evangelical critique remains that written by John Stott in 1964 – *Confess Your Sins* (Hodder and Stoughton). The book is short, concise and to the point. It is no longer in print, however, although it may be available through libraries or second-hand dealers.

Notes

1 Dudley and Rowell (eds), *Confession and Absolution* (The Liturgical Press, 1990), p. 55.
2 Hollings and Konstant, *Go in Peace* (McCrimmons, 1990), p. 183.
3 Max Thurian, *Confession* (Mowbray, rev. ed. 1985), p. 38.
4 Ibid., p. 33.
5 Dudley and Rowell, *Confession and Absolution*, p. 111.
6 Paul Tournier, *Guilt and Grace* (Highland Books, 1986), p. 205; Leslie D. Weatherhead, *Prescription for Anxiety* (Arthur James, 1985), p. 63.

ABOUT THE AUTHORS

Jonathan Baker is Vicar of Scalby

Adrian Daffern is Vicar of Walsall Wood and Treasurer's Vicar of Lichfield Cathedral

Alison Fry is Vicar of Batheaston with St Catherine

John Goldingay is David Allan Hubbard Professor of Old Testament at Fuller Theological Seminary, Pasadena, California

Keith Hubbard is a research student at Bristol University

Jane Keiller is Chaplain and Tutor at Ridley Hall, Cambridge

Anne Long is Honorary Curate at St Paul's, Camberley, and an Honorary Canon of Guildford Cathedral

Mark Morton is a Chaplain to Her Majesty's Armed Forces

Harold Miller is Bishop of Down and Dromore

David Osborne is Rector of Pilton with Croscombe, North Wootton and Dinder

Ian Paul lives in Poole, Dorset, and is on the staff of St Mary's, Poole. The Managing Editor of Grove Books, he also is Theological Adviser in Salisbury Diocese and a member of General Synod of the Church of England.

Roger Pooley is Lecturer in the Department of English, Keele University

David Runcorn is Director of Evangelism and Pastoral Studies, Trinity College, Bristol

INDEX